Forensic Evidence

Admissibility in Criminal Justice System

When a successful criminal investigation is not possible by the traditional method of eye-witness-oriented criminal justice system, the modern technology relating to forensic evidence helps the judiciary to convict the accused or confirm his acquittal. The advent of forensic science technologies and development of tools made great scientific breakthrough in the decision-making process of criminal cases.

The book is divided into six chapters, beginning with Introduction followed by DNA, Ballistics, Fingerprint, Toxicology & Chemical Analysis and Cyber Forensics. INTRODUCTION provides a road map of the book while the chapter relating to DNA discusses the mechanisms used for DNA fingerprinting technique, admissibility of DNA evidence and how it helps to determine identity, paternity or maternity of a child. The chapter on BALLISTICS provides a comprehensive account of classification of firearms and their characteristics. The next chapter is FINGERPRINT which discusses adequately the classification, principle on which such evidence is based, mechanism for collection of fingerprint and Automated Fingerprint Identification System (AFIS). The chapter on TOXICOLOGY AND CHEMICAL ANALYSIS catalogues the classification of poisons, principle on which toxicology evidence is based, isolation & identification of poison and criminal cases in which toxicology evidence is used. The last chapter is CYBER FORENSICS which is the issue of the day. This chapter deals elaborately with the admissibility of electronic evidence, computer fraud, tampering with computer source code, hacking, etc. which will be very much helpful to solve the problems relating to cyber crimes.

An in-depth study has been made of all the important topics relating to the subject, with the help of the pronouncements of the apex court and different High Courts and accordingly it may be treated as an useful tool for busy legal practitioners, judges and researchers as well.

Kolkata
Eastern Law House Private Ltd.
54 Ganesh Chunder Avenue
Kolkata 700 013

New Delhi
Eastern Law House Private Ltd.
36 Netaji Subhash Marg, Daryaganj
New Delhi 110 002

Forensic Evidence

Admissibility in Criminal Justice System

by

Pratyusha Das LLM, PhD
Assistant Professor, Amity Law School

KOLKATA NEW DELHI
EASTERN LAW HOUSE

Published and processed by
EASTERN LAW HOUSE PRIVATE LTD.
54 Ganesh Chunder Avenue
Kolkata 700 013
Tel: (033) 2215-1989
Email: mail@elh.co.in
www.elh.co.in

ISBN 978-81-7177-346-6

Printed at
Dey's Offset, Kolkata

Preface

The advent of forensic science technologies made dramatic scientific breakthrough in the decision-making process of criminal cases. The work seeks to analyze the exact impact of such evidence on the administration of justice. The book deals with forensic evidences like DNA, ballistics, fingerprints, toxicology and cyber forensics. Scientific investigation of crime with the aid of forensic evidences has no less probative value than direct evidence in deciding criminal matters.

In India, the adversary system is followed for the administration of criminal justice. Administration of criminal justice is not possible without the presentation of proper evidence before courts. Examination of available evidence by the means of forensic science is thus very important to the judge who attempts to determine the truth and pass the judgment accordingly.

This book has been written chiefly for the persons who opt for specialized knowledge in forensic evidence. It is also hoped that it will prove to be useful to those scholars who pursue their research in the field of forensic evidence. The book is also expected to be helpful to the practitioners as the cases discussed portray the loopholes from the point of view of either of the parties (prosecution as well as defence) in criminal trials which either resulted in acquittal or conviction. Thus it is expected that the practitioners would avoid such pitfalls while arguing their matters.

I would thank Almighty, who has provided all strength to complete this work. I would remain grateful to my teachers Prof. (Dr.) N.K. Chakrabarti, Dr. D.P. Das and Prof. S.K. Nandy, for extending always their support and co-operation. I am obliged to my grandparents, parents, husband and daughter for their sacrifice and encouragement which always became a source of inspiration for me. I owe much to Eastern Law House Private Ltd. for constantly motivating/supporting me for the work.

Kolkata
2nd January 2019 PRATYUSHA DAS

Contents

Chapter 4 **Fingerprint**—*continued* PAGE

Chapter 4 **Fingerprint**—*continued* PAGE

Chapter 5 **Toxicology and Chemical Analysis**—*continued* PAGE

Chapter 5 **Toxicology and Chemical Analysis**—*continued* PAGE

Table of Cases

Chapter 1

Introduction

> "Wherever he steps, whatever he touches, whatever he leaves, even unconsciously, will serve as silent evidence against him. Not only his fingerprints or his footprints, but his hair, the fibres from his clothes, the glass he breaks, the tool marks he leaves, the paint he scratches, the blood or semen that he deposits or collects – all these and more bear mute witness against him. This is evidence that does not forget. It is not confused by the factual evidence. Physical evidence cannot be wrong; it cannot perjure itself; it cannot be wholly absent. Only its interpretation can err. Only human failure to find it, study and understand it can diminish its value."
>
> —Paul L. Kirk, PhD

The advent of forensic science technologies have made dramatic scientific breakthroughs in the decision making process of criminal cases but study was required to analyze the exact impact of forensic evidence in determining the rate of conviction and acquittal. It was also required to assess in what type of cases, which kind of forensic evidence could be used. Forensic evidence is what kind of evidence, i.e. is it treated as substantive evidence or corroborative evidence? In what circumstances the court accepted the forensic evidence? If forensic evidence is accepted, does it always lead to conviction or in spite of accepting forensic evidence, acquittal was recorded. In this context, the views of different courts of India regarding forensic evidence have been while referring such evidence in the decision making process of criminal cases.

It has been experienced that successful criminal investigation is practically impossible by the traditional method of eye-witness oriented criminal justice system. This method of criminal investigation lowers the quality of criminal justice system. It becomes difficult for the judges to decide a criminal matter or corroborate the fact-in-issue only on the sole basis of evidence of witnesses who might lie or are not dependable (because witnesses fail to appear on the dates fixed by the courts or might not be subject to the process of the court, which delays justice). Moreover, by scrutinizing the examinations-in-chief and cross-examination, the judges fail to reach to a definite conclusion regarding the incident. Nowadays witnesses refuse to come and appear before the court in spite of knowing the truth or witnessing the incidence because of fear of becoming preys to criminals or threats which many a time are life taking. Many a time offences are committed in such a condition or situation where it is impossible even to get a single witness. In such cases the decision making process of criminal cases totally depends on circumstantial evidence like DNA evidence, report of the ballistic expert, fingerprints or report of chemical examination.

Due to lack of evidence or lack of proper evidence most of the heinous criminals are acquitted or goes scot free on the basis of even slightest doubt. Moreover the prosecution spends huge amount of money on the trials of criminal cases. Therefore through conventional investigations mostly public money is wasted and criminals get acquittal on the basis of benefit of doubt.

Crimes are now committed in a technical way, even technical crimes have emerged which can be investigated only through the use of forensic science. Classification of crimes has also changed from conventional or traditional to technical. The definitions of criminals have also changed since the criminals are now technology savvy. Conventional crimes are also committed in a scientific way through computers in which case no option is left except to use cyber forensic. Intelligent criminals started exploiting science for their criminal activities, whereas investigators are unable to rely on the age-old art of interrogation, development of sources and surveillance to detect crime. Therefore the criminal justice system cannot suffice without the aid of forensic science or new technology. The development of forensic science has provided a powerful tool in the hands of the law enforcement agencies and the judiciary.[1]

A scientific investigation of crime and the justice delivery system, with the aid of forensic science efficiently and effortlessly establishes the criminal charge against an accused with much accuracy. Scientific investigation of crime with the aid of forensic science has been accepted all over the world and successful criminal investigation can be done with the help of forensic science.

The pillar of a criminal case entirely lies on criminal investigation. Scientific investigation with the help of forensic science is much more powerful, reliable and fruitful than eye-witness oriented criminal justice system. A victim cannot be left at the mercy of the eye-witnesses. The different branches of forensic science like DNA, ballistics, fingerprinting, toxicology etc. are much reliable than the examination of ordinary witnesses. Some of the questions that are coming in the minds of the researchers are as follows. In everyday life we come across recent developments in forensic science through news papers, television or internet and also training of police personnel on the new forensic techniques but it is still to be revealed whether these developments are of real use in the decision making process of criminal cases?

The value of scientific and technological evidence is three folded. Forensic evidence helps in collecting materials from the crime scene, fingers the guilty and sets the innocent free. But there is no particular legislation on the admissibility of forensic evidence before the court except the Indian Evidence Act which talks about expert evidence, so we usually depend on the decisions and judgments of the higher courts or the apex court.

1 B.S. Nabar, *Forensic Science in Crime Investigation,* 3rd Ed. 2002, p. 1 (Hyderabad: Asia Law House).

A crime scene often is rich in information that reveals the nature of the criminal activity and the identities of the persons involved. Perpetrators and victims may leave behind blood, saliva, skin cells, hair, fingerprints, footprints, tire prints, clothing fibers, digital and photographic images, audio data, handwriting, and the residual effects and debris of arson, gunshots, and unlawful entry.[2] Useful evidence cannot be gathered without the aid of scientific analysis. Without the use of science, it is not possible to convict criminals, ranging from common theft to a homicidal rampage, unless there was an eye-witness present at the crime scene when the crime occurred. Murderers would continue killing, thieves would continue stealing, and drug traffickers would continue dealing. Fortunately, in today's world, science is used in solving crimes.[3] The element of anonymity and lack of territorial borders in cyberspace makes internet an attractive médium for criminals to commit crimes. Not only the conventional crimes such as thefts, extortion, defamation or forgery are committed through computers but also new forms of crime have emerged such as hacking, trojan, phishing attacks etc.[4] Therefore, forensic science and its use have become indispensable for purpose of investigations.

1 Brief insight into the history and development of forensic science

Definition The word '*Forensic*' is derived from the Latin word *forum* for "public" (Oxford English Dictionary 2005). In ancient Rome, the Senate met in the Forum, a public place where the political and the policy issues of the day were discussed and debated; Technically, "forensic" means as applied to public or legal concerns. Together, "forensic science" is an apt term for

2 In The Spotlight, available at https://www.ncjrs.gov/spotlight/forensic/summary.html (last visited on 10th January 2015).

3 The Imporatnce of Forensic Science in Criminal Investigation, available at http://www.criminalistica.com.mx/areas-forenses/criminalistica (last visited on 10th January 2015).

4 Karnika Seth, *Computers Internet and New Technology Laws*, Ed. 2012, p. 333 (Nagpur: LexisNexis Butterworths Wadhwa).

the profession of scientist whose work answers questions for the courts through reports and testimony.[5] 'Forensic science' would, therefore, mean the science which is used in the courts of justice. The National Institute of Justice (NIJ, 1908) defines forensic science as "application of scientific knowledge to the legal system."[6] More broadly it can be defined as that scientific discipline which is directed to the recognition, identification, individualization and evaluation of physical evidence by the application of the principles and methods of natural sciences for the purpose of administration of criminal justice. In other words it is the application of a broad spectrum of sciences and technologies to investigate situations after the fact and to establish what occurred based on collected evidence.[7] A synonym of forensic science is also termed as "Criminalistics". The word "Criminalistics" was imported into English from a German word "kriminalistic".[8] It is also known as the science of individualization (Kirk 1963a). The process of individualization is traditionally called identification, as in fingerprint identification, but is more appropriately termed as individualization or source attribution.[9] "Evidence" means and includes—(1) all statements which the court permits or requires to be made before it by witnesses, in relation to matters of fact under inquiry; such statements are called oral evidence; (2) all documents including electronic records produced for the inspection of the court; such documents are called documentary evidence.[10] Richard Saferstein gives a more specific definition than what was previously given in his book *Criminalistics: An Introduction to Forensic Science*, which says

5 Max M. Houck and Jay A. Siegel, Jay A. Siegel, *Fundamentals of Forensic Science*, 2nd Ed. 2011, p. 4 (Oxford, UK: Elsevier).

6 Kelly M. Pyrek, *Forensic Science under Siege: The Challenges of Forensic Laboratories and the Medico-Legal Investigation System*, Edition 2007, p. 4 (Amsterdam: Academic Press).

7 Forensics, available at: http://www.thefreedictionary.com/forensics (last visited on 20th September 2013).

8 Kelly M. Pyrek, *supra* at p. 4.

9 Tim Newburn, Tom Williamson, *et.al.* (eds.), *Handbook of Criminal Investigation*, Edition 2007, p. 303 (UK: Willan Publishing).

10 Section 3 of the Indian Evidence Act 1872.

that forensic science is the "application of science to those criminal and civil laws that are enforced by the police agencies in a criminal justice system." The origin of this type of science cannot be accurately pinpointed. According to H.J. Walls' article *"Whither Forensic Science?"* it started as a hobby of a few scientists who liked to become mixed up in the proceedings of the police and enjoyed the kind of problems this association brought them.

In India, the growing awareness among the police and the judiciary, regarding the role of science played in scientific evaluation of material clues, led to setting up of forensic science laboratories in the State as well as the Centre. After a considerable thought given by the forensic science fora to build comprehensive forensic science facilities under one roof, most of the new laboratories came up with comprehensive facilities by amalgamating scientific sections and chemical examiner's laboratory into forensic science laboratory. The existing position of the forensic science laboratories and other allied forensic science institutions in the country, offering scientific service in the administration of criminal justice can be studied under two heads. They are (1) Institutions under the Centre (2) Institutions at the State.

TABLE 1

(A) Institutions under the Centre

(i)	The Central Forensic Science Laboratories under the control of B.P.R.&D[11] at		
	(a) Calcutta established in 1957.	(b) Hyderabad established in 1968.	(c) Chandigarh which was originally established in 1961 as F.S.L. Punjab, later designated as Union Territory Laboratory and re-designed in 1978 as CFSL under B.P.R.&D.

11 The Government of India vide Resolution No. 8/136/68-P.I (Pers.I) dated 28.08.1970 formally established as the Bureau of Police Research and Development (BPR&D) (Ministry of Home Affairs).

<table>
<tr><td>(ii)</td><td colspan="12">The Central Forensic Science Laboratory, under C.B.I. New Delhi established in 1968.</td></tr>
<tr><td rowspan="2">(iii)</td><td colspan="12">The Government Examiners of Questioned Documents, under administrative control of B.P.R.&D situated at</td></tr>
<tr><td colspan="4">(a) Simla established in 1906</td><td colspan="4">(b) Calcutta established in 1964</td><td colspan="4">(c) Hyderabad established in 1968</td></tr>
<tr><td>(iv)</td><td colspan="12">The Central Fingerprint Bureau under N.C.R.B.[12] New Delhi.</td></tr>
<tr><td>(v)</td><td colspan="12">The Serologist and Chemical Examiner to the Government of India, Ministry of Health, at Calcutta established in 1910.</td></tr>
<tr><td rowspan="2">(vi)</td><td colspan="12">The General Manager Mints at</td></tr>
<tr><td colspan="4">(a) Calcutta</td><td colspan="4">(b) Bombay</td><td colspan="4">(c) Hyderabad</td></tr>
<tr><td rowspan="2">(vii)</td><td colspan="12">The General Manager, India Security Printing Press at</td></tr>
<tr><td colspan="4">(a) Nasik</td><td colspan="8">(b) Bank Note Press, Dewas</td></tr>
<tr><td>(viii)</td><td colspan="12">The Controller of Stamps and Stationery.</td></tr>
<tr><td rowspan="2">(ix)</td><td colspan="12">National Institute of Criminology and Forensic Science under M.H.A.[13]</td></tr>
<tr><td colspan="12">New Delhi established in 1971 which imparts training to police, Judicial and Correctional Service Officers including Scientific personnel from the States and Central Forensic Laboratories.</td></tr>
<tr><td rowspan="2">(x)</td><td colspan="12">Office of the Chief Controller of Explosives established in 1898 in Nagpur. Today there are several circles and sub-circles located in different parts of the country, headed by Deputy Chief Controller, Controller or Deputy Controller at 4 circles and 13 sub-circles. The 4 circles are noted as:</td></tr>
<tr><td colspan="3">(a) East Circle, Calcutta, headed by Dy. Chief Controller</td><td colspan="3">(b) West Circle, Bombay, headed by Dy. Chief Controller</td><td colspan="3">(c) North Circle, Agra, headed by Dy. Chief Controller</td><td colspan="3">(d) South Circle, Madras, headed by Dy. Chief Controller</td></tr>
<tr><td rowspan="2">(xi)</td><td colspan="12">Central Detective Training Schools are training institutes for imparting specialized detective training to investigating police officers on modern scientific methods of investigation. They are situated at:</td></tr>
<tr><td colspan="4">(a) Calcutta</td><td colspan="4">(b) Chandigarh</td><td colspan="4">(c) Hyderabad</td></tr>
</table>

12 National Crime Records Bureau under the Ministry of Home Affairs.
13 Ministry of Home Affairs.

TABLE 2

(B) Institutions at the State Lavel

The State Forensic Science Laboratories exist in 19 States as mentioned below:

(i)	Calcutta, West Bengal established in 1952.
(ii)	Bombay, Maharashtra established in 1958.
(iii)	Jaipur, Rajasthan established in 1959.
(iv)	Madras, Tamil Nadu established in 1959.
(v)	Trivandrum, Kerala established in 1961.
(vi)	Bhubabeswar, Orissa established in 1962.
(vii)	Patna, Bihar established in 1963.
(viii)	Srinagar, Jammu & Kashmir in 1964.
(ix)	Sagar, Madhya Pradesh established in 1964.
(x)	Gauhati, Assam established in 1967.
(xi)	Bangalore, Karnataka established in 1967.
(xii)	Lucknow, Uttar Pradesh established in 1969.
(xiii)	Madhuban, Haryana established in 1973.
(xiv)	Ahmedabad, Gujarat established in 1974.
(xv)	Hyderabad, Andhra Pradesh established in 1976.
(xvi)	Chandigarh, Punjab established in 1981.
(xvii)	Shillong, Meghalaya established in 1986.
(xviii)	Simla, Himachal Pradesh established in 1987.
(xix)	Delhi, established in 1993.

States like Maharashtra, Tamil Nadu, Andhra Pradesh, Gujarat, Uttar Pradesh, Odisha, Jammu & Kashmir have further extended their forensic science facilities by establishing laboratories at regional and District level. Some of the States like Goa, Arunachal Pradesh, Mizoram, Nagaland, Sikkim and

Tripura do not have their own organized laboratories. Similarly, Union Territories like, Pondicherry, Chandigarh, Andaman & Nicobar Islands, Daman & Diu and Lakshadweep do not have their own laboratories. They avail the facilities of the neighbouring States or the nearest Central Forensic Science Laboratory.

2 Divisions and facilities provided by the laboratories

Both the State and Central laboratories may have all or most of the divisions:

(1) Ballistics (2) Biology (3) Chemistry (4) Documents (5) Lie-Detector (6) Physics (7) Serology (8) Toxicology.

The work and functions of some of the divisions are discussed hereunder to co-relate with the forensic topics dealt in herewith:

• Ballistic Division

This division deals with :

(i) Examination of all types of firearms and ammunitions to connect bullets and spent cartridge cases with a particular firearm to the exclusion of all others.

(ii) Determine the serviceability of firearms and ammunitions.

(iii) Determine the time range and angle of firing.

(iv) Nature of gunshot injury and a host of other problems associated with offences involving firearms and ammunitions.

In most of the laboratories, cases related to the identification of explosives, their handling and examination of residue materials, after the explosion, are also handled. In some laboratories there are separate division to undertake examination of explosive cases.

• Chemistry Division

The following items of evidence are dealt with in the Chemistry Division:

(i) Examination of Petroleum products like petrol, diesel and kerosene.

(ii) Examination of sub-standard construction material like bricks, cement, concrete etc. besides adulteration in these materials.

(iii) Determination of alcohol in blood and urine in cases of suspected drunkenness and analysis of fermented wash, illicit liquor, varnish etc. in prohibition and excise cases.

(iv) Examination of inflammable material in suspected cases of arson, dowry deaths etc.

(v) Analysis of pesticides for their identification.

(vi) Analysis of narcotics, dangerous drugs such as opium, ganja, bhang, LSD, heroin, pethidine, methadone etc.

(vii) Analysis of dyes, paint, ink and other chemicals with a view to ascertain their identity, quality and composition.

(viii) Examination of metal alloys and metal fragments for identification and comparison.

- **Serology Division**

The serology division undertakes the following examination:

(i) Examination of articles stained with blood, semen, sweat, saliva to determine their nature, origin, grouping, DNA profiling etc.

(ii) Determination of paternity through blood groups.

(iii) Individualization of blood and bloodstains based on enzymatic studies using latest techniques.

(iv) Determine origin and grouping of fragments of muscle, skin, bones etc. on objects like bullets, fingernails, etc.

- **Toxicology Division**

The division deals with:

(i) The examination of viscera, stomach wash, vomit etc. to determine poisons of vegetable origin, inorganic salts and metals, synthetic drugs, pesticides, alcohol and other general poisons.

(ii) Examination of powders, pills, capsules, syringes, vials etc.

(iii) Determination of alcohol in blood and urine in drunken driving cases.[14]

2.1 Facilities Offered by other Expert Institutions

Now let us study the specialized functions provided by some of the particular institution of the centre except the Central Forensic Science Laboratories and the State Fingerprint Bureau.

- **The Serologist and Chemical Examiner to the Government of India**

This institution, which was first established for serological examination is concerned with the identification, analysis, origin and grouping of blood and blood stained articles referred to by police agencies throughout the country. The articles are sent to through the State Forensic Science Laboratory or the Chemical Examiner Laboratory. This institution is capable of giving advice in a variety of cases involving actual bloodshed like murder, hurt, suicide cases, cases of disputed paternity by identifying blood group or other criminal cases in which other body fluids may be involved. Recently, most of the Central and State Laboratories have developed serological expertise within their set up. Some of these laboratories have discontinued sending articles for serological examination to this institute at Kolkata. Besides, serological examination, it also serves as a production and supply centre for serums, for blood analysis.

- **Central Fingerprint Bureau, Kolkata**

This bureau was set up in 1957, under the control of Intelligence Bureau. It was later brought under the control of Central Bureau of Investigation. It is now under the control of

14 Central Forensic Science Laboratory (CBI). available at: http://cbi.nic.in/aboutus/manuals/Chapter_27.pdf (Last visited on 11th May 2015).

N.C.R.B. It is a national bureau maintaining fingerprints of convicts from all States and Union Territories of India. It has the largest collection of fingerprint records in our country. When a criminal from one State operates crime in another State, his previous conviction records can be obtained from the Central Fingerprint Bureau to secure enhanced punishment. The bureau also maintains the records of international criminals. The fingerprint records are now computerized to facilitate faster retrieval.

- **The State Fingerprint Bureau**

Every State has a fingerprint bureau on the lines of the CFPB.[15] These bureaus have the following functions:

(i) Maintain a record of fingerprint slips primarily of criminals convicted for certain offences specified in the Indian Penal Code.

(ii) Assist in searching the crime scenes for chance prints for suspect identification. Some States have established these bureaus in regions and districts also, most of which are for single digit records. A few States have started using computers for speedy processing of fingerprint records.

3 Types of forensic evidence

Although, 'Forensic Science' clinches all branches of physical and natural sciences, chief among them being chemistry, biology, physics, broadly there are two areas of forensic science. They are Identification and Individualization. In Identification the parent field is mostly chemistry, though principles are drawn from physics or biology. The goal of these specialties typically is to identify a substance and to quantitate it. So the method is also called quantitation. For example, what chemical is certain powder, and how much of it is present? Does a cadaver contain poison, what kind, and how much? These fields

15 Central Fingerprint Bureau available at: http://164.100.44.112:8888/English.aspx (last visited on 11th May 2015).

based on conventional science, are considered highly reliable and are rarely challenged in court unless a new technique is presented or evidence of negligence or fraud exists. The individualization on the other hand seeks to associate an item of evidence found at a crime scene with its unique source, to the exclusion of all others and it is not derived from conventional sciences. Rather the methods and principles employed by the individualization includes, comparison of such things as bite marks, bullets, fingerprints, footwear, hair, handwriting and so on. DNA typing is the exception. It is the first individualization science derived from traditional science.[16] The term "forensic science" encompasses a broad range of forensic disciplines, each with its own set of technologies and practices. Some of the forensic science disciplines are Chemical examination, Fingerprints and Footprints, Mobile phone data, DNA test (Forensic identification), Identification by photograph, Identification by voice, Ballistics, Toxicology.[17] Except these there are also various other classification of Forensic Science. They are, Forensic Entomology, Forensic Odontology, Forensic Pathology etc. In the present book only four topics are dealt with such as DNA, Ballistics, Fingerprints and Toxicology, only those four topics are discussed at length.

3.1 DNA Profiling Technique (DNA tests)[18]

DNA is the abbreviation of Deoxyribo Nucleic Acid. It is the basic genetic material in all the living cells of the body. It is contained in white blood corpuscles and not in red blood corpuscles. It carries the genetic code. Hence the DNA structure determines human character, behavior and body

16 Jane Campbell Moriarty, Michael, J. Saks, *Forensic Science, Grand Goals, Tragic Flaws & Judicial Gatekeeping*, p. 44, Judges Journal 17 (2005).

17 Supreme Court Digest, 2011, 2010 and 2009.

18 Adarsh M. Dhabarde, *Forensic Evidence in Criminal Trial: The Need of the Hour*, Edition 2012, pp. 4-7 available at http://ssrn.com/abstract=2111995 (last visited on 7th February 2015).

characteristics. Each individual, consequently, is unique and is different from all others. In monozygotic twins, DNA structure is the same because they come forth by the division of a single fertilized egg. Monozygotic twins are generally identical.[19] In 1984, Sir Allec Jeffrey discovered the method of identifying individuals from DNA and in 1985 UK police first used forensic DNA profiling.[20]

3.2 Ballistics

Ballistics is the use and study of firearms. The science of ballistics has been developed to facilitate the examination of firearms, ammunition and other related matter. As a term of art, ballistics technically refers to the study of a bullet's path from the firearm, through the air, and into a target. In criminal investigations, however, ballistics is a shorthand term for firearms identification: the art of matching recovered bullets and their casings to the firearm from which they were fired. Firearms identification is often treated as a subspecialty of tool mark identification. A tool mark expert attempts to match tools like screwdrivers and crowbars to the marks they make when used on objects. Ballistics experts are more than tool mark specialists. They are generally experts in many aspects of firearms and testify about topics ranging from whether a specific object is, legally, a firearm, to intricate reconstructions of crime scene evidence.[21] Forensic ballistic was first invented by Calvin Goddard, a pioneer in this study.

3.3 Fingerprints

"Fingerprints are God's own seals, given to us that we may recognize his greatest creation-MAN." The best and certain method in identification was fingerprints which were

19 B.R. Sharma, *Forensic Science in Criminal Investigation & Trial,* 4th Ed. 2003, p. 1123 (New Delhi: Universal Law Publishing Co.).

20 History of Forensic Science, available at http://forensicscience central.co.uk/history.shtml (last visited on 16th May 2015).

21 Ballistics, available at http://apps.americanbar.org/abastore/products/books/abstracts/5450051chap1_abs.pdf (last visited on 22nd April 2015).

discovered during the fag end of the nineteenth century till the advent of a similar method DNA Fingerprinting. Pattern and impression evidence is one of the most common forms of evidence that can be detected and collected from a crime scene. Impression evidence is created when two objects come in contact with enough force to cause an "impression". Typically it is either two dimensional such as finger print or three-dimensional such as marks on a bullet caused by the barrel of a firearm.[22] The fingerprints as evidence are important because of the following features of the fingerprints. They are unique, they are permanent, they are universal, they are inimitable, they are classifiable, and they are frequently available in crime situations as evidence. Latent fingerprints are crucial pieces of evidence used in criminal investigations that can link a suspect to a crime. They are extracted from crime scene by experts by using chemical or physical methods. The fingerprint images could then be photographed, marked up for distinguishing features by latent fingerprint examiners, and used to search an automated fingerprint identification system (AFIS). An AFIS is a computer system (not available in India) that stores fingerprint images in an organized, searchable data structure that is widely used by criminal justice agencies to maintain databases of the fingerprints of individuals who are arrested or incarcerated.[23] There is a controversy regarding the inventor of fingerprint. It is accepted by many that Henry Faulds is the true inventor of Fingerprint. Although evidence were found that the use of fingerprint existed from the pre-historic times, the English first began using fingerprints in July, 1858, when Sir William Herschel, the Chief Magistrate of the Hoogly District, first used fingerprints made during that period.[24]

22 Impression and Pattern Evidence, available at http://nij.gov/topics/forensics/evidence/impression/pages/welcome.aspx (last visited on 22nd April 2015).

23 Fingerprints: An overview, available at http://nij.gov/topics/forensics/evidence/impression/pages/fingerprints.aspx (last visited on 20th April 2015).

24 U.S. Marshals Service for Students, available at https://www.usmarshals.gov/usmsforkids/fingerprint_history.htm (last visited on 30th June 2016).

3.4 Forensic Toxicology

Forensic toxicology is the use of toxicology and other disciplines such as analytical chemistry, pharmacology and clinical chemistry to aid medical or legal investigation of death, poisoning, and drug use. The primary concern for forensic toxicology is not the legal outcome of the toxicological investigation, but rather the technology and techniques for obtaining and interpreting the results. A toxicological analysis can be done to various kinds of samples. The first comprehensive work on forensic toxicology was published in 1813 by Mathieu Orifila. He was a respected Spanish chemist and the physician who is often given the distinction of "Father of Toxicology". His work emphasized the need for adequate proof of identification and the need for quality assurance. It also recognized the application of forensic toxicology in pharmaceutical, clinical, industrial and environmental fields.

4 Existing Indian Laws

Section 45 of the Indian Evidence Act 1872, deals with 'opinion of expert, when relevant'. But the opinion of expert is admissible by evidence only after scrutinization under Art. 21 and Art. 20(3) of the Constitution of India and s. 161(2) of the Code of Criminal Procedure 1973. Section 293 of the Code of Criminal Procedure 1973, specifies under what circumstances certain reports of Government scientific experts may be used in any evidence. Sections 53 and 53A of the Code of Criminal Procedure 1973, is also very much useful for DNA profiling of the accused. The law relating to 'fingerprints' is specifically covered by different sections of the Identification of Prisoners Act 1920, s. 73 of the Indian Evidence Act 1872 and s. 293 of the Code of Criminal Procedure 1973 along with the general laws applicable to other forensic techniques. The laws relating to toxicology is specifically dealt with under certain sections along with the general laws. Section 284 of the Indian Penal Code, levies the punishment for 'negligent conduct with respect to poisonous substance'. Sale of Poisons Act 1919, prohibits except under a licence, the import of any specified poison and may by rule regulate the grant of licences.

5 Nature and trend of scientific evidence

To ascertain the nature of forensic evidence and classify it, an "Appreciation of Evidence"[25] is required. Section 3 of the Evidence Act reveals when a fact is "Proved", "Disproved" and "Not Proved". Section 56 states 'Facts judicially noticeable need not be proved'. According to s. 58, 'Facts which are admitted need not be proved. After considering to such judicially noticeable facts and admitted facts, a reference is required to be made to as to how disputed facts are to be proved on the basis of produced evidence. There might be different types of evidence produced before the court, but in the book since Forensic Evidence is dealt specifically, the focus is shifted to how facts are to be proved on the basis of forensic evidence. Therefore, to classify forensic evidence we need to dissect the different kinds of evidence.

5.1 Evidence

Section 3 of the Indian Evidence Act 1872 (In respect of fact in issue and relevant fact).

Evidence can be oral evidence (ss. 59 and 60) and documentary evidence (ss. 61 to 90A). Further, oral evidence may be classified into direct and circumstantial. Both oral evidence and documentary evidence may be substantive and corroborative.

Forensic evidences are usually documentary in nature, since they are reports of experts according to s. 45 if the Indian Evidence Act 1872. Now, the question is that how can they be categorized in the category of substantive or corroborative. To know the answer it is necessary to know what substantive and corroborative evidence is.

25 What is the trustworthiness of the evidence produced? Whether it is believable or not or whether it is actuated by any evidence or not?

(a) SUBSTANTIVE EVIDENCE is the evidence on the basis of which a fact is proved and which requires no corroboration. Substantive evidence is either direct or circumstantial or both.

(b) CORROBORATIVE EVIDENCE is the evidence used to corroborate substantive evidence to bring home the charge of the accused. If there is no substantive evidence, corroborative evidence loses its significance. In other words in absence of substantive evidence, corroborative evidence is no evidence. [Sections 7, 27, 156, 157 of the Evidence Act, FIR, injury certificate, panchnamas, etc.] Corroborative evidence is either direct or circumstantial or both.

6 Nature of forensic evidence and future trends

A study of various cases on different forensic or scientific evidences or expert evidences reveals that normally scientific evidences are corroborative in nature. Cases on Ballistics, Fingerprints, and Toxicology have revealed that they are corroborative in nature subject to an exception in case of DNA Evidence. DNA evidence is treated as substantive evidence in cases for Determination of Paternity. Automatically, the question which knocks at the forefront is why? Whenever, expert evidence establishes new facts on the basis of pure and absolute scientific investigation which is relevant to the trial it is held to be an useful, important piece of substantive evidence.

6.1 Trends

It is very surprising that in other criminal cases like murder, rape etc. even DNA evidence has been treated as a corroborative evidence like the others. The point to be considered in every piece of scientific evidence is whether the scientific evidence establishes new facts on the basis of pure and absolute scientific investigation which is relevant to the trial. If such is the case, scientific evidences as well as expert evidences should be treated as substantive instead of corroborative. Suppose, if by an expert report, connectivity between victim and assailant is established, it should be treated as substantive evidence. Days are not very far when such considerations would be readily accepted by courts.

7 Indirect evidence

HEARSAY EVIDENCE is indirect and derivative, which is not received as relevant evidence. It is inadmissible. The term 'hearsay' is used with reference to what is done or written as well as to what is spoken and in its legal sense, it denotes that kind of evidence which does not derive its value solely from the credit given to the witness himself, but which rests also, in part, on the veracity and competence of some other person. The word 'hearsay' is used in various senses. Sometimes it means whatever a person is heard to say. Sometimes it means whatever a person declares on information given by someone else and sometimes it is treated as nearly synonymous with irrelevant. The sayings and doings of third person are, as a rule, irrelevant, so that no proof of them can be admitted. Every act done or spoken which is relevant on any ground must be proved by someone who saw it with his own eyes and heard it with his own ears.

7.1 Illustrations

(i) 'A' is charged of commission of murder of 'B' by stabbing him. 'C', 'D', 'E', 'F', 'G', 'H', 'I', 'J' & 'K' are witnesses called by the prosecution.

'C' says that he saw 'A' stab 'B'. His evidence is purely direct and substantive he being an eye witness.

(ii) 'D' says that he heard 'B' cry out that 'A' was stabbing him. His evidence is direct, but circumstantial and substantive in respect of relevant fact and not hearsay even though he actually did not witness the incident of stabbing.

(iii) 'E' says that he saw 'A' running away with a blood stained knife and blood stained clothes. His evidence is direct as he saw A while running away,, but circumstantial (ss. 7 & 8) in respect of relevant fact, it being effect of stabbing under s. 7 and subsequent conduct of the accused under s. 8 to run away.

(iv) 'F 'says that he saw A washing his blood-stained clothes. Evidence of F accordingly given is direct, but circumstantial (ss. 7, 8 & 60 first part) in respect of relevant fact, it being effect under s. 7 & subsequent conduct under s. 8

(v) 'G' is a medical officer, who says that the knife found in 'A's possession might have caused wounds found on 'B'. His evidence being opinion is circumstantial, but direct and corroborative (s. 60 fourth part) in respect of relevant fact.

(vi) 'H' says that he heard from 'C' that 'C saw 'A' stabbing 'B'. His evidence is hearsay & not admissible so far as proof of truthfulness of what 'C said to him is concerned.[26]

8 Principles of admitting scientific evidence by United States (US) courts

Now it's required to know on what principles the criminal cases relating to forensic evidence are dealt with by the courts abroad. A revolution has taken place in the last decade for the admissibility of scientific evidence in federal courts.[27] *Frye* v *United States*[28] was the first important judgment in America regarding the admissibility of scientific evidence. The Frye test had two aspects. First, the principle of scientific technique and secondly, the acceptance. The aspects of the test were criticized on two different grounds: (*i*) That there will have to be a considerable time lag for the scientific method to be accepted by the community; (*ii*) More faith is reposed on the scientific community than in the Court of Law. Hence, the Federal Rules

26 Evidence—Kinds of evidence—Kinds of available at http://mja.gov.iivsite/Upload/GR/EVIDENCE_K_D_PATIL_.PDF, accessed on 29.6.2018.

27 Paul W. Grimm, Chief Magistrate Judge, United States District Court, District of Maryland 1, available at http://www.msba.org/uploadedFiles/MSBA/Member_Groups/Sections/Construction_Law/Expert%20Witness%20Admissibility%20Federal%20Courts.pdf (last visited on 16th June 2015).

28 *Frye* v *United States* 293 F 1013 (DC Cir 1923).

of Evidence was enacted in 1975. Rule 702, of which stated that if scientific, technical or other specialized knowledge will assist the trier of fact to understand the evidence or to determine a fact in issue, a witness qualified as an expert by knowledge, skill, experience, training or education may testify thereto in the form of an opinion or otherwise.[29] But the enactment did not settle the dispute as it neither included the Frye standard nor made a mention of the general acceptance standard. So, the United States Supreme Court laid down the guidelines in the remarkable judgment of *Daubert* v *Merrell Dow Pharmaceuticals, Inc.*[30] The court concluded by saying that the Federal Rules of Evidence superseded the Frye Rule and that the rigid general acceptance rule should not conquer the way of a reasonable minority scientific opinion in the form of new and emerging research based on reliable studies. It also laid down factors for the basis of scientific evidence which are also known as the *Daubert* Guidelines. The Guidelines are as follows:

(1) The content of the scientific testimony which has already been tested, can be tested using the scientific method;

(2) The technique has been subject to peer review, preferably in the form of publication in peer review literature;

(3) There are consistently and reliably applied professional standards and known or potential error rates for the technique;

(4) Considers general acceptance within the relevant scientific community.

Later the *Kumho Tire* case,[31] expanded the *Daubert* Analysis, to technical and specialized subjects that do not fall within the category of "science". After the *Daubert* Guidelines were

29 Federal Rules of Evidence 1975; 2000 available at https://www.law.cornell.edu/rules/fre (last visited on 16th June 2015).

30 *Daubert* v *Merell Dow Pharmaceuticals, Inc* 509 US 579 (1993).

31 *Kumho Tire Company, Ltd.* v *Carmichael* 526 US 137 (1999).

framed, the Federal Rules of Evidence were then amended in the year 2000. The Rule 702 now provides that scientific, technical or specialized evidence (i.e. "Expert testimony") may be admitted if: (a) the expert is qualified; (b) the expert's testimony will help the jury to decide issues in the case or understand the evidence; and (c) the expert's testimony is based on sufficient facts or data; is the product of reliable methods and principles, and if the expert reliably has applied the methods and principles to the facts of the case in trial.[32] As a result of this revolution, federal trial judges are now required to perform as so-called "gatekeepers" to determine at the threshold whether expert testimony will be allowed to be heard by the jury in civil and criminal trials before it helps the jury to decide issues in the case or understand the evidence according to Rule 702 of the Federal Rules of Evidence. In *Daubert*, Justice Blackmun, writing for the majority, expressed the Court's confidence in the ability of federal trial judges to function as gatekeepers of admissibility of scientific and technical evidence to insure that only qualified experts are permitted to testify on these subjects, based on sufficient facts or data, and reliable methodology that properly has been applied to the facts of the particular case. He said: "Faced with proffer of expert scientific testimony, then, the trial judge must determine at the outset, pursuant to Rule 104(a), whether the expert is proposing to testify to (1) scientific knowledge that (2) will assist the trier of fact to understand or determine a fact in issue. This entails preliminary assessment of whether the reasoning or methodology underlying the testimony is scientifically valid and whether that reasoning or methodology properly can be applied to the facts in issue. We are confident that federal judges possess the capacity to undertake this review.[33]

In the *Joiner* case[34] which discussed about the admissibility of scientific evidence, Associate Justice Stephen Breyer, has

32 Dr. M.P. Kantak, Dr. M.S. Ghodkirekar & Dr. S.G. Perni, *Utility of Daubert Guidelines in India*, 26(3) JIAFM 110 (2004).

33 *Daubert* 509 US 591.

34 *General Electric* v *Joiner* 522 US 136 (1997).

offered the following observation on the role of science in court cases:

> "In this age of science, science should expect to find a warm welcome, perhaps a permanent home, in our courtrooms. The reason is a simple one. The legal disputes before us increasingly involve the principles and tools of science. Proper resolution of those disputes matters not just to the litigants, but also to the general public – those who live in our technologically complex society and whom the law must serve. Our decisions should reflect a proper scientific and technical understanding so that the law can respond to the needs of the public".[35]

Justice Breyer, also noted that federal judges typically are generalist, not specialists and few are having training or experience in science and technology.[36]

Chief Justice Rehnquist, in his opinion concurring in part and also dissenting in part from the majority opinion, was not less confident about the ability of the federal trial judiciary, but was less certain that the Court's ruling would provide them with the means to the job assigned. He observed: "The Court speaks of its confidence that federal judges can make a 'preliminary' assessment of whether the reasoning or methodology underlying the testimony is scientifically valid and of whether that reasoning or methodology properly can be applied to the facts in issue. The Court then states that a 'key question' to be answered in deciding whether something is 'scientific knowledge' 'will be whether it can be (and has been) tested.' Following this sentence are three quotations from treatises, which not only speak of empirical testing, but one of

35 Stephen Breyer, *Introduction to Reference Manual on Scientific Evidence*, 2nd Ed. 2000, pp. 1 & 2.

36 "[M]ost judges lack the scientific training that might facilitate the evaluation of scientific claims or the evaluation of expert witnesses who make such claims. Judges typically are generalists, dealing with cases that can vary widely in subject matter." Stephen Breyer, *Introduction to Reference Manual on Scientific Evidence*, 2nd Ed. 2000, pp. 1 & 4.

which states the 'criterion of the scientific status of a theory is its falsifiability, or refutability, or testability.' I defer to no one in my confidence in federal judges; but I am at a loss to know what is meant when it is said that the scientific status of a theory depends on its 'falsifiability,' and I suspect some of them will be, too. I do not doubt that Rule 702 confides to the judge the gatekeeping responsibility in deciding questions of the admissibility of proferred expert testimony. But I do not think it imposes on the either the obligation or the authority to become amateur scientist in order to perform that role".[37]

9 Laws on expert evidence in US

TABLE 3

Following are the laws regarding admissibility of expert evidence in criminal and civil cases.

Rule of Evidence	Summary
104(a)	This rule requires the trial judge to determine as a preliminary matter before the jury hears the evidence whether experts are qualified and whether their testimony will be admitted.
401	This rule defines what evidence is relevant in a case. It defines evidence as relevant if it has any tendency to make a fact that is material to the outcome of the case either more probable or less probable than it would have been without the evidence.
402	This rule prohibits the admission of evidence that is not relevant.
403	This rule allows the trial judge to exclude evidence that is relevant, if its probative value (its value in proving issues that determine the outcome of the case) is substantially outweighed by certain adverse consequences such as unfair prejudice, delay of the trial, confusion of the jury, or if the evidence is unnecessarily cumulative. It requires the judge to balance the positive qualities of the evidence against the inimical consequences of admitting it.

37 *Daubert* 509 US 600.

Rule of Evidence	Summary
702	This rule provides that scientific, technical or specialized evidence (i.e. "Expert testimony") may be admitted if: (a) the expert is qualified; (b) the expert's testimony will help the jury to decide issues in the case or understand the evidence; and (c) the expert's testimony is based on sufficient facts or data; is the product of reliable methods and principles, and if the expert reliably has applied the methods and principles to the facts of the case in trial.
703	This rule identifies the types of factual information that an expert witness may rely on to support an opinion. Included are facts perceived by the expert through her own study or research, facts provided to her by others (including the lawyer), or facts learned of by the expert from other witnesses during the trial. The rule allows the expert to base her opinion on information that is reliable to practitioners in his field, even if it is not admissible into evidence. (For example, a neuropsychologist may rely on a report by the patient's psychiatrist that might be inadmissible hearsay in forming opinions about the condition of a patient.) If the expert bases her opinion in whole or part on reliable but inadmissible facts, the trial judge must decide whether the jury is informed of these particular facts for the purpose of evaluating the weight to be given to the expert's testimony.
704	This rule allows the expert to express opinions about "ultimate facts"–those that determine which party will win or lose the case. Thus, an expert could express the opinion that a plaintiff's emotional injuries were caused by the harassing conduct of the defendant in an employment discrimination case.
705	This rule allows an expert to testify to the jury about her opinions without first stating all the facts that underlie them, unless the trial judge requires them to be disclosed. Note, however, that under Rule 104(a), the party offering the expert's testimony must already have demonstrated to the trial judge that

Rule of Evidence	Summary
	the expert's opinion was based on sufficient facts; otherwise, the expert would not be qualified to testify before the jury.
706	This rule allows the trial judge to retain an expert witness to act as a court expert, to help the judge deal with conflicts in expert evidence between the parties' experts.
1101(d)(1)	This rule allows the trial judge to disregard all rules of evidence except those dealing with privilege when deciding, outside the presence of the jury, whether to admit expert testimony.

The study of the laws reveals that, expert witnesses are only allowed to testify about subjects that are scientific, technical, or that involved specialized knowledge that is beyond the ability of the jury to understand on its own. The lawyers and experts should understand that Rule 702, as interpreted by the courts which outlines the methodology that the trial judge must follow for resolving challenges to admissibility of expert testimony. The trial judge is required to evaluate whether the expert opinion: (1) is based on sufficient facts or data; (2) was reached by the use of reliable methods and principles; (3) is the product of a reliable application of the methodology to the facts of the particular case. But to make the rulings, the trial judge is entirely dependent on the parties to furnish the information necessary to make the rulings which indirectly means that if the parties want to be successful, lawyers and experts need to be well-versed for providing particulars to the trial judge.[38]

10 Basics for admissibility

While deciding admissibility of expert evidence, the trial judge must look into whether the evidence is "relevant" to the issues in the case, "reliable" as outlined in *Daubert/Kumho Tire* and Rule 702, "helpful" to the jury, and "fit" the issues of the

38 B.S. Nabar, *Forensic Science in Crime Investigation*, 3rd Ed. 2002, p. 14 (Hyderabad: Asia Law House).

particular case.[39] Although they are separate concepts, but do sometimes overlap. A summary of each point is discussed hereunder:

TABLE 4

Relevance	Derived from Rule 401, this factor requires the court to insure that the expert's testimony will help prove or disprove an important fact or issue in the case.
Reliability	Refers to "evidentiary reliability", not "scientific reliability". Evidentiary reliability means trustworthiness, and is analogous to scientific validity.
Helpfulness	Whether the expert testimony will help the jury to understand the evidence and or decide issues of fact relating to the claims the parties have raised.
Fit	Whether the expert testimony relates to the facts and issues of the particular case at hand so that it will assist the jury in doing its job.

From 1923 to 1993, Frye "*general acceptance* test [was] the dominant standard for determining the admissibility of novel scientific evidence".[40] The test draws the line for admissibility based on whether the scientific principle underlying the evidence is accepted by a sufficient portion of the relevant scientific community:

> "Just when a scientific principle or discovery crosses the line between the experimental and demonstrable stages is difficult to define. Somewhere in this twilight zone the evidential force of the principle must be recognized, and while courts will go a long way in admitting expert testimony deduced from a well-recognized scientific principle or discovery, the thing from which the deduction is made must be sufficiently established to have gained general acceptance in the particular field in which it belongs."

39 *Daubert* 509 US at 589-91.
40 *Daubert* 509 US at 585.

In two subsequent cases, *General Electric Co.* v *Joiner*[41] and *Kumho Tire Co.* v *Caemichael,*[42] the Court broadened the reach of trial judges under *Daubert* by insulating their decisions from review, allowing them to consider conclusions instead of only methodology and extending the gatekeeping[43] role to non-scientific evidence.[44] In *joiner,* the Court held that appellate court should review trial judge's *Daubert* admissibility decisions under the abuse of discretion standard,[45] and it concluded that the trial court could exclude testimony based on disagreement with the experts' interpretations of studies, rather than with their methods alone, since "conclusion and methodology are not entirely distinct from one another".[46] In *Kumho Tire,* the court extended the *Daubert* analysis beyond scientific evidence to the "technical" and other specialized knowledge also referenced in Rule 702.[47] The Court supported this conclusion by noting the lack of distinctions made in the statutory language, the equal grant of latitude in testimony to non-scientific experts, and the difficulty of distinguishing between "scientific" and "technical" or "other specialized" knowledge.[48] The most recent development in federal admissibility analysis is the amendment of Rule 702 in 2000.

The Supreme Court emphasized that the factors in *Daubert* are neither exclusive nor entirely dispositive of whether or not the testimony at issue should be admitted. Subsequent decisions have recognized that not all the specific *Daubert* factors can apply to every form of expert testimony.[49] For

41 522 US 136 (1997).

42 526 US 137 (1999).

43 "Gatekeeping" means the federal courts act as stainers.

44 *Admitting Doubt: A New Standard For Scientific Evidence* [2010] 123 Harv L Rev 2021.

45 *Joiner* 522 US 139.

46 *Ibid,* at 146.

47 *Kumho Tire* 526 US 141 (internal quotation marks omitted).

48 *Ibid,* at 147-148 (internal quotation marks omitted).

49 Elliott R Feldman, *Criteria for Admissibility of Expert Opinion Testimony under Daubert and Its Progeny* available at http://www.cozen.com/admin/files/publications/feldman1537289.pdf 2 (last visited on 17th June 2015).

instance, lack of peer review or publication is deemed unimportant where the opinion is supported by "widely accepted scientific knowledge".[50]

A review of the case law after *Daubert* shows that the rejection of expert testimony is the exception rather than the rule. When a trial court, rules that an expert's testimony is reliable, it does not necessarily mean that contradictory expert testimony is unreliable rather it permits testimony that is the product of competing principles or methods in the same field of expertise. Expert testimony cannot be excluded simply because the expert uses one test rather than another, when both tests are accepted in the field and both reach reliable results.[51] The court in *Daubert* declared that the "focus", of course, must be solely on principles and methodology, not on the conclusions they generate.[52] Nonetheless, the Court later recognized, "conclusions and methodology are not entirely distinct from one another".[53] Under the amendment, as under *Daubert*, when an expert purports to apply principles and methods in accordance with professional standards, and yet reaches a conclusion that other experts in the field would not reach, the trial court may fairly suspect that the principles and methods have not been faithfully applied.[54] The amendment specifically provides that the trial court must scrutinize not only the principles and methods used by the expert, but also whether those principles and methods have been properly applied to the facts of the case. As the court noted "any step that renders the analysis unreliable renders the expert's testimony inadmissible. This is true whether the step completely changes a reliable methodology or merely misapplies that methodology".[55]

50 *Kannankeril* v *Terminix, International, Inc.* 128 F3d 802, 809 (3d Cir 1997).

51 *Heller* v *Shaw Industries, Inc.* 167 F3d 146, 160 (3d Cir 1999).

52 *Daubert* 509 US 595.

53 *General Elec. Co.* v *Joiner* 522 US 136, 146 (1997).

54 *Lust* v *Merrell Dow Pharmaceuticals, Inc.* 89 F3d 594, 598 (9th Cir 1996).

55 In re *Paoli R.R. Yard PCB Litigation* 35 F3d 717, 745 (3d Cir 1994).

If the expert purports to apply principles and methods to the facts of the case, it is important that this application be conducted reliably. Yet it might also be important in some cases for an expert to educate the fact finder about general principles, without ever attempting to apply these principles to the specific facts of the case. For example, experts might instruct the fact finder on the principles of thermodynamics, or blood clotting, or without ever knowing about or trying to tie their testimony into the facts of the case. The amendment does not alter the venerable practice of using expert testimony to educate the fact finder on general principles. For this kind of generalized testimony, Rule 702 simply requires that: (1) the expert be qualified; (2) the testimony address a subject matter on which the fact finder can be assisted by an expert; (3) the testimony be reliable; and (4) the testimony "fit" the facts of the case.[56]

11 Principles of admitting scientific evidence in United Kingdom (UK/EU)

In England, the law dealing with the admissibility of scientific evidence is totally different from United States. The English precedential analysis shows that judges are reluctant to impose any stringent standards like 'reliability' test in U.S. The English courts are still following the traditional common law test "helpfulness" developed by Lawton, LJ. in the famous case *R.* v *Turner*.[57] The four requirements of admissibility of expert opinion in England and Wales (common law) countries are (i) assistance (ii) relevant expertise (iii) impartiality and (iv) evidentiary reliability.

11.1 Assistance

The meaning of "Assistance" was explained by the leading case of *Turner*[57] that an opinion of expert "is admissible to furnish the court with ... information which is likely to be outside the

56 Rule 702. Testimony by Expert Witness available at https://www.law.cornell.edu/rules/fre/rule_702 (last visited on 19th January 2015).

57 *R* v *Turner* [1975] QB 834.

experience and knowledge of a judge or jury. If on the proven facts a judge or jury can form their own conclusions without help, then an opinion of an expert is unnecessary".[58] In other words if the opinion of the expert is unnecessary, it becomes inadmissible.[59]

11.2 Relevant expertise

The person claiming expertise must be an expert in the relevant field. This point has been explained in the South Australian case *Bonython.*[60] According to the explanation, expertise is a requirement that an individual "has acquired by study or experience sufficient knowledge of the subject to render his [her] opinion of value". This description has also been favoured in England and Wales. In *R (Doughty)* v *Ely Magistrates Court*[61] it has been suggested that the entry for representing expertise is not very high. The interpretation of threshold can be thus: First, the entry point should not be lower than what is required to prove a fact on the balance of probabilities. Secondly, laymen are not qualified to give some types of expert evidence. Thirdly, guidelines for determining expertise which are formulated for scientific fields must be followed.[62]

11.3 Impartiality

The evidence that is presented by the expert should be unbiased and purposive evidence. In *Field* v *Leeds City Council,*[63] Lord Woolf, the Master of the Rolls, said an expert to be "qualified to give evidence as an expert" he or she must be able to provide an objective, unbiased opinion on the matters to which his or her evidence relates. In *Tooth* v *Jarman,*[64] expert

58 *R* v *Turner, Ibid,* at 841.
59 *R* v *Mohan* [1994]2 SCR 9, 10f (Canadian Supreme Court).
60 *Bonython* [1984]38 SASR 45.
61 *R (Doughty)* v *Ely Magistrates Court* [2008] EWHC 522.
62 *Henderso* [2010] EWCA Crim 1269; [2010] 2 Cr App R 24 (medical experts) and *Weller* [2010] EWCA Crim 1085 (experts on DNA).
63 *Field* v *Leeds City Council* [2000]1 EGLR 54.
64 *Tooth* v *Jarman* [2006] EWCA Civ 1028; [2006]4 All ER 1276.

evidence was recognized by the Court of Appeal (Civil Division) where it was held that expert evidence should provide independent assistance to the court by way of objective unbiased opinion and that where an expert witness has a material or significant conflict of interest, the court is likely to decline to act on his/her evidence, or indeed to give permission for his/her evidence to be adduced. This common law admissibility requirement has been incorporated in Rule 33.2 of the Criminal Procedure Rules 2010. It provides that an expert has an overriding duty to give opinion evidence which is objective and unbiased.

11.4 Evidentiary reliability

The expert opinion evidence must in other respects satisfy a threshold (entry) of acceptable reliability. Except these some common law admissibility requirements has also been quoted by the Court of Appeal (Criminal Division) in different cases. They may be summed up as follows:

In *Dallagher*,[65] it was laid that the field of expertise must be sufficiently well established to pass the ordinary tests of relevance and reliability.

In *Bonython*,[66] the admissibility of expert opinion evidence was cited although in England and Wales, it had not been properly analyzed.

In *Gilfoyle*,[67] a particular type of reliability test had been suggested.

In *Bonython*,[68] this admissibility requirement was described as being "whether the subject matter of the [expert's] opinion forms part of a body of knowledge or experience which is sufficiently organized or recognized to be accepted as a reliable body of knowledge or experience. The common law reliability

65 *Dallagher* [2002] EWCA Crim 1903; [2003]1 Cr App R 12.
66 [1984]38 SASR 45.
67 *Gilfoyle* (No 2) [2001]2 Cr App R 5.
68 [1984]38 SASR 45.

test was confirmed by the court of appeals in *Reed*,[69] for "expert evidence for a scientific nature" but the court did not move from the established position that there is no enhanced reliability test for such evidence. In *Weller*,[70] the Court of Appeal recognized the common law reliability test for evidence of a scientific nature. Here the Court of Appeal referred that it is the trial judge's function to determine whether there is a sufficiently reliable scientific basis for [scientific] expert evidence.

12 Relationship among the four admissibility test

The first limb, i.e. "Assistance" of the common law admissibility test known as "The Turner Test" ensures that the expert evidence should only be admitted when it has sufficient probative value, which means that the evidence must help the court to resolve a disputed issue. The second limb, i.e. "Relevant Expertise" and third limb, "Impartiality" is to confirm that such expert evidence is admitted in criminal proceedings when a minimum threshold of general reliability which is called "reliability in the round" is satisfied. The fourth limb known as "Evidentiary Reliability" is meant to deal with matters underneath the expert's opinion, such as his/her soundness over the field of expertise and methodology and the validity of any assumptions relied on.

12.1 Opinion evidence and evidence of fact

In UK Expert Evidence has been distinguished as two types: One is called (i) Opinion Evidence, and the other is (ii) Evidence of fact. Much of the expert evidence is heavily based on opinion, therefore special rules are required to ensure that it is to inform rather than mislead, particularly in criminal trials dominated by expert evidence. However, an expert witness may be called to give expert evidence of fact. When an expert is called to give an explanation of how an unusual piece of machinery operates, or evidence of a reading provided by an instrument or a

69 *Reed* [2009] EWCA Crim 2698; [2010]1 Cr App R 23.
70 *Weller* [2010] EWCA Crim 1085.

symptom which was observed when a patient was examined. These are called evidence of fact as fact also means truth. If such factual evidence is required by the court, the first three limbs of the common law test must be applied in the same way as the limbs are applied to opinion evidence. The witness giving expert evidence of fact should provide such evidence to the court only if the court requires the expert's assistance or help, the witness is an expert in the relevant field and the evidence provided by the witness is unbiased. Although in the case of *Meads*[71] the expert "Evidence of Fact" is not covered by the common law rules summarized above but in "Phipson on *Evidence*"[72] it is stated to prefer the "Evidence of Fact" as expert evidence where level of expertise required was of a very low order.

13 Background of the Law Commissions Report

It was found that the current law on admissibility of expert opinion evidence was unsatisfactory because in England a *laissez-faire* attitude exist in relation to evidentiary reliability.[73] The expert opinion evidence was admitted without adequate scrutiny because no clear test was being applied to determine whether the evidence is sufficiently reliable to be admitted. This problem was aggravated in two ways:

(1) First, the judges lacked experience particularly in scientific evidence so the possibility is that they either stick to the opinions of experts or may defer from the opinion.

(2) Secondly, the advocates were unable to cross-examine the experts effectively in absence of a clear text to ensure the reliability of expert opinion to unveil the potential flaws in the expert's methodology, data and

71 *Meads* [1996] Criminal Law Review 519.

72 17th Ed. 2010, paras 33-19.

73 V.R. Dinkar, *Scientific Expert Evidence*, 2nd Ed., pp. 172-173 (Kolkata: Eastern Law House).

reasoning. Juries may therefore base their decision on the basis of unreliable decision.[74]

So, for the purpose of promoting the reform of law in admissibility of expert evidence in criminal trials, the Law Commission of England and Wales had set up by s. 1 of the Law Commissions Act 1965, published a Consultation Paper on 7th April 2009,[75] to address the problems associated with the admissibility and understanding of expert evidence in criminal trials. It was the first publication of the commission relating to this field of law. It was recommended by the Committee of the Law Commission that the Forensic Science Advisory Council, judges, scientists and other key players in the criminal justice system should work together to develop a new test for determining the admissibility of expert evidence in criminal proceedings.

Encouraged by the previous Parliament (House of Commons Science and Technology Committee report of 29th March 2005 "Forensic Science on Trial"), the Law Commission published in March 2011 the report "Expert evidence in criminal proceedings in England and Wales" (Law Com No. 325).[76] The Law Commission report was largely based on a public consultation conducted in April-July 2009 and on the Forensic Science on Trial Report and used examples of four high profile appeal cases involving unreliable or conflicting expert evidence (*Dallagher*[77] – ear prints; *Clark*[78] and

74 *Law Commission Reforming the Law: Expert Evidence in Criminal Proceedings in England and Wales*, 2011 available at http://lawcommission.justice.gov.uk/areas/expert-evidence-in-criminal-trials.htm (last visited on 21st January 2015).

75 Law Commission Consultation Paper No. 190 (2009) available at http://www.lawcom.gov.uk/wp-content/uploads/2015/03/cp190_Expert_Evidence_Consultation.pdf (last visited on 21st January 2015).

76 Elliott R Feldman, *Criteria for Admissibility of Expert Opinion Testimony under Daubert and Its Progeny* available at http://www.cozen.com/admin/files/publications/feldman1537289.pdf 2 (last visited on 17th June 2015).

77 *R* v *Dallagher* [2002] EWCA Crim 1903.

78 *R* v *Clark* [2003] EWCA Crim 1020.

Cannings[79] – sudden infant death syndrome; and *Harris* and others[80] – shaken baby syndrome).

In short the Law Commission's key recommendations were:

(a) To introduce a statutory admissibility test, to be applied in appropriate cases, whereby expert opinion is admissible in criminal proceedings only if it is sufficiently reliable to be admitted ("the reliability test");

(b) To provide, by statute, judges with a single list of basic factors to help them apply the reliability test;

(c) To codify (with slight modifications) the uncontroversial aspects of the present law, so that all the admissibility requirements for expert evidence would be set out in a single Act of Parliament and carry equal authority.

14 Principles of admitting scientific evidence by German courts

TABLE 5

The German Code of Criminal Procedure is termed as StPO.[81] Let us study the laws at a glance:

Sections	Content
81a [Physical Examination; Blood Test]	(1) A physical examination of the accused may be ordered for the purposes of establishing facts which are of importance for the proceedings. For this purpose, the taking of blood samples and other bodily intrusions which are effected by a physician in accordance with the rules of medical science for the purpose of examination shall be admissible without the consent of the accused, provided no detriment to his health is to be expected.

79 *R* v *Cannings* [2004] EWCA Crim 1.

80 *R* v *Harris* [2005] EWCA Crim 1980.

81 Code of Criminal Procedure in the version published on 7th April 1987 (Federal Law Gazette [Bundergesetzblatt] Part I, p. 1074, 1319), as most recently amended by Article 3 of the Act, 23rd April 2014 (Federal Law Gazette, Part I, p. 410) [StrafprozeBordnung:stop] available at http://www.ohchr.org/Documents/Issues/Opinion/Protection/Germany.pdf (last visited on 21st January 2015).

Sections	Content
	(2) The authority to give such order shall be vested in the judge and, if a delay would endanger the success of the examination, also in the public prosecution office including the officials assisting it (section 152 of the Courts Constitution Act).
	(3) Blood samples or other body cells taken from the accused may be used only for the purposes of the criminal proceedings for which they were taken or in other criminal proceedings pending; they shall be destroyed without delay as soon as they are no longer required for such purposes.
Section 81b [Photographs and Finger prints]	Photographs and fingerprints of the accused may be taken, even against his will, and measurements may be made of him and other similar measures taken with regard to him insofar as is required for the purposes of conducting the criminal proceedings or of the police records department.
Section 81g [DNA Analysis]	(1) If the accused person is suspected of a criminal offence of substantial significance or of a crime against sexual self-determination then, for the purposes of establishing identity in future criminal proceedings, cell tissue may be collected from him and subjected to molecular and genetic examination for the purposes of establishing the DNA profile or the gender if the nature of the offence or the way it was committed, the personality of the accused or other information provide grounds for assuming that criminal proceedings will be conducted against him in future in respect of a criminal offence of substantial significance. If the person concerned habitually commits other criminal offences, this may be deemed to be equivalent to a criminal offence of substantial significance by reference to the level of the injustice done.
	(2) The cell tissue collected may be used only for the molecular and genetic examination referred to in sub-section (1); it shall be destroyed without delay once it is no longer required for that purpose. Information other than that required in order to establish the DNA profile or the gender may not be ascertained during the

Sections	Content
	examination; tests to establish such information shall be inadmissible. (3) Without the written consent of the person concerned, the collection of cell tissue may be ordered only by the court and, in exigent circumstances, by the public prosecution office including the officials assisting it (section 152 of the Courts Constitution Act). Without the written consent of the person concerned, the molecular and genetic examination of cell tissue may be ordered only by the court. Persons who have consented are to be instructed as to the purpose for which the data to be obtained will be used. Section 81f, sub-section (2) shall apply *mutatis mutandis*. In its written reasons the court shall specify in relation to the particular case concerned— (a) The determining facts relevant to ascertaining the seriousness of the criminal offence. (b) The information giving rise to the assumption that the accused will be the subject of criminal proceedings in the future. (c) An evaluation of the relevant circumstances in each case. (4) Sub-sections (1) to (3) shall apply *mutatis mutandis* if the person concerned has been convicted of the offence with binding effect or was not convicted merely on the grounds that— (a) Lack of criminal responsibility has been proven or cannot be ruled out, (b) He is unfit to stand trial on the grounds of insanity, or (c) Lack of criminal responsibility has been proven or cannot be ruled out (section 3 of the Youth Courts Act); and the corresponding entry in the Federal Central Criminal Register or the Youth Register has not yet expired or been deleted. (5) The data collected may be stored at the Federal Criminal Police Office and used in accordance with the

Sections	Content
	Federal Criminal Police Office Act. The same shall apply— (a) subject to the conditions listed in sub-section (1), to the data obtained pursuant to section 81e, sub-section (1), in respect of an accused person, as well as; (b) to the data obtained pursuant to section 81e, sub-section (2). The data may be transmitted only for the purposes of criminal proceedings, for threat prevention and for international mutual legal assistance in respect thereof. In the case of number 1 of the second sentence, the accused is to be informed without delay that the data has been stored, and is to be instructed that he may apply for a court decision.
Section 85 [Expert Witnesses]	The provisions concerning evidence by witnesses shall apply if experienced persons have to be examined to prove past facts or conditions the observation of which required special professional knowledge.
Section 91 [Suspected Poisoining]	(1) Where poisoning is suspected, the suspicious substance(s) found in the corpse or elsewhere shall be examined by a chemist or by a specialist authority appointed for such examination. (2) It may be ordered that this examination be performed with the assistance, or under the direction, of a physician.

The court in principle in Germany has to choose an expert accredited by a public-law body at State level. The body known as 'Kammern' maintains a register of such experts who are appointed to avoid future problems in appointment of suitable expert in specific area. However, the court may also choose experts outside the experts those who have registered with the 'Kammern' according to the situation and circumstances, in practice which happens very frequently.[82] Experts are also retained by the public prosecutor in the preliminary judicial

82 Section 73 StPO.

investigation. A request can be made by the defendant at the trial hearing, that the expert witness be allowed to furnish evidence. Such request of the defendant cannot be dismissed if the expert witness the defendant wanted to call is manifestly more knowledgeable than the expert retained by the court.[83] An expert can also be challenged by the defendant on different grounds laid in the law.[84] Before the expert is accredited by a 'Kammern' he must go through a selection procedure which covers his personal and professional ability to draft reports and tests whether the candidate has an above-average level of expertise. Accredation is given for five years. Accredited experts are subject to regular screening by the Kammern for which they are registered. As long as they meet the criteria, their accreditation can be extended. The most frequently applied criteria are an above average level of expertise in a specific field, the skills to draw up an expert report and the requirements of impartiality and independence. However, all expertise are found among accredited experts. The German Federal Criminal Office and the various State Criminal Offices have a high level of expertise in specific fields, such as DNA analysis. In Germany expert registrations are not linked to criminal procedure.[85]

The principles of admissibility of expert evidence in Germany are suitability of experts in the specific area. German evidentiary proceedings are governed by the principles of free evaluation of the evidence.[86] With few statutory exceptions both the admission and weighing of evidence are within the discretion of the court. In accordance with the principles of free evaluation of the evidence, German courts do not follow certain evidentiary rules adhered to by the courts in the United States. For example, hearsay evidence is admissible in German

83 Section 244 StPO.

84 Section 74 StPO.

85 Experts and expert registers in Europe. The national and the international level available at: http://www.egalresearchnetwork.eu/.../PaperBerendKeulenNicoKwakmanGroningen (last visited on 16th June 2015).

86 ZPO § 286.

courts and it is up to the court to determine whether or not the evidence is convincing. The 'opinion rule' which precludes the factual statement by lay witnesses and the 'best evidence rule' requiring original documentation to prove the contents of writing is not applicable in German Courts. In Germany judges play an active role in selection of evidence and the court's judgment on the question of admissibility is final. Mostly, expert opinions are submitted to the court in writing. When it is required, the court calls the expert into the court for a hearing to investigate specific aspects of expert's opinion. Through this system of active role of courts demonstrates the more integrated evidentiary proceedings before the German Courts, allocating more responsibility and initiative to the court than the U.S. System.[87]

15 DNA evidence in Germany

The taking of blood samples for genetic fingerprinting or DNA analysis was not recognized in Germany until March 1997. The Code of Criminal Procedure (StPO) allowed the taking of blood samples from a suspect for the purpose of criminal proceeding. Originally s. 81a of StPO was mainly used to establish the blood alcohol level of the accused in cases of traffic offences or to ascertain criminal responsibility at the time of crime or sometimes to ascertain the suspect's competence to stand trial as well. The study of s. 81a of the StPO reveals that the purpose for which blood could be taken is not specified, therefore the taking of blood samples in order to obtain genetic fingerprints was widely regarded as lawful among the police community. Although, the Federal Supreme Court and Federal Constitutional Court acknowledged section 81a as sufficient legal grounds for the taking of blood samples for DNA analysis in criminal proceedings, issues of constitutional law, as well as criminal law were raised from various sectors. The draft amendment of the Code of Criminal Procedure, dated 2nd

87 Burkhard Bastuck and Burbard Gopfert, *Admission and Presentation of Evidence in Germany* 16 Loy LA Int'l & CompL Rev 609 (1994).

March 1995 improved the apprehension as it explicitly addressed the problem. The draft referred to a discussion paper submitted by the Federal Ministry of Justice on 20th December 1989 and a later draft by the Federal Ministry of Justice of November 1991, taking into account a commentary by the Federal Data Protection Authority in May 1991. The Parliamentary Group of the Social-Democrats of Germany (SPD) has had proposed its own draft code. On 6th December, 1996, StVAG 1997, was passed, which was based on the previous drafts by the Federal Ministry of Justice and the SPD, but was ultimately rejected as it did not expressly prohibit the establishment of gene databanks. Subsequently, the Parliamentary Act, that changed the existing system and the Administrative Offences Act, finally came into effect in March 1997.[88]

16 Principles of admitting scientific evidence by Indian courts

In India the principles of admissibility of evidence is relevancy. According to the Indian Evidence Act 1872, section 45, deals with expert evidence. The principles of admissibility in Indian courts are that evidence can be given only of relevant facts and facts in issue. A fact may be relevant but not admissible, like in case of documentary evidence, only under certain circumstances secondary evidence of a document can be produced. If it does not satisfy the legislative provision, although a document might be relevant but it would not be admissible. It might also happen that a document or an expert report might be admissible as it is an original one or otherwise but since it is not relevant, such evidence is not accepted by courts. Therefore, in India, the principle for accepting forensic evidence is relevant and admissible. Under, the broad principles of 'relevancy'comes reliability, helpfulness, fitness which are treated as separate grounds in US. Assistance, relevant expertise, impartiality and evidentiary reliability which

88 Jyotirmoy Adhikary, *DNA Technology in Administration of Justice*, Edition 2007, pp. 178-180 (New Delhi: LexisNexis Butterworths).

are the principles for admission of expert evidence in UK, also comes under the requirement of 'relevancy'. In India, the law regarding expert evidence is guided by sections 45 to 51 of the Indian Evidence Act 1872. In the case of *Mahmood* v *State of U.P.*[89] the Supreme Court has defined the term expert and said that it would be highly unsafe to convict a person on the sole testimony of an expert. Although conviction based on expert evidence is unsafe, yet the incorporation of ss. 53 and 53A of the Code of Criminal Procedure 1973, mandates that in certain cases the expert evidence is indispensible. In *Selvi* v *State of Karnataka*,[90] the Supreme Court held that compulsory administration of forensic techniques like polygraphy, Narco-analysis and Brain-Mapping is unconstitutional if performed without the consent of the accused as it violates Art. 20(3) and Art. 21 of the Constitution of India.[91]

89 AIR 1976 SC 69.

90 (2010)7 SCC 263.

91 Article 20(3) prohibits self incrimination and Art. 21 guarantees right to life and personal liberty.

Chapter 2

Deoxyribonucleic Acid (DNA)

1 Introduction

"DNA" means Deoxyribonucleic Acid.[1] The term DNA called the building block or genetic blueprint of life, was first described by the scientists Francis H.C. Crick and James D. Watson in 1953. Both of them identified the double helix structure of DNA, which resembles a twisted ladder and established the role of DNA as the material that makes up the genetic code of living organisms. It is the basic genetic material in all the living cells of the body. It is contained in white blood corpuscles and not in red blood corpuscles. Hence the DNA structure determines human character, behavior and body characteristics. Each individual, consequently, is unique and is different from all others. In monozygotic twins, DNA structure is the same because they come forth by the division of a single fertilized egg. Monozygotic twins are generally identical.[2] Therefore, DNA profiling technique is used to identify the criminals through the means of criminal investigations. Sir Allec Jeffrey discovered the method of identifying individuals from DNA in 1984 and the UK police first used forensic DNA profiling in 1985. Forensic use of DNA technology in criminal cases began first time in 1987 when

1 Section 2(g) of the Human DNA Profiling Bill 2015.

2 B.R. Sharma, *Forensic Science in Criminal Investigation & Trial*, 4th Ed. 2003, p. 1123.

police asked Dr. Alec J. Jeffrey to verify a suspect's confession that he was responsible for the two rape-murders in the English Midlands.[3]

Although, DNA profiling technique is recognized by law,[4] there is no regulating body which can supervise the method used for DNA profiling. Neither there is any regulation which could be followed to maintain a standard of conformation while implementing the technique which is in existence. Therefore, the Human DNA Profiling Bill 2015 has been drafted for the following purposes:

(i) To regulate the use of Deoxyribonucleic Acid analysis of human body substances for the purpose of making profiles;

(ii) For the establishment of the DNA Profiling Board;

(iii) To lay down the standards for laboratories, collection of human body substances, custody trial for collection to reporting;

(iv) To establish a National DNA data bank and for matters connected therewith and incidental thereto.

Although the Human DNA Bill 2015 has been drafted but the Bill is yet to be passed by the Parliament as debates have been raised on its consequences. One of the points of debate was the privacy issues as DNA analysis offers sensitive information which if misused can cause harm to the person or society and therefore regulation of the Act is required through another Act passed by Parliament. Irrespective of the pending legal formalities to be incorporated still it is astonishing to see that DNA profiling is used by the prosecution in criminal cases and cases for determination of paternity. Moreover, study of various judgments of Supreme Court and

3 Marvin D'Souza & R.P. Kataria, *Forensic Science in Criminal Trial & Investigation*, 2016, p. 80. See Kelly, K.F. J.J. Rankin and R.C. Wink, *Methods and Applications of DNA Fingerprinting: A Guide for the Non-Scientist*, Criminal Law Review, 1987, p. 105 (108). Note, *Stemming the DNA Tide: A Case for Quality Control Guidelines*, Hamline Law Review, (1992)16, pp. 211, 231-214.

4 Section 53A of CrPC.

High Court reveals the importance and the indispensible character of DNA evidence to point the guilt of the accused. In rape cases it has been directed by the Supreme Court to opt for DNA Profiling Test which would help the prosecution to prove.[5]

In February 2009, the prestigious National Academy of Sciences (NAS) of United States, issued a long-awaited report on forensic sciences which concluded: "With the exception of DNA analysis, no forensic method has been rigorously shown to have the capacity to consistently, and with a high degree of certainty, demonstrate a connection between evidence and a specific individual or source."[6] Although forensic science can lead to erroneous convictions and sometimes are not dependable. But scientists have come to the conclusion that DNA typing[7] is the New Model for Scientific Forensic Identification. During the past decade thousands of people who were convicted of heinous crimes and were sentenced to death had been exonerated by DNA analysis.

2 DNA fingerprinting

DNA is the most important chemical compound of living organisms; it is the blueprint of life carrying hereditary information from generation to generation. It carries all the important information for controlling all the biological activities like growth, cell division and protein synthesis. DNA is a nucleic acid which is composed of nucleotides. Nucleotide is a complete unit of nucleic acid which is chemically made up of phosphate (phosphoric acid), pentose sugar and nitrogenous base. Gene is a functional fragment of DNA nucleotide capable of synthesizing a specific protein and acting

5 *Krishan Kumar Malik* v *State of Haryana* (2011)7 SCC 130.

6 A Path Forward: Where are We Now? available at http://wispd.org/attachments/article/246/A%20Path%20Forward-Where%20Are%20We%20Now%20Article.pdf (Last visited on 16th May 2015).

7 DNA profiling (also called DNA testing, DNA typing, or genetic fingerprinting) is a technique employed by forensic scientists to assist in the identification of individuals by their respective DNA profiles.

as the unit of inheritance. Chromosomes are self-reduplicating nucleoprotein filaments composed of hereditary units called genes.[8] Therefore, an unit of chromosome is DNA and an unit of DNA is gene. DNA is unique in every individual, for which it is used as a means for identification. One of the distinguishing features of DNA is that it is also identical in all cells of a human being. DNA of an individual remain in his or her skin cell, hair follicles, muscles, semen, samples from buccal swabs, saliva or other body parts. This becomes an advantage of DNA Typing in Forensic Cases. So, the forensic scientist can use any of the biological samples recovered from the crime scenes. There are a few exceptions. For example, our red blood cells lack DNA. A strand of DNA is made up of tiny building-blocks which are also known as "bases". There are only four, different basic building-blocks. Scientists usually refer to these using four letters, A, T, G and C. These four letters are short nicknames for more complicated building-block chemical names A-Adenine T-Thymine G-Guanine C- Cytosine. The order in which the four bases appear in an individual's DNA determines his or her physical makeup. Since DNA is a double-stranded molecule, it is composed of two specific paired bases, A-T or T-A and G-C or C-G. The sequence of the paired bases is due to the characteristics of the base pairs where adenine only pair with thymine and *vice versa* whereas cytosine only pairs with guanine and *vice versa*. There are no chances of pairing of Adenine and Cytosine or Thymine and Guanine. The pairing leads to the formation of "genes". Every gene has a certain number of the above base pairs distributed in a particular sequence. The sequential arrangement of the individual nucleotides is responsible for giving uniqueness to each individual. This gives a person his genetic code. However, somewhere in the DNA framework, there are sections that differ. The sections that differ are known as 'polymorphic loci'[9]

8 Arup Kumar Mitra, Sailesh Guha, Sumantra Chanda, *A Text Book of Biology*, 4th Ed. 2007, pp. 178, 186, 187, 286.

9 A locus is simply a location in the DNA. The plural of locus is loci. A locus is simply a location in the DNA. Such locations, or loci, reside at specific places on chromosomes.

and are analyzed in DNA Typing. DNA Typing is also called DNA Profiling, DNA Test, DNA Fingerprinting, DNA Analysis or even Genetic Test or Genetic Fingerprinting. Therefore, DNA typing simply means determining the "polymorphic loci".

In other words, DNA fingerprinting in genetics is the method of isolating and making images of sequences of DNA. This technique was developed in 1984 by the British geneticist Dr. Alec J. Jeffrey, after he noticed the existence of certain sequences of DNA called 'minisatellites' that do not contribute to the function of a gene but are repeated within the gene. Dr. Alec Jeffrey also determined that each organism has a unique pattern of these minisatellites except in identical twins.

2.1 Mechanisms used for the DNA fingerprinting technique

DNA evidence has made the most significant contribution in the world on criminal investigations. The matching of DNA profiles by comparing it with a specimen obtained from a crime scene with one obtained from the database of suspect is the most common technique used in criminal investigations[10]. Sir Alec Jeffrey, in 1984 accidentally invented the DNA Fingerprinting method when he used restriction enzymes to identify and classify "microsatellites" called 'Variable Number Tandem Repeats' (VNTR) while was doing his research. VNTR are composed of a stretch of nucleotides which are repeated in parallel, the "core set" of repeated nucleotides[11] can be 15-20 base pairs long. Therefore, using a technique called 'Restriction Fragment Length Polymorphism' (RFLP), Jeffrey was able to demonstrate that VNTR are different from one individual to the next (except in the case of identical twins) and that this pattern was consistent in somatic cells, which meant that any type of cell (except for egg and sperm cell) could

10 Marcus Smith, Monique Mann, *Recent Developments in DNA Evidence*, 11, Australian Institute of Criminology, 56 (2015) available at http://www.aic.gov.au/publications/current%20series/tandi/501-520/tandi506.html, last visited on 21st January 2015.

11 Complete unit of nucleic acid which is chemically made up phosphate, pentose sugar and nitrogenous base. Eg. Adenine, guanine, cytosine and thymine.

be used to carry out the technique and produce the same result.[12]

There have been various modes of Forensic DNA testing according to the various sequence or segments of the components available in the DNA. They are often called RFLP, PCR, STR etc. testing. In RFLP the fragments of DNA are separated according to their various sizes, in STR the components are separated according to its short repeating sequence. Generally, RFLP testing requires larger amounts of DNA and the DNA must be undegraded. Crime-scene evidence that is old or that is present in small amounts is often unsuitable for RFLP testing. Warm moist conditions may accelerate DNA degradation rendering it unsuitable for RFLP in a relatively short period of time.

2.1.1 RFLP (Restriction Fragment Length Polymorphism) process

For the purpose of DNA profiling, DNA is first extracted from a specimen by an elaborate chemical process, which is then mixed with a special enzyme called "restriction endonucleasis" which functions as molecular scissors to cut the DNA at specific sites. This technique of analysis is known as Restriction Fragment Length Polymorphism (RFLP). The restricted fragments are then separated according to size using gel electrophoresis technique. Then the DNA fragments are transferred from the gel to a nylon membrane, which process is called as "Southern Blotting". This is followed by a hybridisation process, which involves bringing in contact a radioactive labelled probe. The probe bound fragments, being radioactive, can then be recorded on an X-ray plate, which process is known as autoradiography. The X-ray plate will show dark bands appearing very much like bar code. In nutshell, this is a process of DNA profiling. The comparison of the bands in the DNA profiles of different specimen from the same individual will show similarity, whereas DNA specimen of two different individuals will show different DNA band profiles. The following steps are followed in the process:

12 Marvin D'Souza, R.P. Kataria, *Forensic Science in Criminal Trial & Investigation*, p. 93.

- First, extraction and purification of DNA from specimen.
- Secondly, fragmentation of DNA using "restriction enzyme".
- Thirdly, arranging the fragments on the basis of their length by agarose gel electrophoresis.
- Fourthly, transfer of separated fragments to nylon membrane by "Southern Blotting".
- Fifthly, hybridisation with a radioactive labelled probe.
- Sixthly, visualising the bands of DNA by autoradiography.
- Seventhly, interpretation of results and statistical conclusion.

2.1.2 PCR (Polymerase Chain Reaction) technique

Recently, another technique known as "Polymerase Chain Reaction" (PCR) has been developed for DNA profiling. This method is specifically recommended where DNA is insufficient (as little as 50 molecules) for analysis or it is in degraded form. The PCR technique takes into account polymorphic DNA segments present in the specimen and by polymerase chain reaction (PCR) produce multiple copies of a particular polymorphic DNA segment, sufficient to meet the requirements of DNA profiling test.[13] Once a sufficient sample has been produced the pattern of alleles from a limited number of genes is compared with the pattern from reference sample. Although a non-match is conclusive through this technique but the technique provided less certainty when a match occurs.[14]

2.1.3 STR (Short Tandem Repeats) technique

Repetitive sections of DNA are called Short Tandem Repeats (STR) which varies between individuals. A DNA profile may also be created by analyzing the number of STR's that occur at specific points in an individual's DNA. STRs are the type of DNA used in most of the currently popular forensic DNA tests. STR is a generic term that describes any short, repeating DNA

13 B.R. Sharma, *Forensic Science in Criminal Investigation & Trial*, 4th Ed. 2003, pp. 351, 352.

14 DNA Fingerprinting available at http://www.infoplease.com/encyclopedia/science/dna-fingerprinting-methods.html.

sequence. For example, the DNA sequence ATATATATATAT is an STR that has a repeating motif consisting of two bases, A and T. It turns out that our DNA has a variety of STRs scattered among DNA sequences that encode cellular functions. For reasons that are not entirely understood, people vary from one another in the number of repeats they have, at least for some STR loci. For example, person #1 may have ATATAT at a particular locus while person #2 may have ATATATATATAT. Thus, STRs are often variable (polymorphic) and these variations are used to try and distinguish people. The term, STR doesn't necessarily imply PCR. PCR is one of many methods that might be used to help to analyze STR's. The PCR technique can be used to amplify STR Typing with highly polymorphic DNA sequences of repeating 2-7 base pairs. These STR loci are considered polymorphic due to being unique to each individual. In particular, 5-10 alleles[15] of particular STRs are often the focus of forensic profiling. The amplification of STR, *via* PCR, starts with targeting loci by sequence-specific primers. Electrophoresis is used to separate the DNA fragments. The STR markers used in human identification need to exhibit the highest variability among individuals and are measured by the lengths of the different alleles. STRs are generally classified by the length of their repeat: mono-, di-, tri-, tetra-, penta- and hexa- nucleotides. STR loci can even be obtained from maggots removed from a corpse. STR detection at this time involves the use of fluorescence with a gel or capillary electrophoresis (CE) and ABI gel-based DNA sequences. STRs are most informative with samples that involve well-preserved soft tissue and bone.[16] STRs have also been analyzed by DNA sequencing for example. To understand PCR-assisted STR typing, it is useful to briefly consider how such PCRs are designed.

15 A pair of genes that represent contrasting alternative of a character placed at the same locus in the homologous chromosomes (pairing of two chromosomes) are designated as allelomorphs or in short alleles.

16 Romeika JM, Yan F, *Recent Advances in Forensic DNA Analysis*, 2013 J Forensic Res S12: 001. doi: 10.4172/2157-7145.S12-001 available at https://www.omicsonline.org/recent-advances-in-forensic-dna-analysis-2157-7145.S12-001.pdf.

Suppose that laboratory data revealed the following DNA sequence:

*—ATGCTAGTATTTG*GATAGATAGATAGATAGATAGATAGA TA*AAAAAATTTTTTT—*

The STR is underlined and consists of the sequence, GATA repeated 7 times. The dashes at the beginning and end of the overall sequence shown indicate that there is more sequence available both upstream and downstream of the region shown. Remember, DNA is relatively very long and linear and we are just going to look at a small region of it.[17]

Since the advent of forensic DNA analysis in the 1980s, it has gone through several stages of development. The first generation of DNA analysis — Restriction Fragment Length Polymorphism (RFLP) profiling is no longer used by the forensic community, as it requires relatively large amounts of DNA and degraded samples could not be analyzed with accuracy. The second generation of DNA analysis was based on PCR and mainly involved dot-blot techniques. However, it is not suitable in the analysis of longer strands of DNA. The third generation of DNA analysis or the current method of choice is short tandem repeats or STR analysis. Despite its undoubted advantages, it does not work well for highly degraded DNA samples, such as in cases of mass disaster situations or accidents where an individual is too badly damaged to identify. More effective, faster and cheaper DNA analysis techniques are continually being developed, which are addressing different targets for forensic applications. Some of the recent progresses made in the analysis of DNA are STP (Short Tandem Repeats), SNP (Single Nucleotide Polymorphism), low-template DNA, mitochondrial DNA, and DNA methylation, and illustrates how microfluidic devices and nanotechnology can be integrated to develop a new generation of DNA.

17 DNA Testing: An Introduction for Non-Scientist An Illustrated Explanation available at http://www.scientific.org/tutorials/articles/riley/riley.html.

TABLE 1

Targets of DNA Analysis, Definitions and Major Limitations

Target of DNA Analysis	Definition	Major Limitations of Analysis
Short Tandem Repeats (STP)	Short Sequences of DNA that contains short segments consisting of 2-7 repeating base pairs.	1. Unsuitable for the analysis of highly degraded or low copy number DNA samples. 2. Inconsistency of number of STR markers in different DNA databases.
Single Nucleotide Polymorphism (SNP)	DNA sequence variations that occur when a single nucleotide (A,T, C or G) in the genome sequence is altered.	1. Less informative per locus than STR. 2. Unsuitable for DNA mixtures.
Low Template DNA	Less than 200 picogram of DNA found in a sample.	1. Ease of contamination and amplification of contaminants. 2. Mixed profiles being produced and wrongful accusations.
Mitochondrail DNA	A circular molecule of DNA 16,569 base pairs in size, obtained from the mitochondrion organelle found within cells.	1. Less discrimatory (material inheritance). 2. Relatively time consuming and expensive.
DNA methylation	DNA methylation is a biochemical process involving the addition of a methyl group to the cytosine or adenine DNA nucleotides.	1. Large amount of samples needed. 2. Labour intensive and time consuming.

3 Admissibility of DNA evidence in criminal cases

Standards of admissibility have been fixed by different courts to create their own benchmark. Some states have adopted vaguely worded statutes regarding admissibility of DNA typing results without specifying the methods intended to be covered.

Such laws were obviously intended to cover only conventional RFLP analysis of single locus probes on Southern blots[18] the only method in common use at the time of passage of the legislation. In India there is no uniform legal standard either fixed by legislation or judicial decisions for the admission of Forensic DNA evidence. The principle of admissibility of evidence in India is relevancy. Whether particular DNA evidence is relevant or not depends on facts and circumstances of each case to be decided by the court. But there is a paradigm shift in the interpretation of DNA evidence by Indian Courts which also indicates the increasing value of such evidence in the administration of criminal justice. Presently in India DNA analysis has become a common form of evidence in criminal trials. It is also used in civil litigation, particularly in cases involving the determination of paternity or identity.[19] In 1991 for the first time DNA fingerprinting evidence was presented in Indian courts and was accepted as infallible evidence in the court of law.[20] In *Kamti Devi's*[21] case for the first time Supreme Court judicially noticed the acceptability of DNA typing result. In this context, K.T. Thomas, J., held that the result of a genuine DNA test is said to be scientifically accurate. This judicial declaration was later considered by the courts as a judicial notice for receiving the DNA evidence. In *Kamalanatha* v *State of Tamil Nadu*,[22] the Supreme Court for the first time considered the reliability and admissibility of DNA Test in India. DNA Profiling technique apart from being relied upon by Courts as corroborative evidence, has also received legislative recognition. There were cases where the court commented on the relevancy and legal aspects of DNA test and the situations in which it can be conducted. The court discussed the admissibility of DNA profiling technique and held that DNA

18 *DNA Technology in Forensic Science*, p. 52, National Research Council.

19 *Nirmaljit Kaur (2)* v *State of Punjab* (2006)9 SCC 363.

20 *Kunhiraman* v *Manoj* II(1991) DMC 499 (Ker).

21 *Kamti Devi (Smt)* v *Poshi Ram* 2001(2) CTC 625 (SC); (2001)5 SCC 194.

22 AIR 2005 SC 2132; (2005)3 SCR 182.

profiling technique has been expressly included among various forms of medical examination in amended *Explanation* to s. 53, CrPC. DNA profile is different from a DNA sample which is usually obtained from bodily substances. Moreover the court opined that "Conducting DNA profiling is not a violation of Fundamental Rights under Article 20(3) of the Constitution of India and s. 161(2) of CrPC.[23] Court also gave an explanation of the circumstances when DNA test is required to identify the dead body.[24]

It is noteworthy that DNA evidence has a dual nature. In criminal cases DNA evidence is treated as corroborative evidence except in rape cases and in determination of maternity or paternity. In cases where rape has been committed the court strongly relies on the DNA evidence and commented that that after the incorporation of s. 53A in the Criminal Procedure Code, w.e.f. 23.06.2006, it has become necessary for the prosecution to go in for DNA test in such type of cases, which would facilitate the prosecution to prove its case against the accused. Prior to 2006, although it was not incorporated in the Code but still the prosecution could have resorted to the procedure of getting the DNA test or analysis and matching the semen of the accused with that found on the materials collected from the prosecutrix to make it a fool proof case. The court was of the view that if the prosecution fails to perform such kind of investigation, they themselves must face the consequences.[25] The Supreme Court stringently deprecated the prosecuting and investigating agencies for the lapses committed by them by not conducting DNA test, when it was required. In such cases directions were issued for the purposeful and decisive investigation and prosecution. The court ordered that training programme to be fixed within six months to ensure that those persons who handle sensitive matters concerning investigation or prosecution are fully trained to handle the case. The Home Department of every

23 *Selvi* v *State of Karnataka* (2010)7 SCC 263.
24 *Jarnail Singh* v *State of Punjab* (2009)9 SCC 719.
25 *Krishan Kumar Malik* v *State of Haryana* (2011)7 SCC 130.

State Government was advised to formulate procedure for taking action against all erring investigation or prosecution officials or officers. The court had also mandated that the direction should be given effect to within six months. All the Home Secretaries were directed to look into the compliance of the directions and maintain the records for consideration.[26] Nonetheless, there were cases, where the courts recorded convictions in rape cases on the testimony of the prosecutrix, if it was trustworthy.[27] Therefore in rape cases DNA evidence must be placed before the court as a matter of prudence as in most cases it is treated as like a substantive evidence.

Regarding the relevancy of DNA evidence excluding rape cases, the Supreme Court opined that, DNA examination might result in identifying the remains of the dead victim, still the involvement of the respondent in the commission of the crime has to be established. Some definite evidence has to be established to indicate that the victim had been done to death of which the respondent was aware or must be aware of and also at the proximate time of death of the victim and the respondent were last seen together. Even in the absence of *corpus delicti*,[28] it would be possible to establish a crime if the appropriate materials are made available to the court.[29] This observation of the court proves the corroborative nature of DNA. The circumstance of the 'last seen together' is normally taken into consideration for finding the accused guilty of the offence charged with when it is established by prosecution that the time gap between the point of time when the accused and the deceased were found together alive and the deceased was found dead so small that the possibility of any other person being with the deceased could completely be ruled out.[30]

26 *State of Gujarat* v *Kishanbhai* (2014)5 SCC 108.

27 *State of Kerala* v *M. Ayoob* (02.08.2004 – KERHC) MANU/KE/0510/2004.

28 Concrete evidence of a crime, such as corpse.

29 *State of Karnataka* v *M.V. Mahash* (2003)3 SCC 353.

30 *Vansha Lakama Gangad (through jail)* v *State of Maharashtra* (05.04.2010-BomHC) MANU/MH/0319/2010.

Although DNA test result acts as an corroborative evidence, it has been considered as the blueprint of an individual. DNA decides the characteristics of persons such as colour of skin, type of hair, nails etc. The identification of individuals by the aid of DNA test is considered to be hundred per cent precise expert opinion by the court, provided the samples are collected in the proper way maintaining the quality control. The court observed that there is a need of quality control, so precautions are necessary to be taken to ensure preparation of High Molecular Weight DNA, complete digestion of the sample with appropriate enzyme, and perfect transfer and hybridization of the blot to obtain distinct bands with appropriate control. If such chain of quality control is maintained by the expert during investigation, then the expert evidence becomes admissible in accordance with s. 45 of the Indian Evidence Act.[31] The requirement of quality control has been reiterated in different cases where DNA profiling was conducted by experts. In such cases the experts revealed that the samples had been tested as per the procedure developed by the laboratory, that the samples were sufficient for the purposes of comparison and that there was no possibility of the samples having being contaminated or tampered with. In another case, the Supreme Court said that DNA report must be accepted as it is scientifically accurate and an exact science. An issue was raised by the trial court that the semen swabs on the slides and the blood samples of the appellant had not been kept in proper custody and had been tampered with. This issue was countered by the Supreme Court, by considering it as an 'error' of the trial court as it was properly explained. In the case under discussion, 20ml. blood were taken from the appellant's body, for DNA profiling and transferred into four vials, each containing 5ml. The vials were also sealed and signed by hospital doctors under whose supervision the blood samples were taken. Although arguments were raised on behalf of the appellant that the blood samples were tampered but it resulted as baseless as the expert who conducted DNA profiling in the CCMB deposed that due to

31 *Pantangi Balarama Venkata Ganesh* v *State of Andhra Pradesh* (2009) 14 SCC 607.

some leakage found in the vials, traces of blood appeared on the material with which the vials were sealed. Only 3ml. blood was found in each vial which amounted to total 12ml. blood and the loss of 8ml blood was thus accounted for. Even the proper custody was explained by the experts that before handling over the vials to CCMB, blood was stored in a refrigerator in Government hospital and therefore there was no possibility of evaporation of blood. In this case itself, the Supreme Court explained the philosophy of the "rarest of rare" principle as it commuted the death sentence of the appellant to life imprisonment.[32]

The fate of the admissibility of the DNA test in cases in which it was conducted not only depends on experts but also the investigating personnel who collect materials from the crime scene. Therefore the sample should be collected, preserved and transported carefully to minimize the resultant error or to make the expert evidence reliable.[33] Regarding the acceptability of DNA evidence, the Supreme Court reiterated that DNA forms a natural barrier against exogenous DNA contamination and are resistant to environmental assaults when the identity of the deceased is in question and it has to be determined from the bones. In the present case the blood sample of the father of the deceased was taken in accordance with the set up precept and procedure for DNA isolation test and the same was sent along with taken out femur and humerus bones of recovered skeleton to the Centre for DNA, Fingerprinting and Diagnostics (CDFD), Ministry of Science and Technology, Government of India, Hyderabad. The court also said that the question regarding whether DNA Tests are virtually infallible may be a moot question, but the fact remains that such test has come to stay and is being used extensively in the investigation of crimes and the Court often accepts the views of the experts, especially when cases rest on circumstantial evidence. Samples of DNA are being used in the Criminal Justice System since more than half a century.

32 *Santosh Kumar Singh* v *State (through CBI)* (2010)9 SCC 747.

33 *Sandeep* v *State of Uttar Pradesh* (2012)6 SCC 107.

Although debate remains over the safeguards which should be required in testing samples and presenting evidence in Court. DNA profile, is consistently held to be valid and reliable but it depends on the quality control and quality assurance procedures in the laboratory. So far as applicability of DNA evidence in this case, the DNA sample from the skeleton matched with the father and all sampling and testing have been done by experts whose scientific knowledge and experience have not been doubted in these proceedings. Therefore the court had no reason to discard the evidence since the prosecution succeeded in showing that the skeleton recovered from the house was that of the deceased and none other than the accused had strangulated her to death and buried the dead body in the house.

In *Nithari* murder case, the court held that the identity of the deceased girl was established by matching DNA extracted from pieces of her body with the DNA extracted from her parents and brother. Such kind of matching can establish identity to a certain degree of probability but not absolute identity of deceased person. There is absolutely no discussion in any of the Supreme Court Judgments or High Court judgments regarding what degree of probability was found in the present case when her DNA was matched with DNA of her parents and her brother, and whether the degree of probability found in the case is judicially acceptable. The court also referred a foreign judgment on DNA fingerprinting of the Supreme Court of Florida and commented as "very lively discussion on DNA fingerprinting".[34] In USA, Scientific Working Group on DNA Analysis Methods (SWGDAM) has developed "Interpretation Guidelines for Autosomal STR Typing by forensic DNA Testing Laboratories".[35] Hence the DNA evidence was accepted in this case but the degree of probability is yet a matter of concern.

34 *Thomas Mitchell Overton* v *State of Florida*, decided on 29.11.2007 available at http://www.floridasupremecourt.org/decisions/2007/sc04-20/1.pdf, last visited on 16th June 2015.

35 SWGDAM-Interpretation-Guidelines available at http:www.fbi.gov/about-us/lab/codis/swgdam-interpretation-guidelines, last visited on 16th June 2015.

4 Admissibility of DNA evidence in determining paternity and maternity

In determination of paternity or maternity DNA evidences were also treated as substantive evidence.[36] The Supreme Court held that where the purported father denied paternity but refused to undergo DNA Test, such a person was disentitled from disputing paternity.[37] The Kerala High Court differentiated between legitimacy and paternity. The court opined that DNA test need not be ordered as a matter of routine in all cases where the legitimacy or paternity of a child is in issue. A distinction had to be drawn between 'legitimacy' and 'paternity' of the child. Legitimacy can be established by legal presumption, while it is desirable to establish paternity by DNA test, particularly when both parties agree.[38] The current situation regarding the application of DNA test in determining paternity can be summarized from the case of *Muniappan* v *Ponni.*[39] In this case an application was filed by the husband for the dissolution of the marriage as he suspected the paternity of his son. He also filed an application to direct the blood test upon the son which was dismissed by the trial court on the ground that the marriage is proved and it would intervene into the fundamental rights of the mother. Relying on the case of *Sharda* v *Dharmpal,*[40] the High Court reversed the findings of the Trial Court and observed that directing blood test does not violate fundamental rights.

The inception for interpretation of applicability of DNA test was first observed in the case of *Goutam Kundu* v *State of West Bengal*[41] where it was observed that DNA test should not be directed as a matter of routine or as a matter of course and no one can be compelled to give blood sample for analysis. *Goutam Kundu's* case was overruled by the case of *Sharda* v

36 *Nirmaljit Kaur (2)* v *State of Punjab* (2006)9 SCC 363.
37 *Dwarika Prasad Satpathy* v *Bidyut Prava Dixit* (1999)7 SCC 675.
38 *Jayaprakash* v *Nisha* (21.03.2013 – KERHC) MANU/KE/0617/2013.
39 2011(2) CTC 635.
40 2003(2) CTC 760.
41 (1993)3 SCC 418.

Dharmpal[42] where it was held that directing DNA test cannot be held to be violative of one's right to privacy, and is also not in violation of right of personal liberty guaranteed under Art. 21 of the Constitution. A compilation of the two propositions forwarded by the Supreme Court, results that DNA test should not be directed as a matter of course but in cases of "eminent need" after consideration of pros and cons such test is desirable.[43] The court has the power to give directions for DNA test but should exercise such power if the applicant has a strong *prima facie* case supported by sufficient materials which are presented before the court. Therefore, the Supreme Court did not completely prohibit the power of the court to order for DNA test but the court was of the view that such direction would not be granted as a routine practice by the courts. If despite the order of the Court, the respondent refuses to submit himself to such test, the court will be entitled to draw an adverse inference against him, on the basis of preponderance of probabilities with available evidence.[44] On the other hand the adverse inference policy has been reversed now after the incorporation of s. 53A, CrPC, where reasonable force can be used on the accused to collect his blood samples for DNA test. This policy was followed in the case of *Narayan Dutt Tiwari* v *Rohit Shekhar*.[45] In *Dipanwita Roy* v *Ronobroto Roy*,[46] the Supreme Court held that s. 112 of the Evidence Act is not strictly attracted in the present case. As without DNA test it would be impossible for the husband to establish the alleged infidelity of the wife, the said test which is the most legitimate and scientifically perfect means, could be used by husband to establish his assertion of infidelity.

Moreover, it has to be remembered that s. 112 of the Evidence Act 1872 was enacted at such time when the modern scientific advancements like DNA test was not into existence

42 2003(2) CTC 760.

43 *Banarsi Dass* v *Teeku Dutta (Mrs.)* 2005(3) CTC 227 (SC).

44 *Premasundari* v *N.Vanathi* (11.11.2010 – MADHC) MANU/TN/3155/2010.

45 (2012)12 SCC 554.

46 (2015)1 SCC 365.

and were even not in contemplation of the legislature. Presently, the result of a genuine DNA test is considered to be scientifically accurate. But such accuracy is not enough to escape from the conclusiveness of s. 112 of the Act. It means that if the husband and the wife is living together during the time when the child was conceived but the DNA test revealed, that the child was not born to the husband, still the conclusiveness of law will remain unrebuttable.[47] The principle underlying the conclusiveness of s. 112 is that apparently although from the point of view of the husband, he might be compelled to bear the fatherhood of a child who might not be his child at all but in such case the innocent child would be protected from being bastardized taking into consideration the mother and her spouse were living together during the time of conception.[48]

Matters of cheating requires special reference as s. 112 of the Indian Evidence Act was not applicable to cases where there was no relationship of husband and wife between the complainant and the accused. Naturally, this type of case becomes an easy ground to disown the paternity of the child. Therefore, the court correctly observed that in this type of cases under s. 417 of IPC, DNA typing test is mandatory, as there are no other means to determine paternity of the child.[49]

While considering the cases of paternity determination a distinction has to be drawn between 'legitimacy' and 'paternity' of a child. Legitimacy can be established by legal presumption, while it is desirable to establish paternity by DNA test, particularly when both parties agree.[50] In maintenance claims under s. 125 of the CrPC, legitimacy of a child is not primary issue as maintenance can be awarded both for legitimate and illegitimate minor child but paternity is required to be proved.

47 *Kamti Devi (Smt.)* v *Poshi Ram* 2001(2) CTC 625 (SC).

48 *Babita Devi* alias *Babali* v *State of Jharkhand* 2011 CrLJ 3643.

49 *Sabur Hossain Biswas* alias *Paltu* v *State of West Bengal* Cal LT 2008(1) HC 349.

50 *Jayaprakash* v *Nisha* (21.03.2013 – KERHC) MANU/KE/0617/2013.

5 Grouping of cases

5.1 Rape and murder cases

Petitioner along with seven others were chargesheeted for offences punishable under ss. 120(B), 302 read with ss. 34, 376, 376(2)(c) read with ss. 109, 201, 202 read with ss. 114 and 506(ii) of IPC. Hence this petition for bail was filed. Held, all particulars required under s. 173(2) of CrPC, viz. statement of witnesses examined during course of investigation were produced except further statement of victim girl, DNA report and abortion certificate into court. However when petitioner approached Magistrate to provide copies of chargesheet and copies of documents Magistrate declined to grant copies and passed order stating that scientific reports are awaited after receipt of which only chargesheet to be prepared and furnished to petitioner. Prosecution had examined 109 witnesses and there were statements recorded under s. 164 of CrPC. Medical evidence and DNA certificate. However keeping in view position of petitioner and status of victim and nature of evidence so collected, release of petitioner on bail would have an impact in tampering with material collected by investigating agency. Thus release of petitioner was not conducive to fair trial. Hence the petition was dismissed.[51]

The accused were convicted under ss. 376, 302 and 120B, IPC. A serious charge of rape of 13 girls was made. The DNA Test revealed that he had fathered the terminated foetus of the victim. Further allegations were that since the deceased protested against this act, he was brutally murdered by the accused. Prosecution established that accused caused bodily injuries on deceased with stick on left upper limb and lower limb. Deceased was confined in kudil without being provided with food or water. Deceased was starved to death. Prior and subsequent conduct of the accused and circumstances of case including motive and their intention to murder was established.[52]

51 *Swami Premananda* v *State* 1996 CrLJ 3884.

52 *Chandradevi* v *State of Tamil Nadu by Inspector of Police*, C.B., C.I.D. Appeal (Crl.) 611-612 of 2003.

In *Santosh Kumar Singh* v *State through CBI*,[53] DNA profiling was conducted from several articles like the clothes and underwear of the deceased, underwear of the appellant/ accused and vaginal swabs of the deceased. DNA profile of the semen matched the DNA profile of the appellant's blood. The accused was convicted but the Supreme Court commuted the death sentence of the appellant to life imprisonment as it appeared before the court that the sentencing part is difficult as the court had to choose between life sentence and death sentence.

The appellant in the present case was accused for murder and rape of a young girl. On being arrested, the accused confessed that he had committed the murder along with three other co-associates, whom he named. The three co-associates were also arrested. The trial court acquitted the three people but the appellant was found guilty for the commission of the offences punishable under s. 302 read with s. 34 and s. 201. DNA test was used in the case for identifying the person from the recovered skeleton. The Supreme Court convicted the accused who worked as a guide.[54]

The victim and her friend had reposed complete confidence in occupants of a bus while boarding same to reach destination. The convicts misused confidence and faith of victim and her friend, made them to board the bus so as to overpower them on way and satisfy their lust. Crime was pre-planned and executed by restoring to diabolic method, exhibiting inhuman conduct in a ghastly manner. Convicts behaved in barbaric and inhuman manner by inserting rods and hand in victim's private parts and taking out her internal organs. Convicts also pulled victim with hair, dragged her from rear portion of bus to front gate and threw her out of bus along with her friend in nude condition on the road side. DNA test of the accused was conducted and accepted by the court and the trial court granted death penalty to convicts. Not only to deter others from

53 (2010)9 SCC 747.

54 *Dharam Deo Yadav* v *State of U.P.* (2014)5 SCC 509; (2014)6 CrLJ 2371.

committing such atrocious crimes but also to give emphatic expression to society's abhorrence of such crimes. death penalty was confirmed.[55]

The accused aged 32 years came to the house of his neighbour, and stayed with his four children, as the neighbour and his wife went to irrigate agricultural fields in the night. At midnight the accused raped the victim and caused grievous injuries consequent to which she died. The next morning when the father of the victim along with his wife returned, they found the victim aged about 14 years was dead. Immediately after which they went to the police station and lodged the complaint. DNA test report established the presence of semen of accused in vaginal swab of prosecutrix. The specimen of the blood of the accused was obtained to conduct DNA fingerprinting after taking permission of the Judicial Magistrate and sent for analysis in the State Forensic Science Laboratory. Conviction was awarded.[56]

The victim girl was helpless and innocent child of less than seven years when accused brutally and inhumanly raped her and caused her death in a violent manner. DNA test was conducted. DNA report showed that the semen was detected in the vaginal smear of the victim. Thus the accused was convicted and death sentence was awarded.[57]

In a case of rape and murder, the dead body of the victim was recovered. The blood stained weapon and blood stained clothes were also recovered. The medical evidence and the DNA report clearly established the commission of rape and murder of the victim. Death sentence was awarded to the accused.[58]

55 *State through Reference* v *Ram Singh* 212(2014) DLT 99 (Nirbhaya case).

56 *Rajkumar* v *State of MP* (2014)5 SCC 353.

57 *State of Maharashtra* v *Babasaheb Maruti Kamble* Criminal Appeal No. 167 of 2013.

58 *Kalu Khan* v *State of Rajasthan* Criminal Appeal No. 1891-1892 of 2014.

5.2 Kidnapping, rape and murder

Since 2005 till a period of two years several children went missing. It was alleged that the accused killed, chopped and ate the body parts after cooking them. Accused and his servant lived together. In a confession made by the accused under s. 164, CrPC before the Magistrate which was voluntary, he admitted in great detail that he used to kill the girls after luring them by strangulating them, and he would then chop up and eat up their body parts after cooking them. DNA fingerprinting was used to establish the identity of the dead bodies or the body parts found. The appellant was convicted. The court convicted the appellant as guilty of murdering and upheld the death sentence.[59]

Two minor children were kidnapped, one of them was gang raped and both of them were given poison and pushed into the canal alive where they suffered a watery grave. DNA test was conducted and accepted by the court. Death sentence was confirmed by the Supreme Court.[60]

The offence was committed by the accused deserved severe condemnation and was heinous crime but on looking to cumulative facts and on balancing aggravating and mitigating circumstances of the case, it did not fell in category of rarest of rare cases. From the evidence of the doctor and other evidence on record, especially the DNA reports, it was proved beyond reasonable doubt that the accused committed rape on the victim girl and thereafter throttled her to death. Conviction of the accused was maintained by the conversion of the death sentence to life imprisonment.[61]

In Re *Kamlesh*[62] DNA test was conducted and its report was presented as evidence. Keeping in view, the totality of the circumstances and the legal principles, the court was of the

59 *Surendra Koli* v *State of UP* (2011)4 SCC 80 (Nithari Murder case).

60 *State by the Inspector of Police* v *Manoharan* Criminal Appeal No. 1461 of 2010.

61 *State of Maharashtra* v *Sadashiv Jetappa Kamble* Criminal Appeal No. 1261 of 2013.

62 2016 Cri LR 1171.

considered view that the crime in question was committed by the appellant in a pre-determined and cold blooded manner on a small child without any provocation. Accused was convicted and accordingly death sentence was awarded.

The fact that the accused was last seen with deceased was proved beyond reasonable doubt. Evidence proved that accused after committing murder the deceased took gold ornaments for her body, thus, motive was established. DNA test was conducted to establish the evidence. Conviction of the appellant was justified.[63]

5.3 Unnatural offence and murder

A boy aged about 10 years had gone to school in the morning. Normally he used to return in the evening, but on that day he did not return. Since the whereabouts of the boy were not known, the mother of the boy, who was a maid servant, lodged a complaint, after running here and there anxiously for several days, before, the Sub-Inspector of Police, attached to Crime Branch, Nagpur. In the mean time Mary, a lady, residing near the house of the accused, informed that the dead body of a boy aged about 9-10 years was seen floating in a well near the old cemetery. Sub-Inspector of Police then proceeded to the spot and with the assistance of fire brigade took the dead body from the well and sent the same for conducting post-mortem examination. With the help of DNA evidence the accused was convicted.[64]

5.4 Murder

Rajiv Gandhi, former Prime Minister of India, was assassinated by a human bomb. The incident was a result of a conspiracy. DNA profiling not only assisted in identifying the victims but also established the identity of the perpetrators mainly by the belt being recovered from the scene of crime which was carrying paltry body flesh tissue. Seven accused who were alive and were involved in the conspiracy including a woman were convicted under s. 302 read with s. 120B of IPC. Death sentence

63 *Mahanand Naik* v *State* Criminal Writ Petition No. 51 of 2014.
64 *Anil* v *State of Maharashtra* (2014)4 SCC 69; (2014) CrLJ 1608 (SC).

was awarded to 4 of the seven convicted accused (including the woman) were confirmed. Sentence of the remaining 3 convicts altered to life imprisonment.[65]

In a murder case, the husband of the victim was the accused. Although DNA examination was conducted on the recovered bones which proved that the bones belong to the wife but since the involvement of the respondent in the commission of murder could not be proved, Supreme Court recorded an acquittal.[66]

Murder of a pregnant lady was a result of conspiracy. DNA test of the foetus was conducted which proves that the accused was the father of the foetus in the womb of the victim and finally it was held that the accused was one of the conspirator of the murder of the victim.[67]

Appellant filed the present appeal against his conviction under s. 302 and s. 201 of IPC. Held, there was no hesitation in accepting evidence of witness to effect that appellant had taken them up to well and on his pointing out, a dead body was recovered from that well. DNA test of the dead body got conducted by the prosecution. Prosecution had also succeeded in establishing that dead body recovered at instance of appellant was that of complainant's son. All that which was required to be shown was that something belonging to deceased was recovered pursuant to information given by appellant and which prosecution had succeeded in establishing. Therefore the case of the prosecution was established beyond any shadow of doubt. The court did not find any infirmity in findings of trial court holding appellant guilty and consequently this appeal was liable to be dismissed. Conviction upheld.[68]

In a murder case of a lady whose husband was convicted by both trial court and the High Court. DNA fingerprinting was done to identify the skeleton of the victim and help to convict

65 *State* v *Nalini* (1999)5 SCC 253.
66 *State of Karnataka* v *M.V. Mahesh* (2003)3 SCC 353.
67 *State through CBI* v *Amarmani Tripathi* (2005)8 SCC 21.
68 *Sachin* v *State (NCT of Delhi)* 2007 CrLJ 3947.

the husband of the victim who was awarded death sentence.[69] Finally awarded life imprisonment.[70]

Accused was convicted under various sections of IPC and Arms Act. Dissatisfied with the judgment of conviction and sentence, an appeal was preferred by the accused before the High Court. Whereas the appeal of the accused was dismissed for which the accused again appealed before the Supreme Court. DNA fingerprint was conducted for the identification of the accused from a pink colour shirt which was seized from the abandoned car used by the accused to escape. Result of DNA fingerprinting gave affirmative answers. The appeal was dismissed and the conviction of the Trial Court was upheld.[71]

The sole surviving terrorist of Mumbai terrorist attack Ajmal Kasab was captured among ten terrorist. He made bold confession under s. 164 of CrPC which was corroborated with ocular evidence of eyewitnesses who had life and death encounters with the terrorists and it was further corroborated with forensic evidences like DNA etc. The court upheld the conviction of Kasab and thus was sentenced to death.[72]

The deceased was the Chief Track Engineer, South Central Railway. He was living in the Bungalow of Railway Officers along with his wife, son and daughter. The entire family of the deceased were killed and the dead bodies were shifted to the car putting the body. After taking the car near the railway tracks, one of the accused purchased petrol. Then the accused persons jointly had put petrol on the car and burnt the dead bodies with the car. DNA test confirmed that it was deceased family which was found burnt in car. Although there was no eyewitness the attendant circumstances had been fully

69 *Swamy Shraddananda* alias *Murali Manohar Mishra* v *State of Karnataka* (2007)12 SCC 288 (Swami Shraddhananda case).

70 *Swamy Shraddananda* alias *Murali Manohar Mishra* v *State of Karnataka* (2008)13 SCC 767 (Swami Shraddhananda case).

71 *Pantangi Balarama Venkata Ganesh* v *State of Andhra Pradesh* (2009)14 SCC 607.

72 *Mohammad Ajmal Amir Kasab* v *State of Maharashtra* (2012)9 SCC 1 (Mumbai Terrorist Attack case).

established by the prosecution. The forensic expert's view corroborated the circumstances and the appellant was convicted.[73]

The accused along with his companion was charged with having killed his girlfriend by taking her from Delhi to U.P. on pretext of marrying her in Haridwar. On being interrogated the injured girl revealed her name, parent's address and that she developed friendship with the accused while she was working in a mobile shop and she was pregnant. The crime was committed as the girl refused to abort pregnancy caused by the appellant. DNA test was conducted for determining the paternity of the foetus which was found in the womb of the deceased. The conviction of the accused was confirmed and was awarded life imprisonment.[74]

A pair of human legs were found floating in the backwaters of a Lake by a person thereafter lodged a complaint to police department. DNA test was conducted to dismembered parts of the body to determine whether the same was the dead body of one *P*. The DNA analysis made it clear that the blood samples of the parents of *P* matched with the DNA of the dead body and the same proved and established the identity of the dead body as the DNA had also been extracted from the portion of the limbs recovered from the lake and compared with that of DNA of the parents.[75]

The chopper used in the murder was recovered. The Maruti van used in murder was recovered on the basis of disclosure. The forensic surgeon deposed that dismemberment of body parts of the victim could have been possible with the said chopper. DNA report stated that hair and bloodstains found in Maruti van matched with those of victim. Dismembered parts of the body of the victim was identified by the DNA report. Thus, the case was solved with the help of DNA test.[76]

73 *Munna Kumar Upadhyay* v *State of Andhra Pradesh* (2012)6 SCC 174.

74 *Sandeep* v *State of Uttar Pradesh* (2012)6 SCC 107.

75 *R. Shaji* v *State of Kerala* (2013)14 SCC 266.

76 *Sahib Hussain* v *State of Rajasthan* (2013)9 SCC 778.

The Superintendent of Police received anonymous letters and phone calls to the effect that some unidentified dead bodies were lying dumped on the hillocks of village Nandos. A search operation was organized on the same day in course of which dead bodies were recovered. Along with the dead bodies, articled like clothes, trouser hooks, two bloodstained diaries were also recovered. DNA fingerprinting was used to identify the deceased from their decomposed dead bodies. The investigation led to the arrest of the accused and subsequently were convicted.[77]

A young lady was brutally killed by her husband as he was suspecting that she was having some affair with her friend. After killing her the appellant, with the help of other person burnt her body in the tandoor of his restaurant. DNA test was conducted to determine the identity of the dead body recovered from the tandoor. Husband of the victim was convicted for the offences punishable under ss. 302, 120B and 201 of IPC.[78]

Former Chief Minister of Punjab and Haryana was assassinated using human bomb. The accused persons were convicted under ss. 302 and 307 read with s. 120B, s. 306/109 of IPC. DNA test was conducted on the parts of the body of the victim. Conviction of the accused was confirmed and sentenced them to death.[79]

The appellant was convicted under ss. 302 and 201 of IPC. Held the prosecution case entirely based on circumstantial evidence, relying on the last seen theory and failure of the accused to explain some material circumstances. On internal examination of the dead body of the victim, the doctor noticed a fracture of the 7th rib. The DNA report also indicated that the rib fracture was not ante mortem. The circumstance of last seen together would normally be taken into consideration for finding the accused guilty of the offence charged with when it

77 *Mahesh Dhanaji Shindhe* v *State of Maharashtra* (2014)4 SCC 292.

78 *Sushil Sharma* v *State (N.C.T. of Delhi)* (2014)4 SCC 317.

79 *Central Bureau of Investigation* v *Jagtar Singh Hawara and Balwant Singh* Criminal Appeal No. 731-DB of 2007.

is established by the prosecution that the time gap between the point of time when the accused and the deceased were found together alive and when the deceased was found dead is so small that possibility of any other person being with the deceased could completely be ruled. In the instant appeal, the prosecution case stands established based on re-appreciation of the evidence as adduced before the trial court that it was the accused which caused the homicidal death. The order of conviction recorded by the Additional Sessions Judge was confirmed and the appeal was dismissed.[80]

5.5 Dowry death and cruelty by husband and relatives of husband

All sorts of incriminating materials were confronted to appellant so adduced on behalf of prosecution during course of trial, which was not at all answered or explained by the accused. Allegations made by prosecution witness against accused was found fully corroborated. The decomposed body of the victim was subjected to DNA test. The victims was identified. The accused was convicted.[81]

5.6 Kidnapping, abduction and murder

As regards medical evidence, the doctor opined that although it was not possible to determine the cause and time of death, the age of human skull and mandible provided showed that the same was of a boy of less than six years of age. In regard of report of DNA test, the learned judge relied upon the evidence of Doctor who made the DNA test and also the evidence of others who collected the blood samples of the parents of the deceased and sent them to C.D.F.D., Hyderabad. Doctor who made the DNA test opined that the remnants were that of deceased. The learned judge also relied upon the recovery of articles and other burnt clothes from the scene of offence which was pointed out by way of corroborative evidence by the appellant. He also relied upon the recovery of the bones in furtherance of the disclosure statement made by the accused

80 *Vansha Lakama Gangad (through jail)* v *State of Maharashtra* Criminal Appeal No. 618 of 2002.

81 *Rajiv Singh* v *State of Bihar* Criminal Appeal No. 1169 of 2011.

in his confession leading to the recovery of the bones. Reliance was also placed on the confession of the accused. Noticing that there was no direct evidence, the following circumstances were held to be sufficient to prove his guilt.[82]

Prosecution case clearly suggested that accused had kidnapped deceased with a view to demand ransom from his parents and since grandfather of deceased called him accused pressed his nose and mouth which resulted in his death. Then accused burnt the dead body of the deceased by taking it to jungle in a gunny bag and setting it on fire after pouring kerosene on it. DNA test was conducted to identify the dead body of the deceased and answered positively. The court held that the accused was also liable to be convicted for offence of kidnapping as it was clear that he was kidnapped by the accused for ransom.[83]

Prosecution had successfully established guilt of the accused by adducing evidence of extra judicial confessions made by him. Prosecution had also successfully established that the dead body was of deceased by tattoo marks and also by DNA report. In view of evidence, prosecution had successfully proved guilty of accused.[84]

A young medical student was murdered by another senior medical student of the same college. After murder the dead body was disposed of after cutting it into different pieces which was very gruesome and ghastly. DNA test was conducted from the recovered skull, torso and some other limbs of the dead body. The accused was convicted.[85]

There was no evidence to prove that family members of deceased had any enmity towards appellants so as to falsely implicate them. Therefore, motive of abduction of deceased to extort money from his family members was clearly proved.

82 *Anil* alias *Raju Namdev Patil* v *Administration of Daman and Diu, Daman* 2006 Supp (9) SCR 466.

83 *Deepti Anil Devasthali and Leena Anil Devasthali* v *State of Maharashtra* 2009(111) Bom LR 3981.

84 *High Court of Karnataka* v *Madhu* AIR 2014 SC 394.

85 *Inspector of Police, Tamil Nadu* v *John David* (2011)5 SCC 509.

Prosecution witnesses had supported case of prosecution. At instance of the accused persons, recovery of headless dead body and weapon of offence was effected. After the body was recovered, its identity was established by the family members and also by sampling the blood of the deceased with the blood samples of parent by DNA fingerprinting. Offence against accused was proved beyond reasonable doubt.[86]

It was established that appellant enticed the deceased from his place of employment. Accused could not escape liability for offence punishable under s. 364 of IPC as there was evidence to show that he had knowledge of deceased skeleton being buried in fields of his uncle. It was also proved that accused made disclosure statement exhibiting his knowledge of the skeleton and there was discovery of skeleton confirming appellant's knowledge of burying the skeleton. Identity of the skeleton was also established by DNA fingerprinting. Therefore circumstances established unerringly towards the guilt of the accused.[87]

5.7 Kidnapping and rape

DNA report showed that the blood on the frock of the deceased tallied with DNA of semen on underwear and pant of accused. DNA report was accepted and the accused was convicted.[88]

When it was found that prosecution had been unable to establish its case beyond reasonable doubt. Even in expert evidence, i.e. the DNA report of FSL, there was no match of semen found on clothes of prosecutrix with that of accused. Appeal was allowed and the appellant was acquitted.[89]

5.8 Kidnapping and abduction

Evidence on record proved that there was plan to abduct victim. Appellants were identified by prosecution witness. Bloodstains were recovered from specified locations. The police produced

86 *Mohd. Javed* v *State (Govt. of NCT)* (06.04.2011 – DELHC) MANU/DE/1084/2011.

87 *Pati Ram* v *State (NCT of Delhi)* Criminal Appeal No. 298/2011.

88 *State of Maharashtra* v *Sadashiv* Criminal Appeal No. 1261 of 2013.

89 *Sashi Kumar* v *State of Himachal Pradesh* 2013 CrLJ 4301.

the CFSL report relating to the DNA test of the bloodstained clothes found from where the victim was confined. Bloodstains matched with the victim's blood. The circumstances proved prosecution case beyond all reasonable doubt. The accused was convicted under ss. 364A and 120B of IPC.[90]

5.9 Dacoity and murder

The accused persons assaulted the accountant of a petrol pump and fled away jointly with the booty of ₹1,61,800. In committing this plunder, one of the accused persons murdered the owner of the petrol pump by firing a shot from the gun. DNA test was conducted from the hair recovered from the nails of the deceased. The accused was convicted.[91]

The report by the expert indicated that the source "C", i.e. femur bone of the dead body yielded partial DNA profile and thus the result was inconclusive. According to the view of the Supreme Court, since the DNA report is inconclusive, the court has to consider the other evidences to find out if the identity of the dead body was established.[92]

5.10 Theft and murder

Accused was sentenced to death for the offence under s. 302, IPC. In his appeal before the Supreme Court, accused challenged his conviction on various grounds like failure of prosecution to complete the chain of circumstantial evidence, lack of motive, unreliableness of the recoveries effected by the prosecution etc. and irregularity in the judicial confession. The Apex Court held that there was no irregularity in the judicial confession given by the accused voluntarily while he was on bail and dismissed the appeal. As there was no direct evidence, the prosecution relied on circumstances to fasten the guilt of the accused.

90 *Abdul Rahaman Kunji* v *State of West Bengal* Cal LT 2015(1) HC 318 (Abduction case of Khadim owner Partha Roy Barman).

91 *Amin Khan* v *State of Rajasthan* (2009)3 SCC 776.

92 *Manju Kumar* v *State of NCT of Delhi* Criminal Appeal No. 702 of 2007.

Accordingly, the conviction was recorded. The High Court confirmed the conviction and sentence was imposed. It has come in the evidence that human spermatozoa was detected in the pubic hair and vaginal swab of one of the deceased. These swabs were subjected to DNA test after taking the blood samples of the accused. Although the DNA evidence was in favour of the accused but the other evidences like fingerprints etc. proved the guilt of the accused. Thus the conviction of death sentence awarded to the accused was upheld.[93]

5.11 Rape

The accused preferred the appeal before the Supreme Court against conviction and sentence under s. 376, IPC. DNA test on dead foetus was performed and established the paternity. The sentence and conviction as recorded by the trial court and High Court were confirmed by the Supreme Court.[94]

Accused was convicted for wrongful confinement and rape upon the victim. There were no mitigating circumstances at all in favour of the accused for reduction of sentence. Deterrence remained as one of the objects behind the imposition of punishment. The medical evidence proved that rape was committed on the victim. The Senior Scientific Officer, carried out the DNA test on the basis of the materials forwarded to him. He confirmed that the accused is the contributor of the semen which was collected by doctor, in the form of vaginal swab. The injuries inflicted on the victim although might heal, but nevertheless the scars left by the said injuries, which were physical, emotional and psychological and may never heal and she might have to live with them for a long time to come. Appeal was devoid of any merit and was dismissed by upholding the conviction.[95]

The accused persons were convicted for rape. Conviction was based on the testimony of the prosecutrix and DNA report. Appellants contended that in view of the totality of evidence,

93 *M.A. Antony* alias *Antappan* v *State of Kerala* AIR 2009 SC 2549.

94 *Kamalanatha* v *State of Tamil Nadu* (2005)5 SCC 194.

95 *Raghubir Dessai* v *State* 2007 CrLJ 829 (Bom).

the impugned judgment of conviction and sentence was not sustainable. Held, the evidence on record clearly showed that the accused persons entered into the room of the prosecutrix, forcibly pressed cloth on her mouth and they laid her on the bed and thereafter committed rape one after another. The evidence of prosecutrix was convincing and it is the settled principle of law that evidence of prosecutrix itself is sufficient to warrant conviction. On perusal of the evidence on record, the court held that the trial court properly appreciated the evidence, facts and law and rightly recorded the order of conviction and sentence.[96]

Trial judge convicted the appellant for an offence of rape. Age of prosecutrix was 18 years according to her own statement in FIR. So, on the date of occurrence prosecutrix must had been about 17 years. Moreover, according to her, appellant had sexual intercourse with her only with her consent. Admittedly, victim was more than 16 years of age on date of occurrence. It was also the case of the prosecutrix, that she became pregnant only because of the accused. To rebut this part of the evidence of the prosecutrix, the accused had produced report of the DNA test conducted for the prosecutrix and the accused. The result of the report revealed that the accused is not the father of the child born to victim. Hence, offence under s. 375 IPC could not be said to be made out against appellant.[97]

Evidence of victim was sufficiently corroborated not only by her father but also by Doctors and this evidence itself was more than sufficient to prove charge against accused. Presence of semen stains on the clothes of the victim was a piece of corroborative evidence and this had been confirmed being that of accused by DNA testing. Prosecution had proved its case beyond reasonable doubt. The appeal was dismissed and conviction was upheld.[98]

96 *Ajit Barman* v *State of West Bengal* 2007(3) CHN 747.

97 *Soundarrajan* v *State of Tamil Nadu represented by the Inspector of Police* 1997(2) CTC 665.

98 *Subhash Swami Naik* v *State of Goa* (2012)8 SCC 365.

Evidence of child witness could not be rejected *per se*, but court as a rule of prudence was required to consider such evidence with close scrutiny. Prosecutrix in her testimony in Court, described in sufficient detail incident of rape which happened with her and also identified accused as person who had ravished her. Presence of blood of prosecutrix on clothes of accused corroborated testimony of prosecutrix. DNA test was also conducted and relied by the court. Therefore, prosecution established guilt of accused.[99]

Statement of complainant had given clear statement of evidence with regard to role of appellant in crime. Complainant had not been shaken from her evidence in cross-examination. Complainant was admittedly minor, so matter of cohabitation with her by appellant did not attract element of consent. Complainant by expressing willingness in court to undergo DNA test for her child read with her cogent evidence with regard to details of incident on fateful night, left little iota of doubt with regard to complicity of accused. Oral testimony of victim which was found to be cogent, reliable, convincing and trustworthy must be given credence by court. Therefore, appellant was not entitled to extended benefit of doubt. Appeal was dismissed and conviction sustained.[100]

Appellant was convicted under ss. 376 and 417, IPC. During course of trial, a petition was filed for conducting DNA test of victim and her child. Trial court allowed the petition holding that DNA test would conclusively determine paternity or otherwise of the accused. Hence this revision application is by appellant. Held, under s. 362 of CrPC when an order of rejection of prayer of holding DNA test was passed when eight witnesses were already examined, contrary order on renewal of prayer of prosecution is impermissible. The issue before the trial court was not whether the child was fathered by the present petitioner but whether the petitioner had committed the

99 *State* v *Sujeet Kumar* Criminal Appeal No. 1190 of 2014.
100 *Gautam Chowdhury* v *State of West Bengal* (2015)1 C Cr LR (Cal) 690.

offence of rape. Therefore, holding of DNA test will not be relevant to the consideration of the charge. As held in *Goutam Kundu* v *State of West Bengal*,[101] courts in India, cannot order blood test as a matter of course. DNA test cannot escape the conclusiveness under s. 112 of the Evidence Act. If the evidence of the prosecutrix and any other witnesses supporting in the prosecution are found by the trial court sufficient to indicate that offence under s. 376, IPC has been committed by the petitioner then the result of the DNA test by itself would be of no avail. Therefore it is not a deserving case where DNA test should be held. Impugned order of the trial court was set aside. Revisional application was allowed.[102]

5.12 Denial of paternity

The judicial Magistrate allowed petition of prosecution and granted permission to police to perform DNA typing test on accused as well as complainant and her child. Hence, this petition was filed. Held accused and complainant was factually not married and complainant had given birth to a child. However, s. 112 of the Act was not applicable to case as there was no relationship of husband and wife between the complainant and accused. Therefore accused disowned paternity of the child. Further trial court passed an order that DNA typing test was must for case under s. 417, IPC. Thus, there was no infirmity in finding of trial court.[103]

6 Cases in which DNA evidence was used in determining paternity or maternity

Petitioner claimed to be the son of the respondent. DNA test was conducted. Test concluded that that the respondent was the father of the petitioner.[104]

101 *Goutam Kundu* v *State of West Bengal* AIR 1993 SC 2295; (1993)3 SCC 418; 1993 CrLJ 3233.

102 *Sabur Hossain Biswas* alias *Paltu* v *State of West Bengal* (10.01.2008 – CALHC) MANU/WB/00332008.

103 *Ravichandran* v *Sub-Inspector of Police* 2006(2) CTC 827.

104 *Anil Kumar* v *Turaka Kondala Rao* 1998 CrLJ 4279.

Respondent wife filed an application under s. 125 of CrPC before the Judicial Magistrate, for her and her daughter's maintenance. The Judicial Magistrate allowed the said application and granted a monthly maintenance of ₹400 to her and ₹200 to her daughter. The order was challenged by the husband before the Sessions Court. The revision application was heard by the 1st Additional Sessions Judge who by his judgment and order partly allowed the revision application of the appellant and set aside the maintenance granted to respondent. The order granting maintenance of ₹200 per month to the minor daughter was maintained. Against the judgment and order the appellant filed another case before the High Court. Respondent wife had also filed Revision Petition before the same High Court. The High Court heard both the revision applications together, dismissed the revision application filed by the appellant and allowed the revision application filed by respondent wife. Hence the present appeal was filed by the husband before the Supreme Court. The court held where the purported father denied paternity but refused to undergo DNA test, such a person was disentitled from disputing paternity. The appeal of the appellant husband was dismissed.[105]

Result of DNA test by itself could be taken as conclusive in deciding paternity. It was the duty of the court before making the order under s. 125, CrPC to find the paternity of the child in a summary manner. Both the courts below did not appreciate the evidence in the right perspective. Therefore the orders of the courts below were set aside.[106]

Accused cohabited with victim by giving assurance of marriage. Consequently two children were born. Accused denied marriage. Petitioner filed suit and SDJM took cognizance against the accused for commission of offence under ss. 376 and 506 of IPC. Thereafter case was committed to Court of Sessions. The victim filed an application before the Sessions Judge for direction to make further the investigation

105 *Dwarika Prasad Satpathy* v *Bidyut Prava Dixit* (1999)7 SCC 675.
106 *Modi (Smt.)* v *Latoor Lal* RLW 2004(3) Raj 1766.

of the aforesaid case stating therein that the investigating officer had not taken any step for medical examination with regard to her age and had not conducted DNA test regarding paternity of the children born. The application was rejected. Hence the present petition with prayer for direction to IO to conduct DNA test and blood grouping test for determination of paternity of the children. Hence the IO was directed to collect blood samples from the accused and two children to conduct DNA test and submit the said report to the Sessions Judge who will consider the said report for proving or disproving the guilt of the accused.[107]

Report of DNA fingerprinting issued by the DNA Fingerprinting and Diagnostic Centre, Hyderabad, which is a Central Government Undertaking, can be admitted in evidence without examination of the expert under s. 293, CrPC. Hence DNA fingerprinting cannot be rejected on the sole ground that the Government Scientific Expert who issued the same is not enumerated under sub-sec. (4) of s. 293, CrPC. On the other hand, it has to be admitted in evidence under sub-sec. (1) of s. 293 as a report which was issued under the hand of Government Scientific Expert. At that time when s. 293 was brought into the Code, DNA fingerprinting might have been an alien theme, and so it did not strike the attention of the Legislature.[108]

The question raised in this matter was whether a person disputing paternity of the child could seek for subjecting the mother and child to DNA test to determine paternity? Held, in the view of the ratio laid down by the Apex Court in *Banarasi Dass* v *Teeku Dutta*,[109] it was to be held that in the maintenance proceedings, the party disputing the paternity of the child has to prove his 'non-access' with the mother of the child during the relevant time in order to dispel the presumption under s. 112 of the Evidence Act 1872 and such presumption should have to be displaced by leading strong preponderance of

107 *Thogorani* v *State of Orissa* 2004 CrLJ 4003.
108 *Geetha* v *State of Kerala* 2006(3) KLT 960.
109 *Banarsi Dass* v *Teeku Dutta* (2005)4 SCC 449.

probability and not by mere filing of petition for determining the paternity by medical tests, i.e. DNA, the impugned order was set aside. Criminal petition of the appellant was thus allowed.[110]

The instant criminal writ petition was filed under Art. 32 of the Constitution of India for the production of her daughter baby Simran in the court with the following prayer:

(i) To issue appropriate writ, order or directions in the nature of *habeas corpus*, directing the respondents to produce baby Simran, in the Supreme Court, enabling the petitioner to meet her being her natural guardian/ mother.

(ii) Issue appropriate Writ, order or direction to the respondents to disclose the whereabouts of baby Simran, and DNA test be conducted to affirm and ascertain the correct identity of baby Simran being the daughter of the petitioner and custody of the child be given to the petitioner.

(iii) Pass such order or other reliefs, as the Hon'ble court may deem fit and proper in the facts and circumstances of the case.

On 15.07.2005, having regard to the nature of the dispute, the court decided to resolve the dispute as far as scientifically accurate, by having the DNA test of the petitioner, the child, respondent 3 and his wife. It was proved by the DNA test that the child produced before the court is not the petitioner's real daughter. The court stated that since it is proved by the DNA test that the child produced before the court was not the child of the petitioner it was the duty of the respondents to produce the child which was forcibly taken by them on the date of the death of the husband of the petitioner.[111]

Result of a genuine DNA test may not be enough to escape from conclusiveness of s. 112 of the Act. When there was

110 *Didde Sundara Mani (Smt.)* v *Didde Venkata Subbarao* 2005 CrLJ 3618.

111 *Nirmaljit Kaur (2)* v *State of Punjab* (2006)9 SCC 363.

apparent conflict between right to privacy of a person not to submit himself forcibly to medical examination and duty of court to reach truth, court must exercise its discretion only after balancing interest of parties and on due consideration whether for a just decision in matter. Held in the present case DNA test was eminently needed.[112]

The court can use reasonable force by taking police assistance if blood sample is not willingly given as putative father was unwilling to subject himself to DNA test. Hence an SLP was filed before the Supreme Court by Narayan Dutt Tiwari, the putative father. The Supreme Court while dismissing putative father's SLP, modifying High Court directions to the extent that confidentiality would be afforded to petitioner by taking sample at his residence instead of requiring him to come to court premises for this purpose. Petitioner's old age was also taken into consideration. Putative son and his mother also permitted to be present at the time of taking sample so that genuineness of sample remains free from controversy.[113]

The learned Magistrate of the trial court accepted the plea of the wife of the appellant and granted maintenance to her and her daughter. The husband challenged the order in revision, and failed. Thereafter, he filed a petition under s. 482 of CrPC for direction from the said court to conduct DNA test of the child which was refused. Against the said order of refusal, the present leave petition was filed before the Hon'ble Supreme Court and the leave was granted subject to the payment of all dues paid in terms of the order passed by the learned Magistrate. Therefore both the parties were directed to make a joint application to the Forensic Science Laboratory at Nagpur for conducting the test. The wife filed an application for maintenance under s. 125 of CrPC, but the same was dismissed by the Magistrate. Thereafter, the wife resorted to a fresh proceeding under s. 125 of CrPC claiming maintenance for herself and her daughter. The husband's plea that he had no access to the wife when the child was begotten stands proved

112 *Babita Devi* alias *Babali* v *State of Jharkhand* 2011 CrLJ 3643.
113 *Narayan Dutt Tiwari* v *Rohit Shekhar* (2012)12 SCC 554.

by the DNA test report and the appellant thus could not be compelled by the court to bear the fatherhood of a child, when the scientific reports prove to the contrary. The court was conscious that an innocent child may not be bastardised as the marriage between her mother and father were subsisting at the time of her birth but in view of the DNA test reports and what had been observed by the court, the court could not preclude the consequence which would be denying the truth. As a result, the court allowed the appeal, set aside the impugned judgment so far as it directed for the payment of maintenance to the respondent. However, it was directed that the payment already made should not be recovered from the respondents.[114]

In this case the illegitimate son was claiming maintenance against his father. Father was not consenting for DNA test. The father had admitted that he had acquaintance with the mother of the son but no reason or explanation was forwarded as to why a false case was brought against him. Hence the claim of maintenance against the father and the paternity of the illegitimate son was proved. With reference to s. 114 of Indian Evidence Act, it was held that an adverse inference can be drawn by the Court in the matter of paternity, where person alleged to be the father of child refuses to undergo DNA test.[115]

114 *Nandlal Wasudeo Badwaik* v *Lata Nandlal Badwaik* (2014)2 SCC 576.

115 *Riyas* v *Haseena* 2014 CrLJ 4588.

Chapter 3

Ballistics

1 Introduction

Firearms and ammunition examination is the field which comes under the discipline of "Forensic Ballistics". The word "Ballistics" has been etymologically derived from the Latin word "*ballistica*" after its first use by Calvin Goddard, who is considered as the father of forensic ballistics and refers to a body in motion. Ballistic means the systematic study of the firearms and ammunitions used in the commission of crimes specially murders for the purpose of investigation and identification. The literal meaning of the term ballistics means the study about the motion of projectiles. Projectile is known as the body projected by force mostly from firearms, especially through air.[1] A firearm is a device by which a projectile or projectiles can be hurled with great force. It includes familiar hand weapons like revolver, pistol, rifle and shotgun, machine gun and an extensive variety of military artillery. The latter type of weapon such as military artillery is the concern of ordinance experts. Ammunition on the other hand, generally means the material fired, scattered or dropped or detonated from any weapon. It also includes weapons like bombs, missiles, grenades, naval mines and anti-personnel mines and the component part of other weapons like bullets and warheads

1 Marvin D'souza and R.P. Kataria, *Forensic Science in Criminal Trial and Investigation*, Ed. 2016, p. 1008.

that create an effect on the target.[2] Usually all mechanical weapons require some form of ammunition to operate. It comes from the French word *la munition,* which refers to the material used for war. The terms ammunition and munitions are often used interchangeably, although the term munition now usually refers to the actual weapons system with the ammunition required to operate it.[3] Moreover, the crimes committed with these weapons are not very common.

The science of ballistics has been developed to facilitate the examination of firearms, ammunition and other related matter. Therefore, when a person is shot the wound and the condition of the victim can tell a lot about the nature of the weapon used. Indeed if the weapon is recovered from the scene of crime or from the perpetrators of the crime, the recovery can provide valuable information as to the kind of person who has committed the offence. Even from the bullets or the residue that is left around it, much information can be gathered. Bullets contain a mixture of gunpowder and cordite which leave burn marks on the skin of the victim who is either wounded or killed. They also leave a fine residue on the fingers and hands of the perpetrator of the the crime. These burn marks can signify the distance from which the shot has been fired, kind of weapon used etc. Each weapon's barrel also contains small ligatures and grooves, from which bullet is fired, make marks on the shell casing, which can be used as a means of identifying the make and model of gun if these shell casings are found at the scene. It is to be noted that an automatic or semi-automatic weapon will expel shell casings as the weapon fires a round whereas a revolver will fire the round but retain the shell casings within the barrel.[4] Ballistic evidence now share the same footing as the fingerprint evidence. Different from other

2 Dictionary.com available at http://www.dictionary.com/browse/ammunition, last visited on 13th May 2017.

3 Dictionary.com available at http://www.dictionary.com/browse/munitions, last visited on 13th May 2017.

4 Ballistics: The Use and Study of Firearms available at http://www.exploreforensics.co.uk/ballistics-theuse-and-study-of-firearms.html, last visited on 22nd April 2015.

forensic identification evidence, ballistic evidence always links to a particular weapon instead of linking a particular person involved in the crime. Therefore, in criminal trials, ballistic evidence can establish the crime or link the assailants only through the weapon. Currently, in forensic science, ballistic is classified into three types (*i*) interior ballistics (deals with the study of the projectile inside the firearm) (*ii*) exterior ballistics (deals with the study about the projectiles when it is fired and comes out the barrel) (*iii*) terminal ballistics (covers the wound and damage it causes to the target after the hit). The significance of ballistics is based on few important principles like (*a*) individual firearms will make unique marks on bullets after firing; (*b*) these marks are based on individual characteristics; (*c*) when two objects come in contact, the material in one object will transfer to the other. The third principle is based on trace evidence and also known as the Lockard Exchange Principle.

2 Principle on which ballistic evidence is based

The principle on which the ballistic evidence is based is known as 'Ballistic Imaging Analysis'. The principle was propounded by Lockard which means that if an object comes in contact with any other object, the materials on one transfers to the other. The role of forensic ballistic expert is to trace the origin of the material from which it comes. So in forensic ballistics, the ballistic experts trace the origin of the bullet from which it was fired and also detects the source of cartridge casings. Thus, forensic ballistics is the study about the path of a bullet inside the firearm, through the air at the target. The term was connected to firearms matching for the first time by Calvin Goddard in 1920. In forensic ballistic examination, tool marks[5] are the major thing that is considered for individualizing a particular case of firing. The sole question which arises in such cases is whether the bullet recovered from the target was fired

5 A firearm leaves its unique 'fingerprint' on components of ammunition fired in that firearm. This 'fingerprint' is in the form of unique impressions or striations also known as tool marks.

from the firearm recovered from the crime scene, accused, suspect or from any other place.

As far as forensic ballistic evidence is concerned, in order to individualize a particular piece of evidence and its source, three characteristics are considered, viz. class characteristics, sub-class characteristics and individual characteristics. Class characteristic includes: (1) the land and groove diameters of the barrel; (2) the direction of rifling; (3) the number of lands and grooves; (4) the width of the lands and grooves; and (5) the degree of the rifling twist. On the other hand individual characteristics are the most important factor in determining the individuality. The individual characteristics are formed as a result of the imperfections during the manufacturing process of every firearm. Such imperfections would be there in every firearm even though it was made by the same machine and utmost care was given during its manufacturing. For example, when a bullet is fired, striation marks will be there on the surface of the bullet due to its contact with the inner surface of the barrel. In rifled arms, the striations will be very clear since the inner surface of the barrel have lands and grooves. The most important task of a ballistic expert is to identify the toolmarks on cartridge casings and bullets. Mainly three types of toolmarks can be found on cartridge casings: (1) firing pin impression; (2) ejector mark; and (3) breech face impression.

2.1 Ballistic imaging analysis technology

Till 1990, the firearm identification was manually conducted by an expert, with the help of a comparison microscope and the expert himself had to recollect the identifying marks and features that individualize each firearm. Due to the advancement in computerized way of identification of ammunitions now it is possible to search the images copied inside a computer system in the form of databases similar to DNA database system. In the United States, the database is the combination of two systems, i.e. the Drugfire system (for cartridge cases) funded by the Federal Bureau of Investigation and Bullet Proof System (for bullets) funded by the Bureau of Alcohol, Tobacco, Firearms and Explosives (ATF). Moreover, due to the networking of the database system of ballistic imaging with all law enforcement agencies throughout the country, it is very easy to link a particular sample database with others. This database networking is known as National Integrated Ballistic Information Network (NIBIN). The ballistic imaging technology in firearm identification is performed by the Integrated Ballistic Identification System (IBIS). The IBIS consists of two main parts, the bullet proof microscope and comparison apparatus which capture images from bullets along with brass catcher which catches images of cartridge cases. For the NIBIN programme, data will be collected by the Remote Data Acquisition Stations (RDASs) with a microscope and two built-in cameras mounted to it. One camera is for bullet imaging and the other one for cartridge cases. The primary step in the functioning of the IBIS is the acquisition of image data of bullets or cartridge case that enters into the system. The bullets and cartridge cases are collected from the crime scenes or the materials that may be test fired by the experts.[6]

IBIS Ballistics imaging and analysis technology installed in India is being used to combat the growing problem of homemade weapons. Quick and easy to produce, these non-conventional weapons are more challenging to identify but the Directorate of Forensic Sciences (DFS) in Gandhinagar has been successful in implementing it.

Till date, the database of countrymade weapons with various agencies was wholly inadequate despite the fact that 85% of crimes were committed by using such revolvers and pistols. DFS has started collating data on 'country-made' weapons and added this category to the existing Integrated Ballistics Identification System-IBIS TRAX-3D (IBIS), a globally accepted system developed in Canada that stores data on standard weapons and can identify them by ballistic marks on bullets. So far, the challenge before ballistics experts was that

6 V.R. Dinkar, *Scientific Expert Evidence,* 2nd Ed. 2016, pp. 303-305 (Kolkata: Eastern Law House).

there was no fingerprinting available for country-made weapons but the DFS has done away with that.[7]

3 Classification of firearms

3.1 Shotgun

Shotgun falls in the category of shoulder arms. All shotguns are smooth bore firearms, that is, the cross-section of the barrel at any point makes a perfect circle. They are known as shotguns because they fire a single ball, slug or a charge consisting of a considerable number of lead pellets (shots). A shotgun may be single or double barreled. SBML (Single Barrel Muzzle Loading), DBML (Double Barrel Muzzle Loading), are examples of shotguns.

3.2 Rifles

All rifled arms fire a single bullet. They have a much longer barrel and can fire a high-powered ammunition. Rifles are characterized by their calibers. The caliber is the actual measure of the bore diameter of the barrel between two opposite lands.

3.3 Revolver

A revolver is a rifled handgun, which has a revolving cylinder having chambers for loading the cartridges. The number of chambers may vary from 4 to 7. On pressing the trigger, the cylinder rotates thereby bringing one of the chambers in line with the barrel for firing. Revolvers of different calibers are available. The size of revolvers also varies from 0.38 to 0.455.

3.4 Pistol

A short-barreled rifled arm, which can be fired by one hand are known as pistols. The revolver also is basically a pistol. But because of a revolving cylinder it is known as a pistol-revolver. Pistols have a magazine, which is enclosed in its grip. These

7 Forensic Technology Blog available at: http://www.ultra-forensictechnology.com/news/bid/69682/IBIS-Used-in-India-in-the-Fight-Against-Homemade-Firearms, last accessed on 15.05.2017.

are available in all calibers from about 5 to 12 mm. The barrel of the rifle in a pistol is known as "Colt Type" and "Smith and Wesson type" with features as discussed herein.

3.5 Improvised firearms

Nowadays in many cases improvised firearms are often used by criminals in India besides the standard firearms discussed above. They are called by different names and commonly known as 'country-made firearms'. The barrels are often made of pipes meant for water lines and often use standard ammunition. Sometimes, discarded cartridge shells are refilled and used. Each such firearm is unique in itself with respect to mechanisms of firing and general make up. Country-made firearm is generally short barreled to facilitate concealment. They are usually smooth barreled and are chambered for different type of cartridges.

4 Characteristics of firearms

A firearm consist of two important parts (1) the barrel which are of two types smooth bore and rifling with lands and grooves (2) the mechanical part which includes the chamber, breech face, firing pin, extractor, ejector and trigger. All barrels are manufactured from drilled solid steel pieces. The solid steel pieces are subjected to drilling process from one end to the other with a uniform diameter. The inner side of the barrel will later bore with a reamer to produce a smooth surface. One of the forensic significance of barrel is that due to the drilling process the inner surface of the barrel gets various scratches and scars which supply the individuality to that barrel. These scratches and scars give distinct marks on the bullets that are fired through the barrel and in forensic ballistics considered as individual characteristics. On the other hand, rifles contain various grooves and lands artificially created for firing accuracy, rotation of bullets, firing to a long distance etc. Barrel grooves are of two types (*i*) grooves which twist towards the left hand side and (*ii*) grooves which twist towards the right hand side. This classification is considered as class characteristics in ballistics. Normally, the barrel contains six to eight grooves but some contains upto twenty four grooves.[8] The bullet when rotates through these grooves will get distinct striation marks on its surface.[9]

5 Classification of ammunition

Ammunition means cartridges composed of shells, propellants, primer and projectiles commonly used in firearms. The standard ammunition is made of the following basic components:

(1) Cartridge case/shell/empty;

(2) Primer cap;

(3) Powder or propellant;

(4) Wads; and

(5) Projectiies.[10]

5.1 Cartridge case/shell/empty

Cartridge case is also known as shell or empty after its contents are discharged. It provides housing for various components of the cartridge. It is usually made of brass for rifle, pistol and revolver ammunition. For shotgun it is made from several layers of thin paper, which are tightly compressed. The base of this paper shell is made of brass. Plastic shells are also manufactured.

5.2 Primer cap

The primer cap contains the primer mixture, which gets sandwiched between the anvil and the firing pin. When the firing pin strikes on it with a force it gives rise to a hot piercing flame, which initiates the main charge. The main ingredient of the primer in the past was either mercury fulminate or lead azide. Safer and efficient compcunds are now replacing these. The primers, which are used nowadays, contain compounds of lead antimony and barium.

8 R.A. Rinker, *Understanding Firearm Ballistics*, 5th Ed., p. 128 (hereinafter Rinker, *Understanding Firearm*).

9 V.R. Dinkar, *Scientific Expert Evidence*, 2nd Ed., p. 292.

10 B.S. Nabar, *Forensic Science in Crime Investigation*, 3rd Ed., p. 174.

5.3 Powder or propellant

To propel the bullet or shot charge through the barrel and then through the air, a certain force is necessary. This force is provided by the powder charge. The powder charge gets ignited through primer and converts into gas at a very rapid rate. The generated gas, under compression, develops pressure in the cartridge and finally forces out of the barrel propelling the projectile. Three types of propellant charge are known as:

- Gunpowder (black powder);
- Smokeless powder;
- Semi-smokeless powder.

• **Gunpowder** Gunpowder or black powder is the oldest explosive known to us. It is an intimate mixture of the three ingredients, namely Potassium Nitrate (KNO_3), Charcoal (C) and Sulphur (S) in the approximate ratio of 75:15:10 respectively.

• **Smokeless powder** The basic components of the smokeless powders are Nitroglycerine and Nitrocellulose (gun cotton). Nitrocellulose is used alone or in combination with Nitroglycerine to form smokeless powder.

• **Semi-smokeless powder** It is an intimate mixture of Nitrocellulose, Potassium Nitrate, Charcoal and Sulphur in the approximate ratio of 20:60:12:8. Unlike gunpowder it develops comparatively less smoke.

5.4 Wads

Wads are used in the cartridge primarily to keep the propellant and shot charge in their respective positions. In addition they seal the barrel to prevent escape of gases and consequently, their respective reduction in velocity.

5.5 Projectiles

In shotgun cartridges the projectile consist of small lead balls or pellets. These pellets are of different size, denoted by numbers and the larger pellets by letters.[11]

11 B.S. Nabar, *Forensic Science in Crime Investigation*, 3rd Ed., pp. 179-183.

6 Characteristics of ammunition

Ammunitions that are used in modern firearms contain three elements integrated inside the cartridge. The elements are bullet, propellant and primer. The bullet is the actual projectile which will come outside the barrel after firing. It is made with different metals like brass, steel, aluminium and also with rubber and wood. Most of the bullets contain lead along with other metals for its good performance and accuracy. The tip of all bullets is pointed for penetrating the air as well as the target. In forensic ballistics the construction and composition of bullets are very important since it is very useful for determining the bullets collected from the crime scene and the target. The other important part is the propellant. The role of propellant is to help the bullet to move towards the target. In the earlier days black powder was used as propellant and it was substituted later by smokeless gunpowder. Presently, the nitrocellulose (powder of cotton, nitric acid and sulphuric acid) is used to create maximum combustion. In fact after igniting, the propellant does not explode, instead of burn creating a huge quantity of gas which will form a high pressure inside the cartridge. The primer will ignite the propellant. Earlier mercury was used as primer. Nowdays, different chemicals like leadstyphnate, trinitrotoluene, lead or copper sulphocyanide, lead peroxide, sulphur, tetryl, barium peroxide, sulphur, tetryl barium peroxide and barium nitrate are used for making primers. The primer is an extremely explosive agent that works when the firing pin strikes and compresses the composition in between the cup and anvil. As a result of the compression, the flame occurs and that flame travels through a vent to ignite the propellant charge.

7 Definition of firearms under Arms Act 1959

According to s. 2(1)(*c*) of the Arms Act 1959, "Arms" means articles of any description designed or adapted as weapons for offences, or defence, and includes firearms, sharp-edged and other deadly weapons, and parts of, and machinery for manufacturing arms, but does not include articles designed solely for domestic or agricultural uses such as a *lathi* or an ordinary walking stick and weapons incapable of being used otherwise than as toys or of being converted into serviceable weapons.

According to s. 2(1)(*e*) of the Arms Act 1959, "firearms" means arms of any description designed or adapted to discharge a projectile or projectiles of any kind by the action of any explosive or other forms of energy, and includes—

(i) artillery, hand-grenades, riot-pistols or weapons of any kind designed or adapted for the discharge of any noxious liquid, gas or other such things,

(ii) accessories for any such firearm designed or adapted to diminish the noise or flash caused by the firing thereof,

(iii) parts of, and machinery for manufacturing, firearms, and

(vi) carriages, platforms and appliances for mounting, transporting and serving artillery.

According to s. 2(1)(*h*) of the Arms Act 1959, "prohibited ammunition" means any ammunition, containing, or designed or adapted to contain, any noxious liquid, gas or other such thing, and includes rockets, bombs, grenades, shells, missiles articles designed for torpedo service and submarine mining and such other articles as the Central Government may, by notification in the Official Gazette, specify to be prohibited ammunition;

According to s. 2(1)(*i*) of the Arms Act 1959—

(i) "prohibited arms" means—

(i) firearms so designed or adapted that, if pressure is applied to the trigger, missiles continue to be discharged until pressure is removed from the trigger or the magazine containing the missiles is empty, or

(ii) weapons of any description designed or adapted for the discharge of any noxious liquid, gas or other such thing, and includes artillery, anti-aircraft and anti-tank firearms and such other arms as the

Central Government may, by notification in the Official Gazette, specify to be prohibited arms.

In UK, the Firearms Act 1968 describes a firearm as "a lethal barrelled weapon of any description, from which any shot, bullet or other missile can be discharged". It includes four main classes of weapons: firearms, shotguns, prohibited weapons and air weapons.

8 Firearms evidence collection and procedures

Firearms evidence is usually collected in crimes against persons such as homicide, assault and robbery but may also be found in other crimes such as burglary, rape and narcotics violation. Comparisons of bullets and cartridge cases to specific firearms are the most common examinations for collection of firearm evidence. But other examinations are possible such as distance determinations based on powder residue or shot spread, examination of firearms for functioning or modification, sequence of shots fired and trajectories, list of possible weapon used, serial number restoration and ownership tracing. Evidence of firing or handling a firearm may be detected through the analysis of gunshot residue collected from a person's hands or other body surfaces.

8.1 Mechanism used for collection of ballistic evidence

The first method for collection of ballistic evidence is to identify the bullet. One of the primary methods of categorising bullets is based on their calibre. Calibre refers to the diameter of the bullet, which can be expressed in various terms, including millimetres, inches etc. Moreover, bullets fired through rifled firearms receive both the class as well as accidental characteristics of the barrel from which they are fired. The bullet will show not only the primary markings left by the lands and grooves of the gun barrel but will also reveal the fine striations in all the marks. To determine whether or not a particular gun has fired the questioned bullet, a detailed comparison is made of markings on the question bullet with corresponding markings on the test bullets fired through the suspected gun. A bullet comparison microscope is used for this determination. The suspect bullet and the test fired bullet are illuminated obliquely in order to create shadows that reveal the ridges and furrows engraved by the gun. The test bullets are obtained by firing the suspected weapon into a water tank or a bullet recovery box filled with cotton or cotton waste, to obtain bullet bearing marks characteristic of the barrel.

When bullets are seized at the crime scene is greatly deformed or when only fragments of it are recovered, comparative chemical analysis of the question and the known bullets by spectrographic analysis may yield useful information. Foreign material in the form of blood, tissue etc. on the fired bullet can often be very useful to link it with the target. Sometimes, lead bullets may carry weave pattern of the intermediate targets, like cloth which may be equally useful.

Direction of fire, time of fire, range of fire are other details which might help in the investigation process. The direction of fire can be of great help in the reconstruction of the events in the firearm offences. Time of fire may often be required to determine the time of fire when a firearm is involved in a crime. Range of fire is important information required in the investigation of a firearm case. It is to estimate the distance of a gun from the target hit by its projectile at the time of firing. This information is particularly useful in connection with self-defence pleas. It may also be useful in probing into a murder or suicide theory. It is often possible to estimate, with considerable certainty, the distance of a gun from the target by a study of patterns and residues left on the latter.

8.2 Detection of residues on hand

When a gun is fired, especially a revolver, powder residue from the propellant and the primer may be blown around the cylinder. Traces of such residues are sometimes transferred on the hands of the shooter. Detection of such residues helps the investigator in identifying the shooter.

8.3 Nature of injuries

Determination of nature of injuries are very important in investigation through ballistic evidence. Firearm injuries greatly varies. Ordinarily they cause punctured wounds. But sometimes explosive, contusion and incised wounds are also caused.

8.3.1 Entrance wound

The entrance wound is recognised by its inverted margins, the presence of scorching, blackening, tattooing, dirt ring, size and the number of wounds. The inversion of the entrance is caused by the projectile, which draws the skin inside.

8.3.2 Exit wound

An exit wound is recognized by the absence of various marks found around the entrance wound such as presence of averted edges of the skin and the shape and size of the wound. The marks due to hot gases, smoke, powder residue etc. will be absent. The size of the exit wound is ordinarily larger than the entrance wound or even the size of the projectile.

8.4 Handling, collection and preservation of evidence

The weapon found at the scene of crime should not be touched until its position has been photographed, sketched and marked. If a weapon is found on the floor, any marks on the floor caused by it must be examined. The position of the cartridges, cartridge cases and bullets is equally important. From their position it is possible to deduce the position of firing, the direction of shot and in certain cases also the path of the bullet.[12]

9 Admissibility of ballistic evidence in criminal cases

The history of firearms evidence can be traced back to 1030's in the United States. As it happened with the other evidences, ballistic evidence also faced an immature dealing when it was first introduced in the courtroom. The judges and the defense lawyers were in dilemma regarding the scientific background of the testimony. For the first time the ballistic evidence was evaluated in *People* v *Fisher.*[13] In this case the Supreme Court

12 B.S. Nabar, *Forensic Science in Crime Investigation*, 3rd Ed., pp. 187-195.

13 340 III 216 (III 1930).

of Illinois pointed out one of the issues as the error committed by the trial court in admitting the ballistic evidence on two grounds in spite of the reasonable explanation provided by the ballistic expert before the trial court. They are, there was no proper chain of custody of the bullet which was recovered from the body of the deceased and the expert testimony was novel and should not have been admitted. But, the trend was changed when the court settled the issues raised previously and answered them in the case of *People* v *Jennings*.[14] After this case, courts in the United States considered it as a valid precedent for admitting expert testimony based on firearm identification evidence. In 1975, a major breakthrough occurred when the Federal Rules of Evidence was drafted. The authentication of the specimen by an expert witness was specifically insisted by r. 901(*b*)(3) of Federal Rules of Evidence for identifying a particular piece of evidence through comparison. In *United States* v *Bowers*[15] although there was an attempt from the appellant's side to set aside the ballistic evidence but the court held that the trial court has wide discretion in determining whether the particular scientific tests are sufficiently reliable and permit expert testimony. Thus the court accepted the trial court's view and rejected the appellant side argument. After the formulation of the *Daubert* guideline, the court relied on the guidelines to proceed in any matter.

In India, a thorough search of judicial decisions pronounced by the Supreme Court and different High Courts, it is difficult to find out any case where the evidential aspects such as reliability based on the technicalities of forensic uniqueness has been analysed in a profound manner. In the case of *Sidhartha Vashisht* v *State*[16] (Jessica Lal murder case) the Supreme Court of India while examining the propriety of the High Court's reversal of the acquittal of the trial court had considered the reliability of the forensic ballistic evidence given by one of the three ballistic experts on the conclusion that two

14 (1911)96 NE 1077; 252 III 534.
15 [1976] 534 F 2d 186.
16 AIR 2010 SC 2352.

cartridge cases came from same .22 pistol without examining the weapon itself. This reliability issue arose in this case due to the unfortunate defense theory named "two weapon" theory was formulated by the defense. According to the defense, in order to reach a definite conclusion that whether two cartridge cases came from the same firearm; there is no need to examine the firearm. This contention was negated by the court stating that "while giving reports after Ballistic Examination, the bullets, cartridge case and the cartridges recovered and weapon of offence recovered are carefully examined and test firing is done by the FSL by the said weapon of offence and then only a specific opinion is given". The negation was based on the proper application of the scientific theory that "when pressure is built inside the cartridge case, which results in the pushing out of the bullet from the barrel, there is difference in the marks to the extent that it may be either clear or unclear and flattened and deepened thus no opinion can be rendered on account of this dissimilarity in the absence of the weapon of offence and test firing". The observation made by the court regarding this is very significant to be mentioned here: "[A]n expert is only an expert if he follows the well accepted guidelines to arrive at a conclusion and supports the same with logical reasoning which is a requirement of law as laid down in the Indian Evidence Act." In fact, the court was forced to deliver this observation due to the conflicting opinions of three ballistic experts whose findings were based without proper reasoning.

In *State of M.P. through C.B.I.* v *Paltan Mallah,*[17] the defense strongly challenged the ballistic expert evidence given by the CFSL, New Delhi. The basis of the challenge was that a forensic ballistic expert who has based his examination on a particular country made 12 bore firearm which was alleged to be involved in the case was not grooved. The contention was that it was not possible for a forensic ballistic expert to come to a conclusion about the identification of the bullets used in a case which was fired from a country-made firearm having no barrel

17 AIR 2005 SC 733; 2005 CrLJ 918.

grooves. But this contention was countered by the expert stating that even though the firearm barrel was not a grooved one, when the pellets are fired, they will get special individual marks due to the friction inside the barrel. For substantiating this, the expert had submitted the micro photograph of one pellet he had taken as evidence. The evidence was also challenged by the defense stating that at least three such photographs should be produced as sufficient evidence was rejected by the court relying on *Ramanathan* v *State of Tamil Nadu.*[18]

Apparently, from the term Ballistic, what strikes our mind is that in cases relating to firearms, the involvement of the Ballistic expert is essential, but this concept has been swayed away by the Supreme Court. While deciding the case of *Prem Kumar* v *State of Bihar*[19] the Supreme Court referred to the case of *Mohinder Singh* v *State*[20] (supra) and laid its opinion. In the case of *Prem Kumar*, the plea of the appellant's counsel was that the cartridges recovered were neither sent to the ballistic expert nor was any ballistic expert examined, the court in this respect invited the decision of the Supreme Court in *Mohinder Singh* v *State*[20] and referred particularly to the observation of the court in this respect. The court opined that the observation which was forwarded in the above mentioned case is applicable where the weapon with which the victim sustained injuries was before the Court and there was doubt whether the injuries could have been caused by using that weapon. Whereas, in this case, the rifles used by the accused were never recovered. So, the prosecution could not, in the circumstances, allege that a particular identifiable weapon was used in committing the crime. In this case there was nothing to be examined by the ballistic expert. Therefore the observations in *Mohinder Singh* v *State*[20] should be understood in the above peculiar context. There was no merit in the plea of the appellant's counsel. On the other hand in the case of

18 1978 CrLJ 1137; AIR 1978 SC 1204.
19 *Prem Kumar* v *State of Bihar* (1995)3 SCC 228.
20 *Mohinder Singh* v *State* 1950 SCR 821; AIR 1953 SC 415.

Sukhwant Singh v *State of Punjab*,[21] the Supreme Court categorically held that, in cases where the injuries are caused by firearms, the opinion of the ballistic expert is of a considerable importance where both the firearm and the cartridge were recovered during investigation to connect an accused with the crime.[21] Therefore, by the decision of *Sukhwant Singh* ballistic report is important if the investigation leads to a recovery of both the firearm and crime cartridge. In the field of Ballistics even possession of unauthorised firearms is an offence. In the case of *Bilal Ahmed Kaloo*,[22] the appellant was in possession of a revolver and two cartridges for which he was booked under ss. 3(3), 4(3) and 5 of the TADA and also under s. 25 of the Arms Act. The ballistic expert conducted scientific test on the articles and reported that the seized articles were in perfect working condition. Particulars of the weapon given in the seizure memo tallied with the weapon on examination by the ballistic expert.[22] In cases where rifle was used for firing and the appellant took the plea of general exceptions, the court was of the view that primordial requirement of the said exception is that the act which killed the other person should have been done "with proper care and caution."

The very fact that the accused shot his own colleague at a close range without knowing the identity of his target smacks of utter dearth of any care and caution. Moreover, there is a condition for claiming the extended right of private defence only in case the property sought to be protected is a building. It should be a building used for human dwelling or for custody of property. If it is not a building of that type the person exercising the right of private defence cannot go to the farthest extent of killing another person unless the threatened mischief has caused a reasonable apprehension that death or grievous hurt would otherwise be the consequence. In this case there was no plea at all that the appellant had any apprehension of death or grievous hurt nor it was the case that the tower was

21 *Sukhwant Singh* v *State of Punjab* (1995)3 SCC 367.

22 *Bilal Ahmed Kaloo* v *State of AP* (1997)7 SCC 431.

either used for human dwelling or custody of property.[23] It is reiterated by the court that when the recoveries were not sent to ballistic expert and the oral evidence were trustworthy and it is not contradictory to the medical evidence, there was no infirmity in the impugned judgment of the court in granting conviction.[24] Where firearm injuries were caused which resulted in the death and according to doctors injuries were individually sufficient to cause death, the Supreme Court was of the opinion that minor contradictions or inconsistencies are immaterial. Non-mention in seizure memo whether the cartridges seized by investigating officer from place of occurrence were wet or dry though it was raining at that time or non-mention in inquest report that dead body was covered with a cloth though on of the witnesses had stated so, were minor omissions are cannot be a ground for discarding the prosecution case.[25] Therefore only medical evidence without ballistic evidence can prove a case. In *H.P.* v *Mast Ram*, the Supreme Court laid some observations regarding Ballistic Evidence. One of the views was that generally the fire range of gun differs from gun to gun but it is not always true that the firing ranges of two different guns are different. Therefore, the court opined that it could not be said that the firing range of DBML gun differed from SBML gun or *vice versa*. Secondly, the Supreme Court, confirmed that the report submitted under the hand of Government Scientific Expert comes within the purview of s. 293(1) of CrPC. The Supreme Court confirmed that it is not the requirement of law that the pellets recovered from the body of the deceased be sent to ballistic expert to determine as to whether the pellets were fired from the exhibited gun or not. The court held on the contrary, the recovery of pellets from the body of the deceased clearly established the prosecution case that the deceased died of gunshot injuries. Moreover, the court was of the view that the

23 *Bhupendrasinh A. Chudasama* v *State of Gujarat* (1998)2 SCC 603.
24 *Ajay Singh* v *State of Bihar* (2000)9 SCC 730.
25 *State of Punjab* v *Mela Singh* (2003)12 SCC 464.

ocular testimony corroborated by the opinion of the doctor proved the prosecution case beyond reasonable doubt.[26] Even on the basis of reliable testimony of rustic straightforward witness which is consistent with the medical evidence on record, conviction can be awarded, no recoveries were made from place of occurrence.[27] In cases of Ballistic, if possession and recovery of the firearm is proved, ownership of the firearm need not be proved.[28] In the *Jessica Lal* case,[29] court opined that an expert is only an expert if he would follow the well accepted guidelines to arrive at a conclusion, which is supported with logical reasoning.[30] It has been studied by the court that when a weapon is fired from a close range, normally gunpowder which comes along with the bullet makes dark burn marks around the wound. The reason is that when the weapon is fired from a close range, normally gunpowder comes along with the bullet and makes dark burn marks around the wound.[31] The court also opined that in cases of Ballistic evidence when ocular testimony receives clear corroboration from medical evidence and as well as from the report of the FSL, minor discrepancies are bound to occur and one cannot expect the witnesses to state with precision. Moreover, judicial evaluation of the evidence should be done by considering the totality of the facts and circumstances of the case and not on scrutiny in isolation and further the concept of proof beyond reasonable doubt cannot be made to appear totally unrealistic. Thus to effect conviction of the accused facts should be established cumulatively.[32]

In *Bastiram* v *State of Rajasthan*,[33] although according to the post-mortem and evidence of the doctor, no firearm injury was found in the body of the deceased, the Supreme Court

26 *H.P.* v *Mast Ram* (2004)8 SCC 660.
27 *Birendra Rai* v *State of Bihar* (2005)9 SCC 719.
28 *Sivakumar* v *State* (2006)1 SCC 714.
29 *Sidhartha Vashisht* v *State* AIR 2010 SC 2352.
30 *Manu Sharma* v *State (NCT of Delhi)* (2010)6 SCC 1.
31 *Gurjinder Singh* v *State of Punjab* (2011)3 SCC 530.
32 *Manjit Singh* v *State of Punjab* (2013)12 SCC 746.
33 *Bastiram* v *State of Rajasthan* (2014)5 SCC 398.

concluded that the ocular evidence undoubtedly showed that deceased was fired by the accused but in view of the unchallenged testimony of the doctor, it was quite clear that the gunshot did not hit the deceased and the cause of his death was the cumulative effect of the various sufferance by him. Thus the Supreme Court upheld the convictions of the appellants.[33]

9.1 Opinion of ballistic expert

In cases where injuries are caused by firearms and empty cartridges were recovered from the spot. Pistol and cartridges were seized from the accused but the prosecution failed to send the empty cartridges recovered and the seized pistol to the ballistic expert, acquittal was recorded. The court opined that failure to produce the expert opinion before the trial court in such cases affects the creditworthiness of the prosecution case to a great extent.[34]

In the other matter acquittal was recorded as the FSL failed to predict with any scientific accuracy as the time when the gun was last fired. In the case in hand, gun belonging to accused had fired at some point of time but that point of time could not with any exactitude, be related to time of incident. It was common that fire arm barrels was not cleaned after every discharge and may be that gun had fired long before its seizure from accused. There was no evidence as prosecution witness had not supported prosecution case, to show that accused had fired gun. No corroboration was available even from seizure of gun from accused as he had a valid licence. Even statement made by the deceased in the dying declaration did not corroborate the involvement of the accused in the case. Therefore conviction was set aside and accused was acquitted of charge.[35]

In another case, due to contradiction of the deposition of the doctor and the prosecution, the case of the prosecution

34 *Sukhwant Singh* v *State of Punjab* (1995)3 SCC 367.
35 *Gajadhar Soni* v *State of M.P.* (04.12.1996 – MP HC) MANU/MP/0786/1996.

was controversial. Although the guns and empties recovered were sent for analysis to the ballistic expert, and they were reported to be in working condition but it was of no use as it did not corroborate the prosecution case. The motive on the part of the accused to kill the deceased could not be proved. Hence, acquittal was recorded.[36]

9.2 Forensic evidence leads to acquittal

Acquittal has also been recorded when, both the ballistic expert's and the medical evidence corroborated each other but both the evidences did not support the prosecution case. Hence acquittal was recorded.[37]

In *State of M.P.* v *Ghudan,*[38] acquittal was recorded, as the Supreme Court was of the view that it is not safe to place reliance on the report of the ballistic expert because it was an admitted fact that the empties which were sent to the ballistic expert after six months were not sealed at the time of seizure. In this case, the identity of the empties seized from the place of incident and those tested by expert could not be safely tallied. If none of the evidences corroborate, it lead to acquittal although the ballistic expert was examined.[39] As the prosecution version is contradictory to the ballistic expert's report and medical report acquittal was recorded.[40] When it was clear from the report of the ballistic expert and the medical evidence that the cartridge in question was not fired from the single barreled 12 bore rifle said to have been used by the accused, acquittal was recorded.[41] When the evidence of the eyewitnesses were in contradiction with medical evidence and ballistic expert's report, the accused was acquitted.[42] For the

36 *Raj Kumar* v *State of Haryana* (13.06.1996 – PN HC) MANU/PH/0916/1996.

37 *State by Aldur Police* v *B.C. Parameshwarappa* (07.06.1999) MANU/KA/0359/1999.

38 *State of M.P.* v *Ghudan* (2003)12 SCC 485.

39 *Jasbir Singh* v *State* (*Govt. of NCT of Delhi*) (29.10.2007 – DEL HC)(MANU/DE/9065/2007).

40 *Ghurey Lal* v *State of U.P.* (2008)10 SCC 450.

41 *Puran Singh* v *State of Uttaranchal* (2008)3 SCC 795.

42 *Mahendra Pratap Singh* v *State of Uttar Pradesh* (2009)11 SCC 334.

same reason in many cases the accused was acquitted.[43] When, the existence of conspiracy could not be established, the recoveries which were examined by ballistic expert become doubtful.[44] Sometimes on the sole basis of the ballistic expert's report, even an accused was acquitted. When according to the ballistic expert's report the pistol which was recovered from the appellant was not in a working condition, the accused may be acquitted.[45] For conviction on the basis of the forensic evidence, corroboration is required but for acquittal it might not require, means when there is no other evidence to convict accused, acquittal may be recorded on the basis of the ballistic expert's report, maintaining the principle for conviction, proof beyond reasonable doubt is required. Independent witness should be called by police at the time of search and seizure. After the seizure is made proper care should be taken to keep the seized arms under safe custody in sealed cover even when it is dispatched and ultimately produced before the court. Moreover, if ballistic expert has tested the firearm, it should be mentioned in the report, which was not done in this case.[46] In spite of the availability of the ballistics expert's report, if the prosecution fails to prove that the crime cartridge was recovered from the accused as alleged, and it could not be linked with the gun in question, the evidence of the expert would be considered as discrepant and not worthy of any credit.[47] If the ballistic expert reports that the cartridge cases recovered does not match with the weapon that was seized from the custody of the accused, on the basis of such report of the ballistic expert, acquittal was granted to the accused.[48] If there is insufficiency of the materials available to the ballistic

43 *State of Punjab* v *Rajinder Singh* (2009)15 SCC 612.

44 *Prakash Chand* v *State of H.P.* (19.07.2011 – HP HC) MANU/HP/1426/2011.

45 *Sapna Talwar* v *State* (12.10.2011 – DEL HC) MANU/DE/3999/2011.

46 *Md. Moinul Haque* v *State of Assam* (06.06.2012 – GU HC)MANU/GH/0350/2012.

47 *State of Himachal Pradesh* v *Suresh Kumar* (27.06.2013 – HP HC) MANU/HP/0383/2013.

48 *Joginder Singh* v *State of Haryana* (2014)11 SCC 335.

expert as it happened that due to insufficiency of characteristics of striation present on the bullet mark, it could not be opined by the ballistic expert from which weapon they were discharged.[49]

In *Gajadhar Soni* v *State of M.P.*[50] as the ballistic expert failed to point out the time with exactitude when the gun belonging to the accused had been fired acquittal was recorded. In *Jasbir Singh* v *State (Government of NCT of Delhi)*,[51] although the ballistic expert was examined but none of the evidences corroborated prosecution case, hence acquittal was given. In *Moinul Haque's* case,[52] the alleged weapon recovered from the possession of the appellant was neither sent to ballistic expert nor tested by the police personnel himself. Failure of the expert to mention the fact properly in the report resulted in acquittal.[52] Sometimes prosecution case remained uncorroborated and conflicted, therefore could not be supported by the views of ballistic expert.[53] Due to doubt in the minds of the court sometimes acquittal was recorded.[54]

10 Grouping of cases

10.1 Murder cases

If all the injuries were caused by shots of firearms which led to the death of the victim. Death of victim had been caused by shock and haemorrhage as a result of firearm injury. The conviction of accused persons was upheld.[55]

49 *State* v *Vinod Kumar Yadav* (19.05.2015 – DEL HC)MANU/DE/1763/2015.

50 *Gajadhar Soni* v *State of M.P.* (04.12.1996 – MP HC) MANU/MP/0786/1996.

51 *Jasbir Singh* v *State* (*Govt. of NCT of Delhi*) (29.10.2007 – DEL HC)(MANU/DE/9065/2007).

52 *Md. Moinul Haque* v *State of Assam* (06.06.2012 – GU HC) MANU/GH/0350/2012.

53 *Raj Kumar* v *State of Haryana* (13.06.1996 – PN HC) MANU/PH/0916/1996.

54 *State by Aldur Police* v *B.C. Parameshwarappa* (07.06.1999) MANU/KA/0359/1999.

55 *Prem Kumar* v *State of Bihar* (1995)3 SCC 228.

In cases where injuries are caused by firearms, the opinion of the ballistic expert is of a considerable importance where both the firearm and the crime cartridge were recovered during investigation to connect an accused with the crime. Failure to produce the expert opinion before the trial court in such cases affects the creditworthiness of the prosecution case to a great extent. The court opined that on critical analysis of the materials on the record, it was found that it would not be safe to rely upon sole testimony of one of the witnesses, the brother of the deceased and to uphold the conviction of the appellant. Therefore, the conviction and sentence of the trial court could not be sustained and consequently, the appeal was allowed and the appellant was acquitted.[56]

The accused had injured the deceased by gunshot. The injury caused by gunshot was corroborated by recovery of gun and cartridges and also by the report of ballistic expert and eyewitnesses. In view of the circumstances, it was ruled that conviction was liable to be affirmed on account of gunshot injury on the vital parts of the body.[57]

The trial judge acquitted the accused who was tried for murder. The Division Bench of the High Court reversed the acquittal and sentenced him to imprisonment for life under s. 302 of IPC. The appellant thus became entitled to file this appeal. Bullet injuries resulted in the death of the deceased. The post-mortem examination of the dead body revealed, *inter alia*, one firearm wound on the back of the right shoulder with blackening of the skin and its exit wound was on the left axilla with a big hollow cavity through which lung tissue protruded. Another entry wound on the right scapula, its exit wound on the 5th vertebra with tearing of skin and muscle, another entry wound below the left gluteal fold with blackening of the skin and its exit wound was on the upper gluteal fold. There was no dispute that the death of the deceased was due to piercing of bullets from a firearm and that it was a close-range firing. In the light of the aforesaid discussion there was no scope to

56 *Sukhwant Singh* v *State of Punjab* (1995)3 SCC 367.

57 *Sunil Kumar* v *State* 1997 CrLJ 3380.

conclude that the appellant had any right of private defence to property. Accordingly, the conviction and sentence was confirmed and the appeal was dismissed.[58]

The accused fired a shot from his gun, striking on the chest of deceased. Thereafter, the accused fired another shot and ran away. The accused was arrested and from his possession one DBBL gun along with 3 live cartridges of .12 bore and a licence in his name was recovered. The empty cartridge along with the gun was sent to the ballistic expert who recorded that the empty cartridges had been fired from the gun belonging to the accused. The Sessions Judge convicted the accused under s. 302, IPC and s. 27 of the Arms Act and sentenced him to life imprisonment. The High Court reversed the said decision and acquitted the accused. The Supreme Court held that it was well settled that any irregularity or even an illegality during investigation ought not to be treated as a ground to reject the prosecution case. Therefore, the judgment of the High Court was set aside and the judgment of the Sessions Judge convicting the accused was restored by the Supreme Court.[59]

Court found no infirmity in the dying declaration of deceased that accused shot him on the instigation of another accused. The shot was fired at vital part of the body and ultimately resulted in death. The death was the direct result of the gunshot injury. Apparently the accused wanted to cause death. Hence appellants had been convicted and appeal was dismissed.[60]

The child witness was trustworthy. Bloodstained kurta of one of the witnesses was produced to corroborate his testimony. There was no conflict between ocular testimony and medical evidence. Deceased suffered two gunshot wounds. Report and opinion of the doctor was never challenged. Six pellets were recovered from the dead body. Minute contradiction between medical and ocular evidence do not

58 *Bhupendrasinh A. Chudasama* v *State of Gujarat* (1998)2 SCC 603.

59 *Leela Ram (Dead) Through Duli Chand* v *State of Haryana* (1999)9 SCC 525.

60 *Vijay Singh* v *State of MP* 2000 CrLJ 650.

travel to the root and nature of offence. Accused was convicted and sentenced.[61]

The two appeals were directed against the judgment of the Patna High Court dismissing a Criminal Appeal and convicting the appellants under s. 302, IPC for murdering a person. Two accused persons came on a motorcycle and after taking fuel from the petrol pump they started firing at the deceased. It was stated that immediately after firing these people left and the deceased while being carried to the hospital was found dead on the way. The deceased died on account of gunshot injury. The accused persons were convicted.[62]

Deceased died of gunshot injuries. Although there was discrepancy in medical evidence with regard to nature of injury on the deceased as to whether edges of the wound were averted or inverted the court held that discrepancies were not fatal to the prosecution case when it was not disputed that deceased died of gunshot wounds. While the learned counsel for the appellants were unable to question the correctness of the ballistic expert's opinion, he stated that there was no evidence to show that the bullet casings sent to the ballistic expert were actually the same casings that were found near the dead body. But such question was answered in the evidence of the investigating officer, who in specific terms stated that he found those bullet casings near the body of the deceased and he seized, sealed and sent them to the ballistic expert which statement of the IO was not challenged in the cross-examination. Accused persons were convicted.[63]

Two brothers were murdered by the accused respondents. The death was caused due to gunshot injuries. Failure to send weapon of offence, the gun, to ballistic expert for examination and get his expert opinion would not demolish the creditworthiness of the prosecution case entitling the accused the benefit of acquittal. IO categorically stated that the guns seized were not in working condition and that no purpose

61 *Zafar* alias *Budhu* v *State of U.P.* 2000 CrLJ 3786.
62 *Ajay Singh* v *State of Bihar* (2000)9 SCC 730.
63 *Rachpal Singh* v *State of Punjab* (2002)6 SCC 462.

would be served by sending the same to the ballistic expert for his opinion. No further question was put to the IO in cross-examination to find out despite the guns being defective, the fire pin was in order or not. Accordingly, the appeals were allowed by setting aside the judgment of the High Court and upholding the judgment of the trial court. Conviction sustained.[64]

Accused wanted to take a particular room fell to the share of informant. He came with his licensed gun to the spot of occurrence with his sons who were carrying lathis and they started demolishing the walls. Deceased and others requested them not to do so. One gunshot was fired by accused to the victim which proved fatal. No contradictions in the evidence of the doctor were found who conducted the post-mortem and the doctor who examined the deceased immediately after he had suffered the injuries. Nothing was found to support High Court's conclusion that the change in timing indicated in the FIR was subsequently done. High Court incorrectly appreciated the facts and held that since there was only one gunshot, the question of the eyewitness rushing to the spot on hearing the sound appeared incredible as the evidence showed that there were two gunshots out of which one proved fatal. Unreasoned reversal of conviction by High Court was therefore liable to be set aside. Accused persons were convicted.[65]

The accused fired at one of the witnesses with the pistol which missed. Then the accused fired three times which caused a gunshot injury on the victim who later succumbed to the gunshot injury. The accused was arrested and on an alleged disclosure statement made by him one .22-bore pistol was recovered and the same was seized. During the course of investigation certain empty cartridges had been seized from the spot of the incident and the pistol then recovered at the instance of the respondent herein was sent for ballistic expert, who opined that the empty cartridges found at the place of

64 *State of Punjab* v *Jugraj Singh* (2002)3 SCC 234.
65 *Ramakant Rai* v *Madan Rai* (2003)12 SCC 395.

incident could have been fired by the pistol recovered at the instance of the respondent. The Supreme Court held that it was not safe to place reliance on the report of the ballistic expert because it was an admitted fact that the empties which were sent to the ballistic expert after six months were not sealed at the time of seizure.[66]

The trial court convicted the respondent under s. 302 of IPC and sentenced him to undergo imprisonment for life. He was further convicted under s. 27 of the Arms Act and sentenced to undergo rigorous imprisonment for a period of two years. The sentences were to run concurrently. The apex court held that firearm injuries were resulted in the death of the deceased. Accused was convicted.[67]

The appellant fired on the deceased. Bullet hit the left eye of the deceased which lead to his death. Defence version regarding attack by the prosecution party was not established. Failure to send bullet for ballistic examination, on facts held was not fatal. The accused was convicted under s. 302 of IPC.[68]

Recovery of the pellets from the body of the victim not required to be sent to ballistic expert to determine as to whether those pellets were fired from the exhibited gun or not. Recovery of pellets from the body of the victim clearly established the prosecution case that the deceased died of gunshot injuries.[69]

Testimony of the eyewitnesses in support of the prosecution case was found reliable. There was no inconsistency between the ocular evidence and medical evidence. The accused was convicted.[70]

According to the medical report it was established that bullet injury was sustained by the deceased. Forensic expert was not examined to prove that the injury was caused by a bullet or that bullet could have been fired from any of the

66 *State of M.P.* v *Ghudan* (2003)12 SCC 485; AIR 2004 SC 797.
67 *State of Punjab* v *Mela Singh* (2003)12 SCC 464.
68 *Surendra Paswan* v *State of Jharkhand* (2003)12 SCC 360.
69 *State of HP* v *Mast Ram* (2004)4 SCC 660.
70 *Birendra Rai* v *State of Bihar* (2005)9 SCC 719.

weapons carried by the accused persons. It is held that as the bullet in the body of the victim is itself conclusive of the fact that deceased has suffered a firearm injury. Question whether the said bullet was discharged from any of the weapon carried by the accused was of no significance since the weapons allegedly carried by the accused were neither recovered nor seized.[71]

Additional Sessions Judge convicted all accused/appellants for offence of murder under ss. 302/34 and 100, IPC. On scanning the entire evidence, oral as well as documentary, placing heavy reliance on the statements of the witnesses banking on the corroborative medical and ballistic report and pinning faith on the seizure of the incriminating articles, the learned Additional Session Judge convicted all the accused persons. Hence this appeal. It was held that consorted efforts of appellants did not come within purview of s. 100, IPC. However, statements of eyewitnesses was that injured deceased desperately tried to wrench himself free from clutches of appellants, although they tried to pin him down was on record. In pursuance of the statement of one of the accused, cartridges could be recovered. Fired cartridges were also seized near a Jeep. Thus, non-explanation of injuries by prosecution could not weaken strong prosecution case. Therefore order of conviction against all appellants was affirmed and their appeals were dismissed.[72]

The deceased was shot by the accused. Post-mortem examination was conducted by a team of doctors, who opined that the death was due to bullet injuries. The ballistic expert reported that the pellets extricated from the body of the deceased must have been fired from the pistol recovered at the instance of the accused. It is held that the evidence of the ballistic expert supported the prosecution case fully. Conviction under s. 302, IPC is justified.[73]

71 *Nirmal Singh* v *State of Bihar* (2005)9 SCC 725.

72 *Sk. Sarfaraz alias Sarfu* v *State* Cal LT 2006(1) HC 150.

73 *State of M.P.* v *Paltan Mallah* (2005)3 SCC 169.

Circumstances proved by direct evidence coupled with the failure of the accused to give reasonable explanation of the inculpatory circumstances completed the chain of circumstances. The ballistic expert examined the gun and found it was a hand gun and was a firearm being a regular .380" caliber revolver and was in normal working condition and it was capable of chambering and firing .380" caliber regular cartridge. Evidence taken together with other proved circumstances on record was sufficient to substantiate that the accused knowingly committed the offence and concealed the weapon. Accused found guilty of offence of murder under s. 302, IPC.[74]

This appeal by special leave was directed against the judgment and order of the High Court whereby the High Court upheld the conviction and sentence passed by the trial court against the appellant who was found guilty of the offence punishable under ss. 302 and 307 of IPC and s. 27 of the Arms Act. This is a case of gunshot injuries received by the victims accused was convicted.[75]

The appeal was filed against the judgment of the conviction and sentence under s. 302, IPC passed by the trial court against the appellant and upheld by the High Court. Ballistics was used to examine the recovered air gun. Autopsy of the deceased also revealed that the injury must have been caused by an air gun. The court was satisfied that the cumulative effect satisfied the test of proof of the guilt of the appellant on the basis of the circumstantial evidence for the commission of the offence under s. 304, Part II of the Indian Penal Code.[76]

Statement given by concerned eyewitness had been fully corroborated by independent witness. Medical evidence also corroborated the statement. From evidence on record, case of prosecution was fully established. The disclosure statement

74 *State of Sikkim* v *Milan Kumar Diyali* (09.08.2005 – SI HC) MANU/SI/0003/2005.

75 *Sada Ram* v *State of Haryana* (2006)13 SCC 528.

76 *Sivakumar* v *State* (2006)1 SCC 714, p. 716, paras 3 & 4, p. 719, paras 18 & 19, p. 720, para 21, p. 725, para 48.

recorded lead to recovery of .12 bore DBBL gun. According to the report of the Ballistic Expert, he was not able to give opinion regarding linkage of crime cartridges in respect of gun on account of tampering with of the fire arm as fire pins of .12 bore DBBL gun had been cut and tampered with. Therefore all reasoning of the trial court were perverse and not sustainable.[77]

Accused was convicted under s. 302 of IPC for causing murder. Firearm injury was caused to the victim. Ballistics was also used to determine the weapon which was used for firing the bullets. There was no enmity between the parties and there was no allegation that before the occurrence, the appellant had premeditated the crime of murder. At the most, it could be said that the appellant had the knowledge that the use of revolver was likely to cause death and as such, the present case would fall within the third clause of s. 299, IPC. So, the court held that the appellant was guilty of culpable homicide not amounting to murder.[78]

Trial court doubting the prosecution story as well as their witnesses, acquitted the accused. However, the High Court by the impugned order, reversed the acquittal and convicted the appeal is filed before the Supreme Court. The injuries of one of the witnesses were caused by firearm and the injuries on the deceased were caused by gunshots. Ballistics were also used to explain the nature of the cartridges and to give an opinion. It was held that the accused was presumed innocent as he is not proven guilty.[79]

The victim died due to firearm injuries. Ballistic expert examined the recovered cartridges and the gun. Depending on the ballistic expert's report and the medical evidence it was held that the accused is entitled to benefit of doubt.[80]

The discrepancies in the evidence of the eyewitnesses were vital for disbelieving and discrediting their evidence. The said

77 *State of Haryana* v *Suraj Mal* (22.05.2007 – PH HC) MANU/PH/0474/2007.

78 *Vineet Kumar Chauhan* v *State of UP* (2007)14 SCC 660.

79 *Ghurey Lal* v *State of U.P.* (2008)10 SCC 450.

80 *Puran Singh* v *State of Uttaranchal* (2008)3 SCC 795.

evidence was in conflict and contradiction with medical evidence and ballistic expert's report in regard to weapon of offence, which was different from the one sealed in police station. In the facts and circumstances, prosecution failed to prove its case beyond reasonable doubt.[81]

This appeal by way of special leave arises out of the judgment and order passed by a Division Bench of High Court of Punjab and Haryana whereby the High Court had allowed the appeal filed by the respondent accused, setting aside his conviction and sentence of life imprisonment and fine under s. 302 of IPC and under s. 27 of the Arms Act 1959 by giving him the benefit of doubt. The firearm injury resulted from a shot fired from the rifle. Ballistics was used as the recovered cartridges and cartridge cases were sent for examination to FSL. The appeal was dismissed as the court opined the judgement of the High Court calls for no interference.[82]

The Additional Sessions Judge held the accused appellant guilty and convicted him for offence of murder punishable under s. 302, IPC. Hence this appeal. Held, version of Head Constable was corroborated by other witnesses. The ballistic expert opined that the firearm under reference could be cocked by entangling with chain provided, if change lever was not at "S" (safety) position and if trigger was pressed in cocked condition, it would fire. Thereby, irresistible conclusion reached after thorough examination of weapon of offence was that the entangling of chain during alleged scuffle between accused and deceased could not lead to make the gun fire accidentally. Lastly, if deceased caught hold of SAF/gun by its muzzle with his right hand, no bullet injury on his right hand would have been possible and if he held gun at mouth of muzzle, entry wound on right hand would have been at front and not at back of hand. Thus when facts were clear it was immaterial that no motive was proved and absence of proof of motive did not break link in chain of circumstances connecting accused with crime, nor mitigated prosecution case. Hence, trial judge rightly

81 *Mahendra Pratap Singh* v *State of UP* (2009)11 SCC 334.
82 *State of Punjab* v *Rajinder Singh* (2009)15 SCC 612.

convicted appellant for murder of deceased under s. 302 of IPC on circumstantial evidence. Appeal was dismissed, conviction upheld.[83]

Trial Judge had convicted the appellant for offence of murder under s. 302 IPC on the basis of an dying declaration made by deceased to the police officials. Hence this appeal. It was held that unless the deceased fell in an extraordinary category, there was every possibility that bullet reached the heart, slowly through venous circulation and till it reached the heart, the deceased remained alive. Therefore, testimonies of police witnesses were true. Thus, oral dying declarations made to police officials were sufficient evidence to convict appellant for murder of his wife. The pistol recovered at the instance of the appellant and the bullet recovered from the dead body were sent to FSL for comparison. As per the FSL report, the country-made pistol had an 8mm bore and the bullet recovered from the body of the deceased corresponded to 8mm cartridge but due to insufficient striation marks no opinion could be given that the bullet was fired from the firearm in question. Appeal dismissed, conviction upheld.[84]

Accused had fired at deceased with country-made pistol from a very close range. Doctor who had conducted post-mortem examination found one wound of entry about 3cm × 2.5 cm with blackening and charring and also recovered 160 pellets from the dead body. Medical evidence clearly suggested use of such a weapon from almost point blank range. Appellant's plea of false implication was rejected. Therefore, conviction of the appellant was confirmed.[85]

The deceased was shot dead by accused. The report of the FSL indicated that the pistol recovered from the site of the incident was found to be in working condition. All

83 *Arvind Kumar* v *State* (*NCT of Delhi*) (02.07.2010 – DEL HC) MANU/DE/4281/2010.

84 *Chattar Pal Singh* v *State* (02.02.2010 – DEL HC) MANU/DE/0292/2010.

85 *Hari Singh* v *State of UP* (2010)13 SCC 756.

circumstances taken together clearly formed a continuous and unbroken chain as to leave no manner of doubt that deceased was shot dead by appellants.[86]

Recovery of weapon of offence (pistol of 7.65mm)) as well as ownership and possession by accused was established. The fact that bullets which had caused injury to the deceased were fired from the said pistol was proved. As per the report of Forensic Science Laboratory the cartridges which had been received from the spot of the crime were fired from 7.65 mm pistol. Thus the crime was proved.[87]

The opinion offered by expert would only show that country-made gun had been used and bullet which was found in body of deceased had been shot only from that weapon. In the considered opinion of court, there was no case for defence to project. Thus, from evidence of witnesses and that of ballistic expert opinion, prosecution had clearly established that it was accused, who really shot deceased and caused his death.[88]

According to the prosecution witness four shots were fired in the course of the incident, only one empty cartridge was recovered from the spot. The weapon of offence also had not been seized. The court was of the view that there was no difficulty in reaching the conclusion that the conviction of the appellant accused Ram Singh under s. 302, IPC and the sentence imposed thereunder was fully justified.[89]

The ballistic expert reported that three live cartridges and the examined cartridges were the same and gun contained the traces of firing of gunshot. There were also traces of firing gunshot on the second gun and the empty cartridge which was marked by him had been fired through the gun. The traces of lead were also found in the hole in net and cotton. Plastic pieces recovered by the doctor from the head of the deceased. No

86 *Santokh Singh* v *State of Punjab* (2010)8 SCC 784.
87 *Gurjinder Singh* v *State of Punjab* (2011)3 SCC 530.
88 *Kandan* alias *Viral Kandan* v *State* (22.11.2012 – MAD HC) MANU/TN/2278/2012.
89 *Ram Singh* v *State of Rajasthan* (2012)12 SCC 339.

definite opinion was expressed. The court opined that the prosecution failed to prove that the crime cartridge had been recovered from the accused as alleged. And further it could not be linked with the gun of the accused. The evidence of the expert thus was discrepant and not worthy of any credit. Hence, from the evidence on record, the acquittal ordered by the trial court was reasonable.[90]

Firearm injury along with the cumulative effect of the various sufferances was the cause of the death of the deceased. Although the belief of the Supreme Court regarding the gunshot injury of the deceased did not have any impact on the final decision of the court since the court were in agreement with the courts below that appellants had the common intention of causing the death of deceased. Wherein one of the victims was survived but was injured. The court therefore upheld the concurrent findings of the courts below and confirmed the conviction and sentence of the appellants.[91]

The accused were charged under ss. 302, 307 read with s. 34 of IPC and ss. 25 and 27 of the Arms Act. The trial court acquitted all the accused. However in the appeal filed there against, the High Court convicted one of them under s. 302, IPC. The benefit of doubt was however granted to two of them. Hence an appeal was filed by the last one. The ballistic report was prepared to tally the cartridges fired from the gun. In view of the aforesaid analysis, the appeal was allowed and the accused was acquitted on the basis of the ballistic report.[92]

10.2 Murder and criminal conspiracy

Considering the entire evidence, identification of accused by concerned witnesses who identified assailant was wearing pink colour shirt. Ocular evidence of concerned witness in respect of accused was reliable. Accused was arrested on the same day with injuries on his stomach. A pink coloured shirt was seized.

90 *State of Himachal Pradesh* v *Suresh Kumar* (27.06.2013 – HP HC) MANU/HP/0383/2013.

91 *Bastiram* v *State of Rajasthan* (2014)5 SCC 398.

92 *Joginder Singh* v *State of Haryana* (2014)11 SCC 335.

The accused was also injured in firing. Entire links in chain were complete to hold the accused guilty of committing murder of deceased persons and causing injuries to concerned witnesses. Pistol was recovered which was examined by the ballistic expert was no positive evidence against the accused who had participated in committing heinous offence. Therefore court gave benefit of doubt to the accused. Therefore appeal filed by accused was dismissed.[93]

In *Manu Sharma* v *State* (*NCT of Delhi*) ballistics was used to determine from which firearm the recovered empty cartridges were fired. Although the laboratory reports in it were vague and ambiguous and could not be relied upon to reach any specific conclusion regarding the incident yet from the discussions and other evidences the court held that the prosecution had established its case beyond doubt against the accused.[94]

The victim, ex-Mayor of Mumbai, along with his 7-8 associates were allegedly sitting in an open place when a car came there and three persons started firing at victim and others indiscriminately. In that incident 3 persons died, while some others including victim sustained grievous injuries. The High Court by its impugned judgment confirmed conviction of accused under s. 3(2) of the Maharashtra Control of Organised Crime Act 1999 read with s. 120B, IPC. Appeal filed by one of the accused was dismissed and his conviction under s. 3(2) and s. 3(4) of MCOC Act 1999 read with s. 120B, IPC was confirmed. Some of the accused were acquitted of all the charges by the High Court. Though conviction of one of the accused was confirmed under s. 302 read with ss. 34, 120B read with s. 3(1)(*i*) of MCOCA etc. his death sentence was substituted with rigorous life imprisonment. Conviction of one of the accused under s. 302 read with s. 34, IPC read with s. 3(1)(*i*) of MCOC Act 1999 read further with s. 109 read with s. 120B, IPC and conviction under s. 307, IPC read with s. 3(1)(*ii*) of MCOCA

93 *Pantangi Balarama Venkata Ganesh* v *State of A.P.* (31.03.2003 – AP HC) MANU/AP/1039/2003.

94 *Manu Sharma* v *State (NCT of Delhi)* (2010)6 SCC 1.

read with ss. 34, 109 and 120B, IPC for attempt to murder etc. were maintained. One 9mm pistol recovered at instance of one of the accused and it established that same was used by him. Further report of the ballistic expert established and proved that weapon and bullets tallied with each other and that one of victims of shoot-out was killed due to a bullet fired from a 9mm pistol. Besides, medical evidence also showed that death of three deceased was caused by injuries sustained due to firearms. Other accused had also used pistols and fired during shoot-out. Moreover, though in case of one of the accused High Court held that evidence did not disclose that bullets fired from AK-56 rifle had resulted in death of any person, it convicted him under s. 27(2) of the Arms Act. Hence High Court erred in holding that conviction under s. 27(3) read with s. 7 of the Arms Act could not be sustained in respect of two accused. Hence, the Supreme Court confirmed the conviction and sentences imposed on three accused reversing the acquittal of other two accused and confirmed the commutation of death sentence to life imprisonment of accused.[95]

These appeals were preferred against the common judgment and order passed by the learned Sessions Judge, Designated Court (TADA), Kanpur wherein a judgment of conviction and order of sentence, was passed against the appellant and others and they were convicted for offences punishable under s. 302, s. 302/34 and s. 302/120B, IPC. They had been sentenced to undergo imprisonment for life and to pay a fine of ₹10,000 each. The accused had filed appeal under s. 19 of the TADA Act against the impugned judgment and order of the court. Bullets were recovered from the dead body and ballistic expert opined that the three empty catridges that were recovered were fired from the same 9mm pistol. The appellant was however acquitted of charges under ss. 3(2) and 3(3) read with s. 3(1) of TADA Act.[96]

On 22.12.2000 at about 9 p.m. some intruders started indiscriminate firing and gunned down three army jawans.

95 *Mohd. Farooq Abdul Gafur* v *State of Maharashtra* (2010)14 SCC 641.
96 *Manjit Singh* v *CBI* (2011)11 SCC 578; AIR 2011 SC 806.

However no intruder was arrested or killed and the intruders were successful in escaping by scaling over the rear side boundary wall of the Red Fort. Subsequent searches lead to the recovery of large quantity of arms and ammunitions including hand grenades at various places in Delhi and Srinagar. Rifle was hidden in thick bushes behind Red Fort. Evidence of ballistic experts proved that empty cartridge cases recovered from scene of crime were fired from two rifles found abandoned at places behind Red Fort. One of these rifles was recovered at accused's instance. Judgment of the Trial Court and the High Court convicting the accused and awarding death sentence were confirmed.[97]

The accused persons led the concerned witnesses and his team to place and pointed out place where site plan was prepared. All articles of seizure were kept in pullandah and sealed. From the incriminating materials and the circumstances, it was clearly established by prosecution that murder of victim was committed by two accused persons. It appeared that concerned witness had last seen victim alive in company of those two accused persons. Prosecution had also established that those two accused persons committed offence under s. 201, IPC because they had caused death of deceased and after having knowledge of said facts, they caused disappearance of evidence by throwing dead body in water. It was also established that both appellants conducted offences under s. 302 and s. 120B of IPC but prosecution failed to establish its case under s. 120B against other accused. No expert's opinion or doctor's opinion was obtained regarding use of alleged 'katta' to commit the offence. There was no evidence on record to connect other accused under s. 120B of IPC. Other accused had denied the suggestion for providing the country-made pistol to the other two accused, as there was no reason to do so. Admittedly, as per the report of the ballistics expert, the said pistol was not in a working condition. Therefore, it makes no sense to hold that the appellant provided the weapon of offence. Therefore

97 *Mohd. Arif* alias *Ashfaq* v *State* (*NCT of Delhi*) (2011)13 SCC 621.

impugned conviction against other accused was set aside and he was acquitted.[98]

The trial court recorded conviction of 10 police personnel under various sections separately. The present accused was convicted under ss. 120B, 302/120B, 307/120B, 193 read with ss. 120B, 193, 201/34 and 203/34 of IPC and sentenced to imprisonment for life, rigorous imprisonment for seven years and two years for different offences separately along with different amount of fines for the different sections. On appeal the Delhi High Court after re-examining the entire evidence concluded that the conviction of the appellants under s. 302/120B, IPC could not be sustained but their conviction under ss. 302 and 307 was liable to be maintained with the aid of s. 34 instead of s. 120B of IPC. Against the conviction of the High Court an appeal have been preferred. Ballistics was used to notify the origin or direction of firing of bullets. The appeal was dismissed and the convictions were upheld.[99]

The appellants were convicted for the possession and supply of large quantity of RDX with detonators which was certainly a preparatory act to aid the commission of terrorist act. On the basis of physical examination, chemical analysis of barrel wash and test firing, he opined that two 7.62 mm/AK 56 assault rifles were firearms as defined in Arms Act and were in working order and these were used and fired. Six 7.62 mm/AK 56 assault rifle magazines were in working order and could be fitted in two 7.62 mm assault rifles. One hundred and eighty (180) 7.62 mm/AK 56 assault rifle cartridges marked were ammunitions as defined in Arms Act and were live ones. The conviction was upheld and the appeal dismissed.[100]

The accused were convicted under ss. 302/120B and 201, IPC. Ballistic expert examined the cartridges which were recovered and used to commit the offence. A metallic sheet was also examined in the laboratory and marked along with

98 *Sapna Talwar* v *State* (12.10.2011 – DEL HC) MANU/DE/3999/2011.

99 *Satyavir Singh Rathi, ACP* v *State* (2011)6 SCC 1.

100 *Firoz Abdul Latif Ghaswala* v *State Govt. of NCT of Delhi* (03.09.2012 – DEL HC) MANU/DE/4582/2012.

the cartridges. The report of the ballistic expert was accepted and it corroborated the prosecution case. The prosecution was able to prove its case beyond reasonable doubt.[101]

Accused murdered his wife by shooting her dead with his revolver. Police recovered empty bullet cartridge, a bullet and an air pistol from accused's flat. Medical evidence established that death was caused by bullet injury in head and neck of deceased. CFSL report established that bullets recovered from flat and skull of deceased were fired from accused's revolver. The Hon'ble Supreme Court confirmed the conviction for the offence punishable under ss. 302 and 120B read with s. 201 of IPC.[102]

10.3 Murder and unlawful assembly

This is a case of firearm injury. The experts opined that the shots were fired from .12 bore shotguns, 9 mm pistols and carbines. The doctor stated that the shots had been fired from a distance of a foot or two. The accused was convicted.[103]

10.4 Murder and dishonest misappropriation of property

It was clear from the witnesses that revolver was recovered from box of bed. Therefore noted contradiction pointed out by appellant was not a contradiction in a real sense. Testimony of concerned witness established that room from which revolver was recovered was in exclusive possession of appellant. No evidence was led by defence to show pullanda containing bullets was tampered. Therefore prosecution had been able to establish that the bullets examined by FSL were recovered from body of deceased. The accused was convicted.[104]

10.5 Murder and attempt to murder

The very fact that accused was present with other accused and was supplying live cartridges to accused to kill deceased showed that prosecution had proved beyond reasonable doubt

101 *Satpal Singh* v *State* (21.10.2014 – JK HC) MANU/JK/0179/2014.
102 *Sushil Sharma* v *State* (2014)4 SCC 317.
103 *Sarvesh Narain Shukla* v *Daroga Singh* (2007)13 SCC 360.
104 *Gajraj* v *State* (18.03.2009 – DEL HC) MANU/DE/1074/2009.

that accused persons had committed offence punishable under s. 302/34, IPC. When the intention to cause murder was proved by the prosecution, the mere fact that victim escaped the gunshot injury was not relevant. The evidence of the ballistic expert was helpful to the prosecution to prove that with the help of the SBBL gun which was seized and examined by him that accused fired at the instigation of other accused, and the shirts which were seized were bearing holes caused due to passage of lead pellets. Thus judgment of conviction and sentence of the trial court was upheld.[105]

In *State by Aldur Police* v *B.C. Parameshwarappa*,[106] ballistic expert's evidence and more importantly the medical evidence were the strongest forms of evidence because the oral evidence was often capable of infirmities. First two heads of evidence were before the court and they ran counter to the prosecution case and that was one of the reasons why the court refused to permit any supplementing of the third head by procuring the records and the evidence of the doctor from the hospital. Additional ground for it was even if evidence was forthcoming, there were too many lacuna and conflicting factors in the prosecution case which would make it impossible to sustain a conviction even with that material.[106]

The doctor, categorically stated that the possibility of receiving injury by firearm cannot be ruled out and also stated that he did not extract any pellet from the wound at the time of operation. The gun and the recovered material were sent for ballistics expert for his opinion and the report of the ballistic expert was obtained. There was no cogent evidence on the file to prove requisite intention of the accused to kill deceased. Mere circumstance that a firearm was used to cause injury to victim would not be sufficient to establish that accused had committed an offence under s. 307.[107]

105 *Changananmad Aiyappa* v *State of Karnataka* (24.09.2010 – KAR HC) MANU/KA/1246/2010.

106 *State by Aldur Police* v *B.C. Parameshwarappa* ILR (1999) Kant 9052.

107 *Inderjit* alias *Jitu* v *State of Himachal Pradesh* (23.06.2011 – HP HC) MANU/HP/1366/2011.

The two appellants were tried before the Learned Additional Sessions Judge for the offences punishable under ss. 302 and 307 read with s. 34 of IPC and sentenced each of them to undergo rigorous life imprisonment and to pay a fine of ₹5000. The High Court affirmed the conviction of the two appellants. Three empty cartridges of .315 bore rifle and two empty cartridges of .12 bore were collected from the spot. The seized articles were sent to FSL for ballistic examination. In view of the above premised reasons, the appeal was dismissed and the convictions were upheld.[108]

10.6 Hurt and culpable homocide not amounting to murder

Death of the victim was caused due to pellet injury caused by accused. Careful scrutiny of evidence clearly revealed that witnesses had given cogent, acceptable and convincing depositions. Evidence adduced through doctors and their certificates corroborated ocular evidence. Recovery of weapon used in offence in pursuance of confessional statement of accused. On requisition by the IO the concerned Judicial Magistrate sent all the material objects along with a covering letter to the Assistant Director of Ballistics, Forensic Science Department. The expert after examination of the said items and materials had given a report. Held, accused attempted to cause death due to sudden provocation caused by a witness, which ultimately resulted in the death of the deceased.[109]

The appellant had been convicted under ss. 302 and 323 of IPC for murder of two persons by causing injuries to them with firearms. The doctor who conducted post-mortem deposed that the deaths were homicidal and caused by gunshot injuries. Although the trial court did not rely on the report of the ballistic expert but the High Court could not agree with the findings recorded by the trial court. Although the police had not sent

108 *Manjit Singh* v *State of Punjab* (2013)12 SCC 746.

109 *Diwana* alias *Settu* v *State* (10.07.2003 – MAD HC) MANU/TN/1130/2003.

the bullet/led recovered from the body of the deceased for FSL examination, it did not mean that the FSL report and the findings recorded therein should be disbelieved. The Ballistic expert had submitted that he had given the report after conducting test of the firearm and ammunition. He was not cross-examined and his report as well as his testimony remained completely unchallenged. Two fired and one empty cartridges were recovered from the spot and the third empty cartridge was found in the country-made pistol when seized. Exhibit recorded that three cartridges of .315 bore were made available to the FSL for test firing. These were test fired. The microscopic examination of the test fired cartridges revealed that they were fired from the same country made pistol which was seized from the appellant. The FSL Report, therefore, clearly corroborated that the empty cartridges found at the spot were fired from the arm which was recovered from the possession of the appellant.[110]

10.7 Sedition

Accused was involved in a prosecution under Terrorist and Disruptive Activities (Prevention) Act 1987 (TADA). Though the designated court under TADA had acquitted him of the offences, he was convicted of sedition under s. 124A of IPC and under s. 25 of the Arms Act. The report of the ballistic expert was used to examine the recovered weapon and the cartridges to solve the case.[111]

10.8 Unlawful possession of arms/attempt to murder/criminal conspiracy

The appellant was convicted under s. 25(1)(*a*) of the Arms Act 1959 which was upheld by the Additional Sessions Judge. Hence this petition. Held, it was found that police officials concerned did not take proper care and steps for keeping seized arms under safe custody in sealed cover till it was produced before

110 *Ram Dass* v *State* (08.04.2013 – DEL HC) MANU/DE/1059/2013.
111 *Bilal Ahmed Kaloo* v *State of A.P.* (1997)7 SCC 431.

SDJM and even in dispatching seized arm to Director FSL. Prosecution had failed to satisfy court that there was no chance of manipulation while seized pipe gun was in custody of police for a long period of 125 days. Scientific expert tested gun on firing but it was not stated so in his report. Prosecution had to prove that at time of raid and search independent witnesses were called by police and they were present at time of search and seizure, which the prosecution failed to prove. Witness, wife of accused person, who according to prosecution was present at time of raid and search but she denied basic fact of recovery/seizure of the articles. Therefore on perusal of case records and evidence on record it was found that prosecution miserably failed to establish case against the convict petitioner. The order passed by the court was set aside and the acquittal was recorded.[112]

The ballistic expert examined the pistol and cartridges recovered and gave his detailed report. The prosecution proved its case beyond reasonable doubt. The accused was sentenced to death for the commission of offence under s. 302 of IPC and sentenced for the offences under ss. 25 and 27 of the Arms Act 1959.[113]

The accused was convicted under s. 25 of the Arms Act 1959, ss. 307/34 and 120B of IPC. The forensic evidence also completely supported the case of the prosecution. The FSL report proved that the pistol carried by the Appellant, was thrown by him on the first floor after it failed to fire, was in fact unable to be even test-fired. As far as the other pistol recovered from the accused was concerned, the ballistics report showed that rounds recovered from the spot, were fired from it. The blood on the clothes of the appellant matched the blood group of prosecution witness. The above evidence established conclusively the involvement of the Appellant.[114]

112 *Md. Moinul Haque* v *State of Assam* (06.06.2012 – GU HC) MANU/GH/0350/2012.

113 *State* v *Navin Ahuja* (20.11.2012 – DEL HC) MANU/DE/5590/2012.

114 *Amit* v *State* (23.12.2014 – DEL HC) MANU/DE/3509/2014.

Complaint disclosed presence of arms and ammunition in vessel and also names of Captain and Crew with their National identities and passport details. Evidence collected by police did not show any material which disclosed commission of grave offences prejudicial to peace, order and interest of India like offences under Unlawful Activities (Prevention) Act 1967 etc. The seized arms were sent to the Ballistics Expert of Tamil Nadu Forensic Sciences Department and a certificate was obtained that those were prohibited arms as classified by the Arms Act 1959.[115]

115 *Mariya Anton Vijay* v *State* (10.07.2014 – MAD HC) MANU/TN/1179/2014.

Chapter 4

Fingerprint

1 Introduction

Human beings have friction ridges on the hands and feet. These friction ridges have a specific detail on the gripping surfaces with an enhanced quantity of nerves and pores. These tiny raised peaks and valleys are located on the tips of the fingers along with the sweat pores. The friction skin has a structured dermis layer with the friction layer of skin that includes the sweat pores. There are extra pores that remain moist and help the skin to remain soft and pliable, which presents better frictional characteristics of the print. There is usually a sufficient amount of moisture on a persons fingertips so that when they come in contact with an object, an imprint is made of the ridges. Experts collect the imprints which are otherwise known as fingerprints for the purpose of criminal investigations. Fingerprints play a significant role in crime scene investigation.[1]

The study of fingerprints is also known as "Dactyloscopy." According to Modi's *Medical Jurisprudence and Toxicology*, "Dactylography" is also known as the fingerprint system and consists in taking the impressions of the pulp of the fingers and thumbs with printer's ink on an unglazed white paper and

1 Rev. ED: Ordway Hilton, *Scientific Examination I of Questioned Documents*, 1982 (New York: Elsevier).

then examining them with a magnifying lens. It is based on the principle that the individual peculiarities of the patterns formed by the arrangement and distribution of the papillary or epidermal ridges on the fingertips are absolutely constant and persist throughout life, from infancy to old age, and that the patterns of no two hands resemble each other. Even the fingerprints of twins are not similar. It has been estimated that the chances of two persons having identical finger impressions is about one in thirty times the population of the world."[2] Identity of persons, living or dead, known or unknown, of things, or handwriting or fingerprints or footprints play important part in criminal matters for establishing the guilt or innocence of the accused and in civil matters in proof or disproof of the case of the parties. Dactyloscopy is based on two principles: (*i*) There are no two identical fingerprints; (*ii*) Fingerprints have two unique characteristics, viz. individuality and persistency and thus it is not changeable.[3]

Sir Francis Galton investigated the persistence of the ridges throughout the period of human life and in the following words recorded the results of his examination of many sets of prints taken at different times and covering the interval from childhood to boyhood, from boyhood to early manhood, from early manhood to middle age and from middle age to extreme old age and he found that there is no sign of change in any of these cases which made him to infer that between birth and death there is absolutely no change in 699 cases out of 700 cases as there was an exception in one case only. Sir Galton also inferred that neither there be any change after death up to the time when the skin perishes through decomposition. He forwarded the example of marks on the fingers of many Egyptian mummies and on the paws of stuffed monkeys which still remain legible in support of his views. So careful inquiry is required to justify the idea of persistence of finger impressions.[4]

2 Modi, *Medical Jurisprudence and Toxicology*, 25th Ed., p. 234.

3 Marvin D'Souza, R.P. Kataria, *Forensic Science in Criminal Trial & Investigation*, Ed. 2016, p. 631.

4 *Parappa* v *Bhimappa* ILR (2008) Kant 1840.

Fingerprint as a method of identification is recognized throughout the world and is accepted by the judiciary. The fingerprints as evidence are important because of the following features of it. They are unique, they are permanent, they are universal, they are inimitable, they are classifiable, and they are frequently available in crime situations as evidence.[5]

The history of fingerprints can be traced back to the Indus Valley Civilization where it was used extensively on clay tables and seals. The use of fingerprints on seals indicates their significance for identification purpose. In West Bengal fingerprints were used along with palm prints known as 'Panja' and it was used for several centuries. Shahjahan's Royal Hand Seal on certain important document is very evident in this respect. The history and development of fingerprint science as a means of identification is noteworthy for which the pioneers who made fingerprints an infallible means of personal identification deserves acknowledgement. They are Dr. Henry Faulds, Sir William Herschel, Sir Francis Galton, Sir Edward Richard Henry, Khan Bahadur Aziz-Ul-Haq and Rai Bahadur Hemchandra Bose.

2 Legal history of fingerprints

Fingerprint evidence had been acknowledged by courts of both India and Argentina in the late 1800. Fingerprint evidence was first offered into evidence in *People* v *Jennings*[6] in the United States. Since Jennings in 1911, the Courts have embraced fingerprints as the "gold standard" for forensic identification and have taken "judicial notice" of the permanence and uniqueness (individuality) of each person's fingerprints. For more than 50 years fingerprint evidence not only enjoyed judicial acceptance, but was rarely challenged also. This idea on fingerprint evidence came into being after the ruling in 1993

5 B.R. Sharma, *Forensic Science in Criminal Investigation & Trial*, 4th Ed., p. 305.

6 [1911]254 Ill. 534; [1911]96 NE 1077; [1911]43 LRA (NS) 1206

of the United States Supreme Court decision in the landmark judgment of *Daubert* v *Merell Dow Pharmaceuticals.*[7]

The first challenge of fingerprint evidence under *Daubert* occurred in 1999 in *US* v *Byron Mitchell*[8] of the US District Court for the Eastern District of Pennsylvania. Fingerprint evidence was obtained from a get away car, used in an armored car robbery. After a five days *Daubert* evidence hearing, the District Court ruled testimony that the prosecution's fingerprint experts to be reliable and the fingerprint evidence admissible.

The District Court ruling was upheld on appeal in *United States* v *Mitchell.*[9] The 3rd Circuit Court of Appeals held that fingerprint identification satisfies the standards for reliability established in *Daubert* and *Kumho Tyre.*

The second *Daubert* hearing challenging the admissibility of fingerprint evidence occurred in Los Angeles Federal Court in Anthony Golden County of Los Angeles, *et. al.* US District Court for the Central District of California case.[10] This was the first challenge in a federal civil rights lawsuit. Golden was shot and killed by Sheriff's deputies. The suit alleged that the deputies planted a gun near the body of Golden. Fingerprint evidence that matched Golden's fingerprints were found on the gun and the magazine inside the gun. After the *Daubert* hearing, the trial court held fingerprint evidence as admissible. Since this case in 1999, there have been approximately forty challenges in State and Federal Courts. None have been successful. Many of these rulings have now been appealed and all appeals have affirmed the admissibility of fingerprint evidence.[11]

7 [1993]509 US 592.
8 Criminal Action No. 96-407.
9 365 F.3d 215 (3d Cir 2004).
10 [1999] CV 97-6140.
11 Marvin D'Souza, R.P. Kataria, *Forensic Science in Criminal Trial & Investigation*, Ed. 2016, p. 648.

3 Classification of fingerprints

3.1 Classification of fingerprints on its availability on the crime scene

Fingerprints left by the culprit at the scene of crime are known as 'chance prints'. These prints are left by the criminal unconsciously, and are rightly called as 'burglars visiting cards.' There are three main classes of chance prints which are described hereunder. They are Visible Prints, Plastic Prints and Latent Prints.

(1) VISIBLE PRINTS. When the fingers are covered with some coloured substance such as paint, ink, dirt, blood or other visible material then the prints which are left are visible to the eye. Prints of this nature do not need any development. They can be easily recorded by taking photographs with or without use of filters.

(2) PLASTIC PRINTS. These prints are generally found on pliable surface and so they are called as plastic prints. They are generally found on objects such as soap, mud, pitch, candles, thick dried blood, melted wax or paraffin, adhesives and so on. Prints of this nature can be photographed by angular illumination.

(3) LATENT PRINTS. The most important of the chance prints are the latent or invisible prints. These prints have very poor visibility and can be made clearly visible after suitable development. Latent prints are formed by the deposition of colourless greasy substance from the palmar surface of the fingers. This greasy substance is formed out of perspiration, dirt and oily matter from the face, hair, skin, tools etc. which is carried by the fingers.[12]

The other types of fingerprint which are collected from the subject is known as Exemplar Print and Patent Prints:

(4) EXEMPLAR PRINTS. Exemplars are generally of higher quality and are collected under controlled conditions from a known subject using ink or paper or digitally with a live scan device.

12 B.S. Nabar, *Forensic Science in Crime Investigation,* Edition 2002, p. 58.

(5) PATENT PRINTS. Patents prints are visible to the naked eye and thus they are easy to locate. Such prints occur when substances like grease, paints blood or ink leaves a usually print found on the palm leaves an impression on the surface. It is collected using the method of photography of high resolution with forensic measurement scale in the image for reference. The quality of the images can be improved by using low angle or alternate light sources and/or certain chemicals/dyes during photography.

3.2 Classification of fingerprints on the basis of its formation on the crime scene

According to this classification there are three types of fingerprint:

(1) INDENTED OR MOULDED FINGERMARK. This fingermark, is a three-dimensional fingertip impression, found in a malleable object such as putty or candle wax. Such impressions can be enhanced using oblique lighting.

(2) VISIBLE FINGERMARK. It can be positive or negative depending on whether the fingers were contaminated with a coloured material, such as blood, or whether coloured material such as dust or soot has been removed from the surface, by the fingerprint ridges. This type of marks can be enhanced optically, depending on the properties of the contaminant in question.

(3) LATENT FINGERPRINT. This is the most common type of fingerprint, and causes most problems for their detection and generally require some physical or chemical treatment, to differentiate them from substrate materials. A typical latent fingerprint deposit is a complex mixture of natural secretions and contaminants from the environment. Knowledge of the major constituents of the deposits are essential for effective fingerprint detection.[13]

13 Dr. Chris Lennard, *The Detection and Enhancement of Latent Fingerprint*, (2001)88 available at http://latent-prints.com/images/specialpresentation.pdf, last visited on 4th July 2016.

3.2.1 Modes of determining the identification of the fingerprint found from the crime scene

A Latent Print examiner compare latent prints to exemplar using their expertise. Latent Print examination is a complex process, they are often small, distorted, overlapped and can be manipulated on the crime scene. For such complexities, experts must be trained, in working with the various difficult attributes of latent fingerprints. During examination a latent is compared with one or more exemplars. In a particular case, exemplars are generally collected from persons of interest, who had legitimate access to the crime scene or it might be obtained from a database known as Automated Fingerprint Identification System (AFIS). AFIS, provides a list of candidate exemplars, for comparison with the latents. Exemplars selected by the AFIS are far more likely to be similar to the latent than exemplars selected by other means and gives much accurate result. The method of comparing latent fingerprints with exemplars selected from AFIS is a method by which FBI conducts investigation.

Further, the method prevalent for comparison of (latent fingerprint with the candidates exemplars) fingerprint is known as ACEV System. In this system of fingerprint examination, analysis, comparison, evaluation and verification is conducted for determination of the latent fingerprint. Such examination can reveal three types of results: (*i*) unsuitable for comparison, (*ii*) suitable for comparison, (*iii*) exclusion or inconclusive which means, it is from different source which is not in question and makes the result neither unsuitable for comparison nor suitable for comparison.

3.2.2 ACEV system

(1) ANALYSIS. The assessment of a print for determination whether it can be used for a comparison is known as analysis. If the print is found to be not suitable for comparison because of inadequate quality or quantity of features, the examination ends and the print is reported as not suitable. If the print is suitable, the analysis indicates the features to be used in the comparison and their tolerances (the amount of variation that

will be accepted). The analysis may also uncover physical features such as recurves,[14] deltas,[15] creases,[16] and scars[17] that help to indicate where to begin the comparison.

(2) COMPARISONS. An analyst performs the comparison who views the known and suspect prints side by side. The analyst compares the minutiae[18] characteristics and locations to determine if they match. Known prints are often collected from persons of interest, victims, others who are present at the scene or through a search of one or more fingerprint databases such as the FBI's Integrated Automated Fingerprint Identification System (IAFIS). IAFIS is the largest fingerprint database in the world and as of June, 2012, held more than 72 million print records from criminals, military personnel, government employees and other civilian employees.

(3) EVALUATION. Where the examiner ultimately decides whether the prints are from the same source or from different sources or is inconclusive. Inconclusive results may be due to poor quality samples, lack of comparable areas or insufficient number of corresponding or dissimilar features to be certain.

(4) VERIFICATION. The process of verification is just like re-examination. When another examiner independently analyzes, compares and evaluates the prints to either support or refute the conclusions of the original examiner. Even the examiner may also verify the suitability of determinations made in the analysis phase.

14 Print that recurve back on themselves.

15 It is a point on a friction ridge at or nearest to the point of divergenge of two type lines.

16 Kind of stripes irregularly crossing ridges and valleys in the fingerprint. It is caused due to factors like aging, manual work, accidents etc.

17 A deep cut through the outer layer of the skin, the epidermis and down to the dermis leaves a scar, that changes a fingerprint. A scar is a mark left on the skin due to various reasons.

18 Specific points in a finger image. There are two main types known as ridge endings and bifurcations. Sometimes other details such as the points at which scars begin are considered minutiae.

Latent-exemplar image pairs collected under controlled conditions are known to be mated when they are match of the same source, or nonmated when they do not match as the sources are different. An individualization decision based on mated print is a true positive. An exclusion[19] of decision based on mated prints is a false negative, but it is true negative, if based on nonmated prints. False positive and false negative, both are termed as 'errors'.[20]

4 Principle on which fingerprint evidence is based

According to criminal investigators, fingerprints follow three fundamental principles:

(1) No two people have been found with the exact same fingerprint pattern from which it can be inferred that a fingerprint is an individual characteristic.

(2) A fingerprint pattern will remain unchanged for the life of an individual but the print itself may change due to permanent scars and diseases.

(3) Fingerprints have general characteristic ridge patterns that allow them to be systematically identified.

In *Jaspal Singh* v *State of Punjab*,[21] the Supreme Court observed that science of identifying the thumb impression is an exact science and does not admit of any mistake or doubt. Therefore, it is settled law that the science of identifying thumb impression is an exact science and does not admit of any mistake or doubt. Fingerprint is a physical evidence which is unlike DNA that is generally found in cells that have a nucleus from which the name nuclear DNA has been derived.[22] Even twins with identical DNA have different fingerprints.

19 When the comparison does not match with the accused, although the comparison is matches with somebody else's, but it is of no use as it reveals a third persons identity which is not in question.

20 Bradford T. Ulery, R. Austin Hickman, *Accuracy and Reliability of Forensic Latent Fingerprint Decisions*, 19 *PNAS*. 108 (2011) available at http://www.ncbi.nlm.nih.gov/pmc/articles/PMC3093498/, last visited on 21st January 2015.

21 AIR 1979 SC 1708; 1979 CrLJ 1386.

22 *Hanumappa* v *Yallakka*, Petition No. 8815 of 2014 (GM-CPC), 3rd September 2014 (Kant).

5 Method/mechanism for collection of fingerprints for criminal investigation

Besides having application in criminal investigation, fingerprints are also useful in the identification of deceased persons and disaster victims. It has been proved that fingerprints are much more dependable method than any other mode of identification as it is infallible and practical. It can be found on any solid surface including the human body. Analysts classify fingerprints into three categories according to the type of surface on which it is found and on the ground of their visibility which are termed as Patent Prints, Plastic Prints and Latent Prints. Any person can make an attempt to change his/her voice or handwriting but it is impossible to change fingerprints because they are unique and permanent. The palmer surface of the hands and the plantar surfaces of the feet have ridges skin and are known as papillary or friction ridge skin. These ridges once are formed in foetal life, except for growing in size remain unchanged throughout life and even after death or till the bodies are decomposed. If the epidermis is injured it re-grows very quickly and till the injury has not penetrated deep into the generating layer of the epidermis, the pattern of the ridges on the healed surface becomes identical with the pattern as it existed prior to the injury.

Fingerprint evidence left behind by a suspect or victim may identify who was at a crime scene and what he or she touched. Nevertheless, it is important to know, and to inform the court, that the techniques used to locate and identify fingerprints are far from a perfect science. A understanding of how fingerprints are located and lifted can help defence recognize whether a flawed analysis was performed by investigators or lab technicians. Further, knowledge of the various fingerprint collection techniques is essential to successful cross-examination of crime scene technicians and fingerprint examiners.

5.1 Locating fingerprint

Locating fingerprint is the first step in the process of identification of fingerprint evidence. It often requires a vigilant and calculated search. It becomes easier to trace a fingerprint, if it is visible to the naked eye. When a fingerprint is present on a surface which is not visible the most intricate search takes place. The type of fingerprint left behind usually determines the amount of time and effort investigators must put into locating the print. Investigators usually follow a two phase process when searching for fingerprints. The first phase involves looking for patent and plastic prints since they are visible. The second phase involves a blind search for latent prints, according to Scientific Evidence. The type of surface being searched for fingerprints often determines the technique employed by investigators.[23]

(1) LOCATING THE FINGERPRINT AND IDENTIFYING FROM NON-POROUS SURFACES. A powder technique is usually used to identify latent prints on non-porous surfaces such as glass, marble, metal, plastic and finished wood. When powder is spread on the surface, it adheres to the residue deposited from the finger's touch, allowing investigator's to find the print.

(2) LOCATING THE FINGERPRINT AND IDENTIFYING FROM POROUS SURFACES. The powder technique is not as effective on porous surfaces such as fabric, unfinished wood and paper. In such cases, investigators often use chemical methods to locate the print such as iodine fuming, silver nitrate or ninhydrin. When such chemicals comes in contact with the chemical present in the fingerprint residue which is comprised of natural gas and fats, the print become visual.

(3) LOCATING THE FINGERPRINT AND IDENTIFYING FROM HUMAN SKIN. Locating and identifying fingerprints left on human skin is incredibly difficult. Further, after a print is left on human skin, the oily residue often disperses and is absorbed into the skin, blurring the print.

(4) LOCATING THE FINGERPRINT AND IDENTIFYING FROM TEXTURED SURFACES. Surfaces that are not flat or have a rough surface such as painting with brush strokes or a golf ball will make the

23 Paul C. Giannelli, Edward J. Imwinkelried, Andrea Roth and Jane Campbell Moriarty, *Scientific Evidence*, 5th Ed., p. 949.

process of identifying and collecting fingerprints more difficult but not impossible.

(5) LOCATING THE FINGERPRINT AND IDENTIFYING BY SUPERGLUE FUMING TECHNIQUE. This technique is used by both lab technicians and investigators at the crime scene. Superglue technique is a chemical process that exposes and fixes fingerprints on a non-porous surface. In the laboratory, the process works by using an airtight tank known as fuming chamber to heat up superglue liquid cyanoacrylate which releases gases that adhere to the oily residue of print, thereby creating an image of the fingerprint. The technique can also be performed at the crime scene. Rather than using a fuming chamber, crime scene investigators may use a handheld wand that heats up superglue and a florescent dye. Superglue fuming performed at the crime scene can be vital to preserve prints on items that are being sent to the lab via mail. One of the drawbacks is that if the evidence is fumed too long, it can distort the print, rendering it useless.

(6) OTHER COLLECTION METHODS. In addition to the methods identified above, there are special techniques for capturing prints from skin, clothing and other difficult surfaces. Amido Black, a non-specific protein stain that reacts with any protein present, is typically used for developing or enhancing bloody impressions on human skin. To reveal prints on clothing, hightech methods such as vaccum metal deposition using gold and zinc are used by the investigator. Accu Trans, a liquid casting compound can be used to lift powdered latent prints from rough textured or curved surfaces.

5.2 Photographing the fingerprint

After the print is located, it is vital that it is photographed before it is lifted. A photograph captures where the print was located in comparison to other objects and captures the orientation of the print. A photograph can serve as key piece of identification of a patent or plastic print and can be used to compare and possibly match the print to its source. Photographing the print's location at the crime scene also guards against tampering of evidence.

5.3 Lifting the fingerprint

"Lifting of fingerprint" means to make a permanent impression of the fingerprint. Lifting of fingerprint can be accomplished on either flat surfaces or round surfaces. It usually involves a rubber tape with an adhesive surface which is applied to the fingerprint, leaving an imprint on the tape. Often a flat object such as ruler will be slowly swiped across the top of the tape to ensure that there are no bubbles or ripples in the tape that will affect the imprint. Next, the tape is carefully peeled off the surface and the plastic cover is placed on the adhesive side of the tape to prevent disruption of the print. Identification information and a description of the location of the print should be written on the back of the tape or card.[24] After the print is lifted it is converted into digital data that can be modified to create a clearer image.

5.4 Comparing the fingerprint

The final step involves a close examination of the characteristics of the fingerprints. The fingerprint examination process utilizes the ACE-V method which stands for Analysis, Comparison, Evaluation and Verification to compare a print collected from a crime scene to a set of known prints. A system called the Automated Fingerprint Identification System (AFIS) was created to find a match to the print using a computer database.

6 Automated Fingerprint Identification System (AFIS)

Automated Fingerprint Identification System (AFIS) is a computerized system capable of reading, classifying, matching and storing fingerprints for criminal justice agencies. It uses computer algorithms to mark all minutiae points,[25] cores and

24 Paul C. Giannelli, Edward J. Imwinkelried, Andrea Roth and Jane Campbell Moriarty, *Scientific Evidence*, p. 949, $ 16.03 (5th Ed. 2012) at 964-965.

25 In biometrics and fingerprint scanning, minutiae refers to specific plot points on a fingerprint. This includes characteristics such as ridge bifurcation or a ridge ending on a fingerprint available at http://www.webopedia.com/TERM/M/minutiae.html accessed on 19.07.2017.

deltas on the print, which are used to find possible matches with fingerprints in the database.

Automated Fingerprint Identification System (AFIS) uses automatic scanning devices that convert the image of a fingerprint into digital minutiae (the ridge characteristics) that contains data showing ridges at their points of termination (ridge endings) and the branching of ridges into two ridges (bifurcations). The scanning converts the spatial relationship of a fingerprint's ridge endings and ridge bifurcations called minutiae points into a digitized representation of the fingerprints. The process of automated fingerprinting works by scanning and storing fingerprints digitally in a computer's memory. The computer then creates a spatial map of the unique ridge patterns of the prints and translates this spatial relationship into a binary[26] code for the computer. As new fingerprints are scanned into the computer, the computer searches for any identical prints and updates the system. This enables law enforcement agencies to identify criminals more quickly and also have access to a large data base with information on fingerprints. This alone has greatly enhanced the efficiency of the criminal justice system and also increased the conviction rate for offenders.

7 Legal provisions under which fingerprint evidence was used/referred

The legal aspect of taking fingerprints is covered by different sections of the Identification of Prisoners Act 1920, s. 73 of the Evidence Act 1872 and s. 293 of the Code of Criminal Procedure 1973.

(1) Section 4 of the Identification of Prisoners Act permits a police officer of the rank of Sub-Inspector or an investigating officer (in offences covered by

26 A bit (short for binary digit) is the smallest unit of data on a computer; each bit has a single value of either 1 or 0. Executable (ready-to-run) programs are often identified as binary files and given a file name extension of ".bin." Programmers often call executable files *binaries* available at http://whatis.techtarget.com/definition/binary.

Chapter XIV of CrPC) above this rank to take fingerprint of an accused, arrested for an offence punishable with at least one year's rigorous imprisonment.

(2) Under s. 6 of the Identification of Prisoners Act, a First Class Magistrate can direct any person to give his fingerprints, if in the opinion of the Magistrate it expedites the investigation of the case. It shall be lawful to use all means necessary to secure the taking thereof.

(3) Section 73 of the Indian Evidence Act 1872 also covers fingerprinting. The court may direct any person present in the court to give his fingerprints, if the same is required for comparison with questioned fingerprint.

(4) By virtue of s. 45 of the Indian Evidence Act 1872, the evidence of a fingerprint expert who is a person especially skilled in fingerprints is relevant.

(5) Under s. 293 of the Code of Criminal Procedure 1973, the report of the Director of the Fingerprint Bureau is accepted as evidence. The court may call the expert for evidence.[27]

The types of cases and legislations in which fingerprints evidence played a significant role in solving the crime:

- THE INDIAN PENAL CODE 1860. Murder, rape, unnatural offences, theft, dishonest misappropriation of property, kidnapping or abducting in order to murder, robbery, dacoity, making preparation to commit dacoity, criminal conspiracy, kidnapping, attempt to murder, rioting, unlawful assembly, causing hurt, grievous hurt, assault or criminal force to woman with intent to outrage her modesty, cheating, forgery, falsification of accounts, dishonestly receiving stolen property, house trespass, lurking house trespass and house breaking by night,

27 Marvin D'Souza, R.P. Kataria, *Forensic Science in Criminal Trial & Investigation*, Ed. 2016, p. 291.

criminal intimidation, acts done by several persons in furtherance of common intention.

- The Prevention of Corruption Act 1988. Section 5 — Procedure and powers of special judge; section 13(1)(*d*) Criminal Misconduct by a public servant.
- The Identification of Prisoners Act 1920. Section 5 — Power of Magistrate to order a person to be measured or photographed.
- The Arms Act 1959. Section 25—Punishment for certain offences; Section 27- Punishment for using arms, etc.
- The Indian Evidence Act 1872. Section 73—Comparison of signature, writing or seal with others admitted or proved.
- The Code of Criminal Procedure 1973. Section 311—Power to summon material witness, or to examine person present.
- The Terrorist and Disruptive Activities (Prevention) Act 1987. Section 5 – Possession of certain unauthorized arms, etc. in specified areas.

An attentive study of the cases reveal that fingerprint evidence is a corroborative evidence but the courts accepted the fact 'Fingerprint evidence is a very valuable piece of evidence in any criminal investigation and its importance can never be underestimated'.[28] It is also a settled principle of law that when the material objects recovered from the place of occurrence were sent for the purpose of comparison with the fingerprints taken from the accused, the fingerprints of the accused must be taken procedurally.[29] Nonetheless, the Supreme Court opined that presence of a fingerprint at the scene of occurrence is positive evidence but the absence of

28 *Ouseph* alias *Johny* v *State of Kerala* (12.08.1987 – KER HC) MANU/KE/0515/1987.

29 *Palanichamy* v *State represented by the Inspector of Police* (26.07.2010 – MAD HC) MANU/TN/2116/2010.

fingerprint is not enough to foreclose the presence of the persons concerned at the scene.[30]

8 Criminal cases in which fingerprint evidence was used/referred for recording conviction or acquittal

8.1 Murder and house trespass

8.1.1 Fingerprint evidence along with other evidences proved guilt of the accused

The appellant was convicted under ss. 449 and 302, IPC for committing house trespass and murder. Fingerprints were lifted from the scene of occurrence and were also taken from the accused. Fingerprint evidence is accepted by the courts on the assumption that no two individuals have identical fingerprints. Scientific research and analysis leads to the conclusion that the probability for the existence of two identical fingerprint patterns in the world's population is extremely small.

In view of the circumstances the guilt of the accused was established.[31]

8.1.2 Fingerprint evidence corroborated other evidences

Appellant was convicted under s. 302 as well as s. 460. One of the witnesses in FIR stated that he had seen appellant leaving house of deceased with knife in his hand. Evidence of other witness implicating appellant who was her husband cannot be doubted as no reasons have been given as to why would wife falsely depose against her husband. In pursuance of statement made by appellant knife was recovered. Fingerprints of the appellant was found on mirror and lock of witness house. Plea of alibi taken by accused falsified by evidence of his wife. The prosecution proved the case against the accused beyond reasonable doubt. On basis of fingerprints available conviction of the appellant was affirmed.[32]

30 *Gade Lakshmi Mangaraju* v *State of A.P.* (2001)6 SCC 205.

31 *Ouseph* alias *Johny* v *State of Kerala* (12.08.1987 – KER HC) MANU/KE/0515/1987.

32 *Smt. Chhanno* v *State of Haryana* JT 1996(4) SC 719; (1996)4 Scale 8.

8.1.3 Circumstantial evidence relating to fingerprints and footprints

By the impugned judgment the High Court upheld the convictions and sentences recorded against the accused under ss. 302 and 460 of IPC. Fingerprints of the accused were found on brass jug seized from the house of the deceased. Prosecution failed to prove that the seized articles were not be tampered with before they reached the Fingerprint Bureau. Seized articles were kept in police station for five days without any justifiable reason. Letter forwarding the seized articles to the Bureau contained an overwriting as regards the date of its dispatch. Specimen fingerprints of accused were not taken. Brass jug in question not produced and exhibited during trial. In such circumstances, conviction of the accused on the basis of evidence of his fingerprints was not sustainable. The fingerprints of the accused were also found on a glass tumbler. Although the glass tumbler was seized but it was not produced during trial. So, link between the identity of articles seized and articles examined by the Fingerprint Bureau was missing. So, evidence relating to fingerprints and footprints of the accused could not be safely relied on.[33]

8.2 Murder

8.2.1 Accused persons pleaded guilty and fingerprint evidence corroborated the fact

One of the witnesses lifted the fingerprint from a bottle which was later compared by the fingerprint expert, with the fingerprints of accused and it tallied with each other. Accused was decided to plead guilty.[34]

8.2.2 Evidence doubtful—fingerprint evidence thus obtained from accused was of no use

It was observed that two respectable persons from the locality were not joined before effecting the search. It was ruled that the joining of one witness was not sufficient. Hence the

33 *Mohd. Aman* v *State of Rajasthan* (1997)10 SCC 44.

34 *State of Maharashtra* v *Sukhdeo Singh* (15.07.1992 – SC) MANU/SC/0416/1992.

recovery was doubtful and could not be believed to be made at the instance of the accused. The case debated on the credibility of the murder weapon that was recovered from an open place as per s. 27 of the Evidence Act 1872. The place was accessible to a number of persons. It was found that there was no proof for the weapon was lying concealed and was not visible to open eyes. Thus it was ruled that said recovery could not be given importance. Fingerprint impressions of the accused were also taken. Thus the conviction was set aside and acquittal was recorded but not on the ground of fingerprint evidence.[35]

8.2.3 Misreading of evidence including fingerprint evidence not proved

In *State of Rajasthan* v *Raksh*[36] fingerprints and photographs were not exhibited. No question was put to accused in statement under s. 313, CrPC in this regard. SDM before whom the specimen fingerprints were allegedly taken were not produced as evidence. Fingerprint evidence was therefore, not reliable.

8.2.4 Chain of circumstantial evidence not complete—fingerprint evidence not obtained in presence of Magistrate

In *Paramasivam* alias *Paraman* alias *Kottiyan* v *State of Tamil Nadu*,[37] the specimen fingerprints were neither taken under order nor in presence of Magistrate. Therefore, evidence of fingerprint expert was inadmissible in evidence.[38]

8.2.5 Circumstantial evidence jointly produced guilt of the accused

The prosecution relied upon the presence of fingerprints of the accused at the spot, the movement of the accused on the next day morning at Mangalore Town and in his village and abscondence thereafter till he was arrested after a week after the date of incident. Chance fingerprints were lifted from the spot and compared with the admitted fingerprints and it

35 *Jaivir Singh* v *State* (*Delhi Administration*) 1995 CrLJ 1477.
36 *State of Rajasthan* v *Rakesh* 2000(3) WLC 368; 2000(2) WLN 191.
37 JT 2002(8) SC 214.
38 *Mahmood* v *State of U.P.* (1976)1 SCC 542.

was found that the chance fingerprint was identical with that of the left thumb fingerprint of the accused. Held, all the circumstances conclusively proved the guilt of the accused.[39]

Fingerprints of the accused were found on household articles of the deceased. The fingerprints were found on the toffee box found in the house of the deceased. The investigating agency during their visit to the house of the deceased had picked up certain chance fingerprints which on analysis were found to be that of the accused. Presence of fingerprints of accused on household articles is common and natural as accused was domestic help and thus not relevant.[40]

8.2.6 Fingerprint evidence formed part of the complete chain without any missing link

A cruel and gruesome murder of an old lady was committed for gain. Entire case rested on circumstantial evidence. The fingerprints of the accused were taken by the Inspector of Police at the Police Station and the same were handed over to the Fingerprint Expert. The fingerprint tallied with that of the accused as per certificate of the Fingerprint Expert. Such circumstances point towards the guilt of the accused.[41]

8.2.7 Further corroboration with fingerprint evidence

Fingerprints were lifted from the mirror lying in the room where the murder was committed. The fingerprints were recovered at the instance of the accused. The court found further corroboration from the fact that the fingerprints lifted from the mirror lying in the room where the murder was committed, had been found to be those of the accused. The accused was convicted.[42]

39 *Praveen Kumar* v *State of Mangalore Rural Circle Police* 2003(3) KarLJ 77.
40 *Kuldip Singh* v *State of Delhi* (2003)12 SCC 528.
41 *Natarajan* v *Union Territory of Pondicherry* 2003 CrLJ 2372 (Mad).
42 *Kulwinder Singh* v *State of Punjab* (2007)10 SCC 455.

8.2.8 Prosecution witnesses failed to establish accusations against accused and fingerprint of other accused was found who was already acquitted

In *Tipparam Prabhakar* v *State of A.P.*,[43] fingerprints were taken from the seized objects. On requisition the fingerprints expert visited the police station and examined the material objects seized for developing the chance prints. He found one fingerprint and he lifted it and got photographed the same. He compared the fingerprint sent by the police with the chance print marked, and found it as identical with the lefted fingerprints. The fingerprints expert gave his opinion.

Although the fingerprint evidence was accepted by the court but according to the learned counsel for the accused, the fingerprint of the accused was not found on the article seized. Only the fingerprints of other accused were collected. The fingerprints of that accused were found on the seized articles and it tallied with the fingerprints taken from that accused. But that accused had already been acquitted by the High Court. So the accused was acquitted.[43]

8.2.9 Fingerprints could not be relied upon as not taken procedurally

Fingerprints were taken from the material objects. Scientific Assistant had given an opinion that the fingerprints lifted from the beer bottles tallied with that of the fingerprints taken from the accused. It is settled principle of law that when the material objects recovered from the place of occurrence were sent for the purpose of comparison with the fingerprints taken from the accused, the fingerprints of the accused must be taken procedurally. It was found that no order was obtained from the Magistrate neither any procedure was followed as to how the fingerprints of the accused were taken. In the absence of compliance of any procedural formalities, the fingerprints taken from the accused, even if they were compared and expert's opinion was obtained, cannot be relied upon.[44]

43 *Tipparam Prabhakar* v *State of A.P.* (2009)13 SCC 534.
44 *Palanichamy* v *State represented by Inspector of Police* (2010) SCC Online Mad 4042.

8.2.10 No reliance place on opinion of fingerprint expert as prosecution failed to point guilt of the accused

Prosecution relied on extra-judicial confession given by accused to Village Administrative Officer who was totally stranger to her. Subsequently prosecution relied on last seen by two concerned witnesses. Both concerned witnesses were total strangers to accused. Both of them identified accused only for the first time before court and prosecution had not conducted any identification parade. Therefore, it was unsafe to place reliance on their evidence as identification of accused before court itself was highly doubtful. Last piece of circumstance put forward by prosecution was fingerprint expert's opinion to effect that fingerprint of accused tallied with the fingerprints found on the beer bottle. Opinion of fingerprint expert could not be construed to be conclusive one and same was to be tested only as a corroborative piece of material along with other material available on record. Therefore, no reliance could be placed on opinion of fingerprint expert. Prosecution failed to point guilt of accused. Thus conviction was unsustainable in law. Accordingly appeal was allowed and acquittal was recorded.[45]

8.2.11 Fingerprint evidence not reliable and could not establish identity of deceased

Fingerprint and palmprint was used to identify the deceased. The learned counsel for the prosecution submitted that the comparison of palm prints found in the house of the parents of the deceased and the palm prints of the body parts found in the rubbish container established the identity of the deceased. But the fingerprint expert was not able to conclude that the evidence produced would connect the palm prints with the palm prints of the deceased. Therefore the report of the fingerprint expert on this aspect was not found definite.[46]

45 *Sagunthala* v *State* (2010)3 Mad LJ 899.

46 *State* v *Mahender Singh Dahiya* (2011)3 SCC 109.

8.3 Fingerprint evidence of no use as there were contradictory evidences

The appellant accused and the deceased were crew members on a ship, sailing from South Africa to Japan. The appellant allegedly confessed before a witness, (Second Officer of the ship) that he had killed the deceased. A bloodstained knife was recovered from him. A day before the incident an altercation alleged to have taken place between the accused and the deceased, which was said to be the motive for the murder of the deceased by the appellant.

The knife and the specimen fingerprints were then sent to the (CFSL) for comparison. The fingerprints of the accused had tallied with the fingerprints which appeared on the knife. Another knife was also recovered but that was not examined to find out the presence of fingerprints on it. The accused was acquitted.[47]

8.4 Murder and criminal conspiracy

8.4.1 Fingerprint evidences corroborated other evidences

Present appeals filed against order of conviction under ss. 120B and 302, IPC for hatching criminal conspiracy to kill the deceased. Held, considering investigation in respect of register, conjoint reading of testimonies of concerned witnesses and seizure memo, tend to suggest that register was seized and at that point of time entry in the said register was in existence. Consequently it would indicate that accused had made said entry in said register. Therefore presence of accused at that apartment would stand established. It appeared that time of death was more or less with visit of accused to deceased's flat. Thus it was clear that evidence on record points in direction of accused as being killer of deceased. Fingerprints of accused were found on the polythene cover of the box of sweets and also on one of the teacups. Hence conviction was upheld.[48]

47 *Majenderan Langeswaran* v *State* (2013)7 SCC 192.
48 *Ravi Kant Sharma* v *State* (2011)183 DLT 248.

8.4.2 When testimonies of eyewitnesses are trustworthy: corroborative fingerprint evidence supports the prosecution case

The accused/respondent were charged for shooting victim dead outside his house. Eyewitnesses (mother and wife of deceased) identified both accused in court. Their testimonies were found cogent, natural and trustworthy. There was no material discrepancy in their testimonies. Further fingerprints raised from place of incident found similar to finger impressions of both accused persons taken in presence of Judicial Magistrate, hence there was no suspicion as to their *bona fides*. The fingerprint expert has conducted the experiment and prepared the report as above. In the aforesaid facts and circumstances, held conviction of both appellants under s. 302, IPC and s. 25 of Arms Act, were confirmed.[49]

8.5 Murder/kidnapping and abduction

8.5.1 Prosecution failed to prove fingerprint evidence

The appellants were accused for the offence of kidnapping and murder and charged under ss. 302/34, 364/34 and 201/34, IPC along with s. 25 of Arms Act read with s. 5 of TADA for illegal possession of country-made pistol and a cartridge. Held on facts that prosecution only established that the victim was kidnapped in a Maruti car. It failed to establish that the appellants were the kidnappers or that they were responsible for the death of the kidnapped persons. Although the prosecution led evidence to prove that fingerprints found on the car were taken by an expert, no attempt was made by the prosecution to prove that those fingerprints were of the appellants. The court opined that "needless to say, evidence of the fingerprint expert in proof thereof would have gone a long way to sustain the prosecution case". Therefore judgment of the trial court convicting the appellants was a perverse one for it was not only based on conclusions drawn from inadmissible evidence but suffered from the vice of non-consideration of evidence which materially impaired the prosecution case.

49 *State of Punjab* v *Jagga Singh* (2015)2 SCC 471.

Accordingly, conviction of the appellants was set aside and they were acquitted.[50]

8.6 Circumstantial evidence corroborated prosecution evidence

The appellants herein were prosecuted for commission of an offence under ss. 364/34, 302/34 and 201/34 of IPC. They were sentenced to death. Against this sentence appeals were preferred by the appellants before the High Court.

The accused persons were convicted for the murder of two children aged about 6 and 8 years. The children went to private tuition. They were supposed to come back by 6.30 pm. As they did not return, and the parents of the children was informed by the teacher that the children left the house at 6.15 pm. The children were continued to be searched and he came to know one scooterist had taken his children on his scooter. An FIR was lodged. During investigation, school bags and dead bodies of the children were recovered. One of the accused was related to the complainant and belonged to the same community. They were neighbours. However, they were said to be belonging to different union of their community being that of washermen.

Fingerprints were found from bottle and glasses recovered from the place of incidence. Fingerprints of the appellants were also taken. The sub-inspector found the traces of fingerprints from the recovered bottle and glasses. He developed the fingerprints on the glasses, which were comparable. Those were sent to the fingerprints bureau. The report revealed that the thumb impression lifted from the glasses by sub-inspector and thumb impression obtained from the appellants herein tallied with each other.

In view of the circumstantial evidences, which had been brought on record, the court was satisfied that all links in the chain were completed and the evidences led by the prosecution pointed out only to one conclusion, which was the guilt of the accused.[51]

50 *Vijender* v *State of Delhi* (1997)6 SCC 171.

51 *Gagan Kanojia* v *State of Punjab* (2006)13 SCC 516.

8.6.1 Fingerprint evidence corroborated other substantive evidences

The appellants were accused for the offences under ss. 302, 364A, 120B and 201 of IPC. Deceased was a young boy aged about 16 years, who was the son of a goldsmith and alleged to have been kidnapped from school and later was murdered. Testimonies of witnesses were found credible and corroborating each other. One of the witnesses stated that his grey-coloured Alto car had been taken by accused who was his son's friend at about 7.30 a.m. and returned at about 10.30 a.m. on the day of occurrence. Said circumstances fitted with the prosecution story that other witness had seen one of the accused in the driver's seat of Alto car and other accused getting in the car with deceased at about 8.30 am. Medical evidence indicated that cause of death of victim was chloroform and pentazocine poisoning. Pursuant to the disclosures made by accused, dead body of victim, Alto car, Chevrolet car and other incriminating articles were recovered. The car was subjected to examination by fingerprint experts who lifted several fingerprints which were duly dispatched to the laboratory. Fingerprints of accused were found on cars, while thumb impression of accused found on chloroform bottle. Mobile number from which ransom calls were made were traced. Hence conviction of the appellants under ss. 302, 364A, 120B and 201 of IPC called for no interference. The appeal was dismissed.[52]

8.7 Murder and receiving of stolen property

8.7.1 Fingerprint evidence corroborated other evidences

When photographs of fingerprint impressions were not clear enough to enable the expert to come to any definite conclusion and therefore second impressions were taken by the photographer. The Supreme Court opined that in absence of any effective cross-examination of the photographer his evidence that he was able to take better photographs on the second occasion could not have been disbelieved by court.

52 *Vikram Singh* v *State of Punjab* (2010)3 SCC 56.

Therefore the conviction of the accused appellants was confirmed.[53]

8.8 Murder, robbery and dacoity

8.8.1 No link between the fingerprint evidences forwarded by the prosecution witnesses

In a murder case the court rejected the evidence of the fingerprint expert for the following reasons: Fingerprint expert has in his evidence stated that on reaching the scene of occurrence, he lifted 5 fingerprints from the iron bureau and compared them with the fingerprints of accused, though the police officer stated that he took the fingerprints of the accused. The same was not marked in the court nor the fingerprint expert stated that the fingerprint of the accused taken by the officer was received by him and that he compared it with the fingerprints lifted by him from the scene place. In the absence of any link between the evidence of police officer and that of fingerprint expert, the court did not find it safe to place reliance upon the evidence of the fingerprint expert.[54]

8.8.2 Corroboration by fingerprint evidence

Appellant was convicted under ss. 302 and 394 by the trial court which was challenged by the appellant before the High Court. Facts suggested that accused killed the deceased by strangulation. After the investigation was set in motion Dog Squad and Fingerprint Expert were called for. The fingerprint expert found three chance fingerprints on the TV stand and two chance fingerprints on the stainless steel cups kept near the dead bodies and took photographs of the same as well as the fingerprints of the deceased and nearby occupants.

The lifted fingerprints when compared with the fingerprints of one of the accused persons, tallied with each other.

53 *Ammini* v *State of Kerala* (1998)2 SCC 301.

54 *Abdul Razak* alias *Razak* v *State Represented by Inspector of Police, Cheranpadi Police Station* 2002 LW (Cr) 673.

Fingerprints, thus, matched with the fingerprints of that of the accused. The conviction was confirmed.[55]

8.8.3 Fingerprint evidence corroborated other evidences

The accused was convicted for murder and robbery. The prosecution had relied upon certain fingerprints taken from the place of incident which on examination by the Fingerprint Bureau was found to tally with the fingerprints of the accused. Motive was also established. Establishing the involvement of the accused in the said offence on the basis of the circumstantial evidence. Therefore conviction of the accused was proper.[56]

8.8.4 Fingerprint evidence a link in the chain of circumstances

The accused was convicted under s. 302 and s. 392/377, IPC. Fingerprints of the accused were found at the spot. The prosecution had also further established from the evidence of the handwriting expert, that he had picked up fingerprints of the thumb which were tallied with the corresponding fingerprints of the appellant which also indicated the fact that the appellant was in the house of the deceased at about the time of the incident in question because those fingerprints were picked up immediately after the investigation of the case started. Each and every link in the chain of circumstances was proved by the prosecution beyond reasonable doubt. Guilt was established and the accused was convicted.[57]

8.8.5 When fingerprint evidence becomes crucial and convincing

In a murder case the chance fingerprints found on the handle of the almirah in the bedroom of the deceased were taken immediately after the occurrence and those were compared with the fingerprints of the deceased and her children but it did not tally with their fingerprints. Eight months thereafter when the accused was arrested and his fingerprints were taken

55 *Krishnamurthy* v *State of Ashok Nagar Police, Bangalore* 2000(6) KarLJ 243.

56 *Dayanidhi Bisoi* v *State of Orissa* (2003)9 SCC 310.

57 *Praveen Kumar* v *State of Karnataka* (2003)12 SCC 199.

and it was compared with the chance fingerprints taken from the handle of the almirah, it tallied, and accordingly accused was convicted for murder of the victim and her children.[58]

8.8.6 Fingerprint evidence as a component helped in completing the chain of evidence

Chance fingerprints were lifted as well as photographs of the same were taken in murder of 2 victims. Fingerprints of the deceased and the nearby occupants, a watchman and a maidservant were taken. Fingerprints of the accused were also taken. The fingerprint expert found three chance fingerprints on the TV stand and two chance fingerprints on the stainless steel cup kept near the dead bodies. All the fingerprints were sent for examination.

The chance fingerprints matched with the fingerprints of the accused and the accused was convicted.[59]

8.8.7 Corroboration of the prosecution version by identification of fingerprints of the accused

Fingerprint impression of accused were found on the articles in house where the crime was committed. Moreover, from ocular evidence of witnesses it was established that appellants had committed lurking house trespass by night and they had committed robbery of various articles in furtherance of their common intention and had voluntarily caused dangerous hurt to victims with intention and knowledge of causing death to them and also caused death of Gaurav Batra.

The ocular evidence was corroborated by the recovery of gold jewellery and other articles from the appellants. There was further corroboration of the prosecution version by identification of fingerprints of the accused on the articles removed from the house of the victim. The accused was convicted.[60]

58 *Ramasubhramanian* v *State of Kerala* (2007)12 SCC 801.
59 *A. Yadav* v *State of Karnataka* (2008)15 SCC 322.
60 *Maya Chanchal* v *State* (2011)185 DLT 209.

8.8.8 Fingerprint evidence scientifically established beyond doubt

The appeal had been preferred by the appellant questioning the judgment and order passed by the High Court rejecting the appellant's appeal and confirming the death sentence awarded to him by the Session's Judge. The appellant was convicted under ss. 376, 302 and 392 of IPC. The circumstances pointed to just only one hypothesis, i.e. he raped and murdered the woman while she was alone in house and committed robbery. Offences, were held, to be proved as accused was seen in house by deceased's seven year old son who had just returned after playing. Two neighbours also saw accused leaving with a bag containing household articles. Rape by violent sexual assault was proved by presence of sperm in deceased's vagina and other injuries on her body, particularly bleeding vagina. Cause of death was determined in post-mortem examination as smothering. Household articles were taken away by accused. He was identified by deceased's sister. Accused's fingerprints were found on handle of almirah.

Although there was no eye-witnesses who actually saw commission of these crimes by appellant but there were witnesses who saw him inside the house and leaving the house along with household articles. His fingerprints however were found on handle of almirah lying in the room.

The fingerprint expert found fingerprints on a wall clock and also on the handle of the almirah in the room which matched with the fingerprint of the accused. The court held that the report of the fingerprint expert strengthened the prosecution case and clearly established his presence inside the house of the deceased. The explanation which was attempted to be given for the presence of the fingerprints on the handle of the almirah situated inside the room of the deceased did not inspire any confidence to the court. The court opined that it was the said evidence which scientifically established beyond doubt that the appellant was present in the room in which the deceased was found after her death and had been identified by the witnesses. The fingerprint of the appellant found on the handle of the almirah in the room of the deceased proved his presence in the house of the deceased and that he and no other caused the death of the deceased. The fingerprint evidence along with other evidence of other witnesses, established that it was accused who committed the crime. The appeal was thus dismissed and the death sentence awarded to the appellant was also confirmed.[61]

8.9 Forgery and cheating

8.9.1 Prosecution witnesses required to corroborate fingerprint evidence

A Branch Manager and a temporary sweeper, in Andhra Bank, entered into a criminal conspiracy to cheat Andhra Bank and pursuance thereof. The Branch Manager sanctioned and disbursed eight loans in the names of non-existing persons and misappropriated ₹85,000 by drawing the amounts towards loans. The Branch Manager falsified the loan documents in the names of different persons. The Branch Manager used the forged documents as genuine and cheated the bank to a tune of ₹85,000. The Branch Manager abused his official position and obtained fictitious loans himself. Since the accused persons in the commission of the offence, both of them are punishable for the offences mentioned in the respective charges.

The Senior Scientific Officer, Grade-II in Fingerprint Division of Central Forensic Science Laboratory, deposed that he examined the questioned fingerprints by comparing them with the specimen fingerprints. He deposed that after comparing the fingerprints, he came to the conclusion that the questioned thumb impressions are identical with the specimens thumb impressions of the accused persons and he prepared comparative charts in the form of Annexure to his report. He further opined that the thumb impressions are identical with

61 *B.A. Umesh* v *State of Karnataka* (2011)3 SCC 85.

the specimen thumb impressions of the Branch Manager. The fingerprints were taken in the presence of the mediators and their signatures were also found on the specimen writings, fingerprints and signatures. Section 5 of the Identification of Prisoners Act 1920, is a provision of caution and not a mandatory provision and so the fingerprint evidence was well admissible.[62]

8.9.2 Taking specimen fingerprints and handwriting of accused not hit by Article 20(3)

Respondents herein were Manager and Field Officer of Chaitanya Grameena Bank. Allegations against them were that they both conspired in the matter of sanctioning and disbursing loans under crop loan in the names of fictitious persons by forging signatures and thumb impressions of the proposed borrowers in the documents resulting in misappropriation of the proceeds of ₹30,000.

Charge against the Bank Manager was that of sanctioning crop loan in the name of fictitious persons and misappropriating the same. He completed all the loan formalities himself and affixed his own thumb impression instead of those of the loanees on the loan document. Handwritings on the loan document and the thumb impressions thereon found by qualified fingerprint expert was to be those of the Bank Manager.

But specimen signature, thumb impression and handwriting of the manager was taken during investigation by the IO on the basis whereof expert opined that the specimen impressions were those of manager, the High Court took the view that the procedure adopted by prosecution specially during investigation by taking signatures and thumb impressions of the Manager was not valid and was inadmissible in evidence.[63]

62 *Chita Narasimha Prasad* v *Sub-Inspector of Police* 2006 CrLJ 336.
63 *State* v *M. Krishna Mohan* (2007)14 SCC 667.

8.10 Theft and murder

8.10.1 Intention when relevant in fingerprint evidence

Present appeal was filed against conviction under ss. 302 and 380 of IPC. Held, from sequence of events and testimony of witnesses, facts which were the outcome were that appellant was expected to come to deceased's flat on relevant date and appellant was seen on relevant date. Gold jewellery and cash belonging to deceased was missing from her person and from cupboard in flat. Other than accused no one else was seen in deceased's flat on the date of occurrence, little before murder of deceased or around time of her death as determined in post mortem report. Some fingerprints were lifted from the flat of the deceased's husband. Fingerprints were lifted from the door of the cupboard from which the cash was stolen and other finger print was lifted from the glass pane of the main door. The fingerprints were compared along with the specimen fingerprints of the accused. The examination report revealed that, fingerprint was actually a partial print and was not identical to the fingerprint of the accused. Another fingerprint was smudged and did not disclose sufficient number of ridge details and was unfit for comparison. Other fingerptint was a sequence of two fingers, that is, the right middle finger and the right ring finger and was found to be identical with the specimen fingerprints of the accused. The accused was convicted.[64]

8.10.2 Circumstantial evidence together with the fingerprint evidence

The relevant circumstantial evidence on which the trial court and the High Court proceeded was that the accused was found in the victim house on the relevant day. The fingerprint expert, found the accused's fingerprint on a plastic cover bearing the inscription 'Canara Bank.' This was taken by the fingerprint expert for comparison and on a comparison having been made,

64 *Jeet Singh* v *State* (*Govt. of NCT*) *of Delhi* ILR (2007)1 Del 19.

the fingerprints thereon matched the fingerprints of the accused.

The fingerprint evidence depended on the evidence of two witnesses. They are the photographer and fingerprint expert. The photographer stated that he had taken a photograph of the bank passbook belonging to the deceased. He also produced in court the negative of a photograph taken by him with the fingerprint of the accused on the pass book. No positive print or photograph was developed from the negative. In his cross-examination, photographer could not say if the fingerprint in the negative was that appearing on the pass book. Thus the acquittal of the accused was recorded.[65]

8.11 Theft and house trespass

8.11.1 Corroboration of fingerprint evidence by circumstantial evidence

One person gave information to the police station that his sister, brother-in-law, their two children, the mother and sister of his brother-in-law were murdered by someone within their house. The photographer had lifted the fingerprints and the fingerprint expert had matched them and it tallied with the fingerprints of the accused. All the circumstantial evidence lead to the guilt of the accused. Moreover the confessional statement recorded by the Magistrate was relied upon by the court since it was made voluntarily and freely by accused when released on bail and was a free-man. Extra-judicial confession was also recorded by doctor while recording history of injuries. The statement made by the doctor, was accepted by both the courts below as he was an independent witness. Conviction of the accused upheld.[66]

8.12 Murder and offences under the Arms Act

8.12.1 Fingerprint evidence irrelevant

The appellants were convicted by the High Court under ss. 302/120-B, IPC and under s. 25(1)(*a*) & (*b*) and s. 27 of the

65 *Prakash* v *State of Karnataka* 2014 CrLJ 2503; (2014)12 SCC 133.
66 *M.A. Antony* v *State of Kerala* (2009)6 SCC 220.

Arms Act. Accused persons alleged to have paid money to two other persons for killing deceased, pursuant whereto they shot deceased from a close range resulting in his death. Prosecution case rested on circumstantial evidence and testimonies of witnesses, who were alleged eyewitnesses to occurrence. However, presence of one of the witnesses at place of occurrence found doubtful. Four accused persons were acquitted by courts below, hence substratum of prosecution case, viz. conspiracy theory knocked off. The learned counsel for the State relied very much on the evidence of fingerprint expert. Regarding this, the Supreme Court opined that evidence of fingerprint expert is not substantive evidence. Such evidence can only be used to corroborate some items of substantive evidence which are otherwise on record. In the instant case it was never alleged that there was any altercation between deceased and accused at place of occurrence, or that accused had any physical contact with deceased. Deceased was fired from point-blank range and he immediately fell down inside a car. Thus, no prosecution evidence to the effect that two accused had any occasion to touch car and that too with ring-finger. Hence, evidence of fingerprint expert on car was irrelevant. Even if evidence of fingerprint expert on scooter accepted, that by itself was insufficient to prove connection with crime. Besides, he failed to give any evidence of fingerprint on alleged weapon of offence which was discovered pursuant to disclosure made by accused. For the aforesaid reasons the appeal filed by the appellants were allowed and those two accused persons were acquitted.[67]

8.12.2 Fingerprint evidence to be properly cross-examined

The appeal was directed against the judgment of the High Court confirming the judgment of conviction and order of sentence passed by the Learned Additional Sessions Judge. Accused was charged under s. 302 and was sentenced to death.

67 *Musheer Khan* v *State of Madhya Pradesh* (2010)2 SCC 748.

Accused was also sentenced to suffer rigorous imprisonment for 3 years for each of the offences under ss. 201, 435, 411 of IPC and ss. 25(1-A) and 27(1) of the Arms Act. The fingerprint expert had visited the site and lifted some chance fingerprints. The investigating officer had taken the sample fingerprints of all the accused persons. The fingerprints were sent to the FSL to be compared with the chance fingerprints that had been lifted by the expert.

The expert clearly stated that the chance fingerprints lifted from the inner lock door of the steel almirah and the back door of the house matched with the fingerprints of other accused. The fingerprint expert was also cross-examined at length but no suggestion was put to him in his cross-examination that he never went to the site, never collected the fingerprints or that the fingerprints of the accused were never sent by the police to him. The court also noticed that these suggestions were even never put to the investigating officer by the counsel of the appellant. The attempt on behalf of the accused to object to the evidence of the fingerprints on the ground that the investigating officer had not told in his examination-in-chief that he had taken the fingerprints of the accused and sent them to the expert did not carry much weight in view of the documentary, ocular and expert evidence. It was expected of the investigating officer to make a statement in that behalf in his examination-in-chief, but absence of such statement would not weigh so much against the prosecution that the court should be persuaded to reject the evidence of the fingerprint expert along with the clinching evidence of prosecution witnesses. The expert was cross-examined at length. The court also held that the submission on behalf of the appellant that the fingerprint of the accused could be there upon the almirah in the normal course of business as accused was the domestic servant working in the bungalow was equally without merit. The presence of fingerprints of other accused found in the house and particularly on the almirah in the bedroom of the deceased remained unexplained and no attempt was made by any of the accused persons to take a stand to explain their conduct.

But the appeal was dismissed as the Supreme Court Judges found no infirmity in the judgment under appeal and found no merit in the submissions raised on behalf of the accused.[68]

68 *Munna Kr. Upadhyay* v *State of A.P.* (2012)6 SCC 174.

Chapter 5

Toxicology and Chemical Analysis

1 Introduction

There is no precise definition of poison in India but under the Indian Penal Code, the law describing the word poison are 'any poison or any stupefying, intoxicating, or any wholesome drug, or other thing' or any corrosive substance or any substance which is deleterious to the human body to inhale, to swallow, or to receive into the blood'.[1] With regard to 'any poisonous substance' used in s. 284 of IPC, all the law requires that the substance is such as, if taken, is likely to endanger human life, or will cause hurt or injury to any person. Again the law takes cognizance of the malicious intention of the individual who administers the drug or other substances, with a view to cause injury or death, irrespective of the quantity or quality of the substance.

The science of poison is known as toxicology. It can be divided into two types:

(1) Clinical Toxicology. The recognition of the symptoms of poisoning and the application of the proper remedial measures;

(2) Chemical Toxicology. The detection of the poison in stomach washings, blood samples, etc. (if the patient or the victim recovers), or in post-mortem material (if he dies).

1 Sections 324, 326 and 328 of the IPC and also ss. 299, 304A of the IPC.

The business of the forensic toxicologists is to investigate all fatal cases of poisoning. The investigation of a poisoning case involves:

(i) the separation of the poison or sometimes its metabolite from the material submitted;

(ii) the identification of the poison extracted;

(iii) the estimation of the total amount present and comparison of this with the known lethal dose.[2]

A study has revealed that in 2006 in United States, 20.8% of the deaths were caused by poisoning, surpassing the death caused by firearms which amounted to 17.3%.[3]

2 Post mortem using forensic toxicology

According to Paracelsus, a sixteenth century scientist, a certain amount of every substance, even water and air, can be toxic and those amounts can differ from person to person and substance to substance. Forensic toxicology applies analytical toxicology to the purposes of the law, and includes the analysis of a variety of fluids and tissue samples to determine the absence or presence of drugs and poisons. After the completion of the analytical component, the toxicologist interprets the finding. Forensic toxicology is used in cases of suspected drug overdoses. Toxicology testing can determine, whether levels of toxic substances may have contributed to the death of any person, irrespective of how he died.

The specimens sent for toxicology testing are usually collected by pathologist who might be a medical examiner or might be called a 'coroner' in some jurisdiction. During an autopsy, he is also called 'mortuary technician'. The specimens

2 H.J. Walls, *Forensic Science—An Introduction to Scientific Crime Detection*, 2nd Ed., p. 101 (New Delhi: Universal Law Publishing Co. Pvt. Ltd.).

3 Forensic Toxicology – Drugs and Chemicals available at http://www.emedicine.medscape.com/article/1680257-overview, last visited on 10th July 2016.

might be blood, urine, liver, vitreous humour,[4] gastric contents, lung fluid, hair, kidney etc. Specimens must be properly identified, labeled and sealed as soon as practicable after collection. All specimens pertaining to a case must be collected and bagged separately in tamper-proof containers. Unique number seals are used to track all evidence for each case. Like any other evidence, the chain of custody must be preserved in all times, from the mortuary through the laboratory testing, reporting and storage, for court purposes. The testing of biological fluids is a complex process requiring sophisticated instrumentation and specially trained analyst. Different types of analytical techniques are used by forensic toxicologist to determine drugs or poisons relevant to a case under investigation. The capacity of a laboratory to conduct routine toxicological analysis will vary depending upon equipment, technical capability and analyst experience. There are also specialty toxicology labs that can test for virtually any potential toxin or metabolite in almost every kind of post mortem sample. A laboratory should be accredited to perform the analytical work and must be subject to regular inspections by approved accreditation personnel. All laboratory tests should be validated, fully documented and fit for purpose, which ensures that laboratory can produce accurate and reliable results for medicolegal investigations. All laboratory test should conform standard operating procedures, results are confirmed to meet standards and reported results are peer reviewed by a second toxicologists before being released. The American Toxicology Community recently completed a two tear effort to improve these standards, under the name of "Scientific Working Group on Toxicology" (SWGTOX), in order to meet more stringent legal and scientific challenges.

A commonly used technique for a drug screening test is known as 'immunoassay technique'. Immunoassays are laboratory tests that use antibodies to detect a reaction with specific substances. Immunoassays screening test are designed

4 It is the clear, gel like substance that fills the eye. It can be a useful fluid to screen for a range of drugs.

to detect whether a sample is positive or negative for the targeted drug. Four interpretations of a screening drug test are possible. A true positive result occurs when the test correctly detects the presence of a drug. A false-positive result is one where the test incorrectly detects presence of a drug where no drug is present. A true-negative result occurs when the test correctly confirms the absence of a drug.[5]

3 Classification of poisons

Poisons can be classified in many ways. The classification may be based on the action of the poison on the body and on the basis of their physical and chemical properties.

3.1 Classification on the basis of action on the body

3.1.1 Corrosives

Corrosives may further be classified into strong acids (Examples are sulphuric, nitric and hydrochloric acid) and strong alkalis (Examples are sodium, potassium and ammonium hydroxide).

3.1.2 Irritants

Irritants may be classified as Inorganic, Organic and Mechanical. Inorganic may further be classified into non-metallic (e.g. Phosphorous, Chlorine, Bromine, Iodine etc.) and metallic (e.g. Arsenic, Antimony Mercury, Copper, Lead, Zinc). Organic may further be classified into vegetable (e.g. Castor, Madar, Croton oil, Aloes etc.), animal (e.g. Snake venom, Cantharides and Insect bites) and mechanical (e.g. Glass Powder, Diamond Dust).

3.1.3 Neurotics

Neurotics can broadly be classified into cerebral, spinal and cardio-respiratory. Cerebral may further be classified into Narcotic (Opium and its alkaloids), Inebriant or Intoxicant (Alcohol, Ether, Chloroform, Chloral hydrate, Organo

5 *A Simplified Guide to Forensic Toxicology* available at http://www.forensicsciencesimplified.org/tox/Toxicology.pdf last visited on 10th July 2016.

phosphorous, Barbiturate) Deliriant (Dhatura, Belladona, Hyoscyamus, Cannabis, Cocaine). Cardio-respiratory may be studied under Cardiac (Aconite, Digitalis, Oleander and Hydrocyanic acid and Asphyxiants (carbon monoxide, hydrogen sulphide).

3.2 Classification on the basis of physical and chemical properties

In this category there can be inorganic poison and organic poisons. Inorganic poisons consist of metals and non-metals. We may study various metals as arsenic, mercury, lead, copper, thallium antimony, radio isotopes. The various non-metals are cyanides, yellow phosphorus, iodine, strong acids and alkalis and gases.

Metals

(a) Mercury

Mercury, mercuric chloride and many organo mercury compounds are highly poisonous. They are used in chemical industry and fungicides. Of all the salts of mercury, the chlorides and the nitrates are commonly used in poisoning.

(b) Lead

Most of the lead compound are poisonous and toxic in nature. This poison is cumulative in nature and if given in small doses it acts slowly. Chronic lead poisoning from accidental and industrial causes is more common. Automobile exhaust contains an organic lead compound called tetra ethyl lead.

(c) Copper

Copper salts used in electroplating, chemical industry and as weedicides[6] are toxic when the doses are high.

(d) Arsenic

Arsenic compounds are marketed as insecticides in the form of arsenic trioxide or metallic arsenates. Sometimes

6 A Chemical Substance used to Kill Weeds available at https://www.collinsdictionary.com/dictionary/english/weedicide accessed on 20.2.18.

arsenic compounds are administered as medicines, in small doses.

(e) Thallium

Thallium salts, which are used as rat poison might be encountered in cases of accidental poisoning.

(f) Antimony

Antimony resembles arsenic. It is often used (abused) for homicidal purposes.

Non-metals

(a) Cyanides

The cyanides of sodium and potassium are extremely poisonous, even in small quantities. The toxicity of cyanides is largely dependent on the release of hydrocyanic acid (HCN) is one of the most deadly poisons. It paralyses the respiratory centre in the brain, poisons (inactivates) respiratory and destroys oxyhaemoglobin. A small quantity can result in death due to respiratory failure.

(b) Yellow Phosphorus

This is a highly poisonous substance. Poisoning by this substance was common when it was used in old days in match industry.

(c) Iodine

Tincture iodine is sometimes found to be the cause of death. Only elemental iodine is poisonous. Iodine is not poisonous in small quantities.

(d) Strong Acids and Alkalis

The action of sulphuric acid, hydrochloric acid, nitric acid, sodium hydroxide, potassium hydroxide and ammonium hydroxide in causing death is based on their corrosive action on skin and mucous membrane. They are seldom used for suicide or homicide in other countries. However, in India some cases are being reported.

(e) Gases

In addition to HCN, carbon monoxide, hydrogen sulphide, arsine, phosgene gases become the cause of death or cause severe injury. Carbon monoxide is one of the major causes of death by gas poisoning in many suicidal, some homicidal and accidental cases. This gas is found in automobile exhaust gases, LPG and in fumes of heating appliances. Carbon monoxide also destroys oxyhaemoglobin as a result of which death occurs by respiratory failure. Highly dangerous gas, 'MIC' (Methyl Iso – Cynate) has been responsible to take the toll of more than 2000 lives and invalidating several others, in a gas leak tragedy, which took place in Bhopal in the year 1984.

(f) Radio Isotopes

Many radioactive isotopes, which are used for research purposes, have injurious effect on human life.

3.3 Organic poisons

Volatile substances

(1) Ethyl Alcohol

It is essentially a stimulant and an intoxicant. It is responsible for causing more deaths than any other single poison.

(2) Other Alcohols

Methyl alcohol, isopropyl alcohol and amyl alcohols are used in chemical industry and they are also poisonous. In India death due to methanol poisoning is very common. "French Polish", "Methylated Spirit" and "Illicit liquors" contain Methanol in appreciable quantities. Methanol poisoning causes paralysis, blindness and death.

(3) Phenol

Phenol or Carbolic Acid is used as a disinfectant and also in chemical industries. Most of the disinfectants contain this substance or related substances. Due to the easy availability of disinfectants it may be encountered in accidental or deliberate poisoning cases. It is rarely used for suicidal purposes.

(4) Miscellaneous substances

A variety of organic chemicals are used in various industries out of which many are toxic. They may cause death if inhaled or swallowed. Common examples are chlorinated hydrocarbons, benzene, chloral hydrate and many others. Chloral hydrate is commonly met in poisoning cases as it is mixed indiscriminately in illicit liquors.

Non-volatile material

(1) Alkaloids

These are substances chiefly derived from plant materials. Many of the narcotics and vegetable poisons contain alkaloids. Common examples are strychnine, morphine, cocaine, nicotine etc. The poisoning due to vegetable alkaloids in India was very common, as the poisonous plants grow abundantly in the countryside. With the advent of the insecticides and the pesticides, poisoning due to vegetable alkaloids is on the decline.

(2) Barbiturates

These are sleep inducing synthetic drugs commonly encountered in suicide cases. In India, however, the use of these drugs in suicide is restricted to medical personnel, pharmacists, nurses and people of affluent class.

(3) Glycosides

These are also of vegetable origin. They bring about death by cardiac arrest. The common examples of this class are Aconite, Digitalis and Oleander.

(4) Insecticides and Pesticides

In the recent years varieties of insecticide and pesticide formulations, under different brand names, are available for agricultural operations. Apart from leaving residues on foodstuffs, they are being abused for homicidal and suicidal purposes. Sometimes accidental poisoning also takes place because of negligence.

(5) Abortifacients

Although abortion has been legalized under certain grounds, there are several instances of abortion, which are performed with criminal intention. Drugs (abortifacients) are used for criminal abortions. Most of the drugs are required to be given in toxic doses, which at times result in death of the mother. The commonly used abortifacients in India are Ecbolics (Ergot, quinine, cotton root bark), Irritants (salts of arsenic, mercury, lead etc.), Vegetable irritants (Juice of Madar, twigs of Lal Chitra, roots of white or pink Oleander, Karela (bitter gourd) etc. Drastic purgative (castor oil, aloe, colocynth, Emetics (tartar emetic).

4 Principle on which toxicology evidence is based

Forensic toxicology covers any application of the science and study of poisons to the elucidation (clarification) of questions that occur in judicial proceedings. The forensic toxicologist is expected to detect and identify poisons. Chemical analyses are used to detect the presence of the poison, measure its concentration and relate this to its known toxicity. If the poison is not specified by name, the request to 'test for poisons' is a major problem for the chemist, because no single chemical method of analysis is able to detect all the various poisons. The forensic toxicologist has scarcely any control over the sampling time or the selection of material for analysis, and no certain knowledge that a poison is present. Most cases that enter a forensic toxicology laboratory start with the suspicion that a drug or poison is present. A fatality might be an accident, suicide or murder, but a toxicological examination must be carried out to assist the investigating officer to decide which of these it might be. Details of the circumstances that lead to the conclusion that a criminal action might have taken place must be supplied to the toxicologist so that the analyses can be planned. It is essential that the appropriate samples be collected as soon as possible, correctly and informatively labelled and stored appropriately. Their acquisition, storage and transportation to the laboratory should be documented adequately (with timings where appropriate) to ensure a safe chain of custody. The presence of a poison must be proved in the blood and organs before it can be considered as a cause of death.

There are four stages in any toxicological examination:

(1) *Detection.* To detect any drugs or poisons in the samples submitted by means of screening procedures.

(2) *Identification.* To identify conclusively any drugs, metabolites or poisons present by means of specific relevant physicochemical tests.[7]

(3) *Quantification.* To quantify accurately those drugs, metabolites or poisons present.

(4) *Interpretation.* To interpret the analytical findings in (2) and (3) in the context of the case, the information given and the questions asked by the investigating officer.[8]

5 Examination and collection of evidence at the scene

(a) The examination of the victim, collection of suspicious material and noting the history of the case are the important functions of the investigating officer at the scene of crime. The signs and symptoms shown by the person should be noted carefully. In the case of death an early management should be made for post mortem examination.

(b) The material to be collected in a poisoning case is of two types, one is biological material includes vomit, saliva, froth, stomach wash, urine, blood, cerebrospinal fluid, stomach and intestine with contents, liver, kidney, spleen, lungs, brain, bones, nails and hair etc. The miscellaneous articles may include any bottle, envelope and paper, containers that might have carried the poison. Glass or cup, which may be used for taking the poison, should also be collected.

7 A method of investigating physicochemical systems that makes possible a determination of the nature of the interactions between the components of a system through a study of the relations between the system's physical properties and composition.

8 *Principles of Forensic Toxicology* by Andrew A. Magembe, Manager, Forensic Science Services available at https://www.slideshare.net/MMASSY/principles-of-forensic-toxicology.

(c) The biological material should be collected carefully in clean containers avoiding contamination. Each type of material must be collected in a separate container without adding any preservation and immediately labeled in a proper manner. The misllеneous articles should also be handled very carefully.

(d) In case of exhumed body, in addition to usual post-mortem samples , the earth surrounding the body, a long bone and a bunch of hair should be collected.

(e) The suspected utensils and the remaining food material or any drink or drug left over should be collected and sent to the laboratory.

(f) In case of snake bite, tissue around the site of bite should be collected. Some procedure should be followed in the case of homicidal injections.

(g) In a suspected homicidal case the prisoner is quite likely to dispose off the container at the earliest opportunity to destroy the evidence. Thorough search of the dustbins, garbage cans and such other area around the house should be made.

(h) The viscera in a case of suspected poisoning should always be sent after the post-mortem examination in standard viscera jars, placed in standard boxes. It should be preserved in saturated solution of sodium chloride. The other material recovered from the scene should also be sent along with the sample of preservative.

(i) Sufficient quantities of viscera material, blood, stomach wash or urine must be collected. In the case of ante-mortem blood, 10 ml. blood must be collected. In the case of post-mortem, 50-100 ml. of blood should be collected. Entire stomach wash or urine can be collected. The viscera should contain whole stomach, 100 cms. of small intestine and its contents, 1 Kg. of liver and half portion of the kidney. Care should be taken to use proper preservative.

6 Isolation and Identification of Poison

The forensic laboratory adopts several methods to isolate, identify and estimate the poison. Inorganic poisons from tissues, stomach contents and other material are isolated by a number of methods. Volatile poisons are first extracted by steam distillation and later identified by chemical tests or by gas chromatograph. The non-volatile organic poisons are first extracted by suitable solvents and later identified by the thin-layer chromatography or gas chromatography. Most modern methods like high performance liquid chromatography, gas chromatography coupled with mass Spectrometry (GC-MS) are in use. More sophisticated techniques are employed for quick and reliable assay of drugs and other toxic in blood, urine, saliva etc.[9]

7 Legal history of toxicology evidence

According to Paracelsus, the grandfather of toxicology 'All things are poison and nothing is without poison, only the dose permits something not to be poisonous. The dose makes the poison'.[10]

Forensic toxicology is an essential component of legal investigations which covers a variety of crimes involving anything from prescription medications to recreational drug use. Police officers and experts use forensic toxicology to collect the evidences against perpetrator/s of crimes.

Forensic toxicology has a history that goes back around for hundreds of years. The prehistoric people were applying poison to spears for hunting animals. This might not fall under forensic toxicology, but gives an understanding regarding its existence since long back.

Mathieu Orfila, was a physician and chemist working in France who is hailed as the "Father of Toxicology". In 1814, he wrote "*Traite Des Poisons*" which described the symptoms of different poisons and outlined poisons used by criminals. He looked at samples such as blood, as well as the different effects of poisons and tested their presence in the body after death. There were numerous criminal cases in which Orfila was asked

9 B.S. Nabar, *Forensic Science in Crime Investigation "Poisons"*, 3rd Ed., pp. 254-262 (Hyderabad: Asia Law House).

10 Principles of Toxicology available at http://www.semmelweis.hu/nepegeszsegtan/files/2015/05/Environmental-medicine-5-Principles-of-Toxicology1.pdf, last visited on 02.05.2018.

to be a medical expert and to testify. This is not too different from the expert witnesses of today.

The 19th-century saw a great deal of work done around forensic toxicology as the field gained traction. These advancements were probably since poison had become an all-too-popular method of murder. The first trial to rely on forensic evidence occurred in 1840. Orfila was an expert witness in this ground-breaking case. He used James Marsh's accurate arsenic detection test. Marsh developed this in England four years prior to the trial. Orfila's and Marsh's research paved the way for toxicology and legal cases. Law, science and medicine were advancing greatly.

The Arsenic Act of 1851 was passed in the United Kingdom. It stated that arsenic had to be colored with indigo or soot. This was in response to the alarming number of accidental (or deliberate) poisonings due to its lack of color. Arsenic sellers had to keep written and signed documentation of who they had sold their products to and what they were being used for. This aimed to lessen cases of poisoning.

Forensic toxicology's history moves closer to home in 1918 when the Medical Examiner's Office and Toxicology Laboratory were established in New York. Dr. Alexander Gettler is known as the father of American toxicology. He was the chief forensic toxicologist at the laboratory and played a significant role in making this a world-renowned toxicology laboratory. After World War II, the American Academy of Forensic Sciences was established, followed by the American Board of Forensic Toxicology in 1975. These developments protected citizens and created improved methods of testing and controlling substances. They also contributed immensely to forensic toxicology in America and the rest of the world.

Forensic toxicology has a rich and fascinating history. For hundreds of years, this interesting area of science has been of great benefit to countless criminal investigations, cases and trials. It brings to light both justice and the truth. Today, advancements in technology have broadened and deepened this scientific area, making it even more valuable to the world.

Forensic toxicology will continue to remain important and relevant for hundreds of years to come.[11]

8 Legal provisions under which toxicology evidence was used or referred

There is no precise definition of poison in India but under the Indian Penal Code, the law describing the word poison are 'any poison or any stupefying, intoxicating, or any wholesome drug, or other thing' or any corrosive substance or any substance which is deleterious to the human body to inhale, to swallow, or to receive into the blood'.[12] With regard to 'any poisonous substance' used in s. 284 of IPC, all the law requires that the substance is such as, if taken, is likely to endanger human life, or will cause hurt or injury to any person. Again the law takes cognizance of the malicious intention of the individual who administers the drug or other substances, with a view to cause injury or death, irrespective of the quantity or quality of the substance.

• SALE OF POISONS ACT 1919. Sale of Poisons Act 1919 extends to the whole of India. Under this the Central Government may, by notification in the Gazette of India, prohibit except under a licence, the import of any specified poison and may by rule regulate the grant of licences. Subject to the control of the Central Government, the appropriate Government, may by rule, regulate within the whole or any part of the territories under its administration, the possession for the sale and sale, whether wholesale or retail, of any specified poison.

• THE NARCOTIC DRUGS AND PSYCHOTROPIC SUBSTANCES ACT 1985. The Act which was promulgated in September 1985, consolidates and amends the existing law relating to narcotic drugs, strengthens the existing control over drugs of abuse, considerably enhances the penalties, particularly for trafficking

11 Okorie Okorocha, *A Short History of Forensic Toxicology* available at https://www.okorieokorocha.com/short-history-forensic-toxicology/, last visited on 02.05.2018.

12 Sections 324, 326 and 328 of the IPC and also ss. 299, 304A of the IPC.

offences, makes provisions for exercising effective control over the psychotropic substances and for the implementation of international conventions relating to narcotic drugs and psychotropic substances, to which India is a party. A narcotic drug refers to cocoa leaf, cannabi (hemp), opium, poppy straw and includes all manufactured drugs.

Section 8 – Prohibition of certain operations; Section 15 – Punishment for contravention in relation to poppy straw; Section 17 – Punishment for contravention in relation to prepared opium; Section 18 – Punishment for contravention in relation to opium poppy and opium; Section 19 – Punishment for embezzlement of opium by cultivator; Section 20 – Punishment for contravention in relation to cannabis plant and cannabis; Section 21 – Punishment for contravention in relation to manufactured drugs and preparations; Section 22 – Punishment for contravention in relation to psychotropic substances.

The Act consolidates and amends the existing law relating to narcotic drugs, strengthens the existing control over drugs of abuse, considerably enhances the penalties, particularly for trafficking offences, makes provisions for exercising effective control over the psychotropic substances and for the implementation of international conventions relating to narcotic drugs and psychotropic substances, to which India is a party. A narcotic drug refers to cocoa leaf, cannabi (hemp), opium, poppy straw and includes all manufactured drugs.

The types of cases and legislations in which toxicology evidence played a significant role in solving the crime:

- THE INDIAN PENAL CODE 1860. Murder, rape, unnatural offences, cruelty by husband or relatives of husband, dowry death, causing hurt by means of poison etc. with intent to commit an offence, abetment of suicide, common intention, voluntarily causing grievous hurt by dangerous weapons or means, causing disappearance of evidence of offence, or giving false information to screen offender, wrongful restraint, voluntarily causing hurt in committing robbery, unlawful assembly, punishment for criminal intimidation, culpable homicide not amounting to murder etc.

- THE EXPLOSIVE SUBSTANCES ACT 1908. Section 3 – Punishment for causing explosion likely to endanger life or property.

- THE BOMBAY CHILDREN ACT 1948. Section 57 – Seduction or outrage of modesty.[13]

9 Criminal cases in which toxicology evidence was used/referred for recording conviction or acquittal

9.1 Rape

9.1.1 Proved facts established the offence of rape

The accused appellant committed rape on the victim and was convicted under s. 376(2)(*g*) of IPC. The prosecutrix was sent for medical examination where the doctor, examined her and prepared a medical examination report. One sealed packet containing two slides of vaginal smear, another sealed packet containing clothes and one sealed vial containing cut pubic hair were advised to send for chemical examination. No injury was found on the private parts of the body but injuries were found on front portion of her body and hands. The doctor had deposed that no definite opinion could be given regarding rape till the report of vaginal smear was received. It was noted by the High Court that till the conclusion of the Sessions Trial, the report of chemical examination had not been received. The question which arose for consideration before the Supreme Court was whether the proved facts established the offence of rape. Testimony of the prosecutrix corroborated the testimonies of two constables who were on patrolling duty near the bus stand. Moreover there was no reason for the prosecutrix to falsely implicate the accused as they were strangers. Held, mere fact that no injuries were found on the private parts, cannot be a ground to hold that no rape was committed or that the entire prosecution story was false. Prosecutrix was a married

13 The Bombay Children Act 1948 available at http://www.bombayhighcourt.nic.in/libweb/acts/1948.71.pdf, last visited on 15th May 2015.

grown-up-lady and absence of injuries on her private parts was not of much significance. Conviction upheld and appeal dismissed although there was no report of chemical examination.[14]

9.1.2 No corroboration between version of prosecutrix and her mother hence conviction recorded on attempt

The appellant was convicted under s. 376(2)(*f*), IPC. On account of medical evidence and evidence of mother of prosecutrix, version of prosecutrix did not appear to be true. There was injury on private parts of the accused but there was no injury on the private parts of prosecutrix. Therefore possibility of blood stains on loongi and underwear could be attributed to appellant alone but their presence did not support the prosecution version. No semen or spermatozoa was found on slides prepared from the vaginal material on chemical examination. Version of prosecutrix was not corroborated by her mother who admitted that prosecutrix had only told her that appellant had laid down over her. Therefore, it was not case of rape punishable under s. 376(2)(*f*), IPC. The conviction of the accused was based upon the testimony of the prosecutrix, her mother and chemical examiner's report. Appeal was partly allowed by modifying the conviction.[15]

9.1.3 Although the victim was in a state of virginity still offence consisted of rape

The petitioner was convicted under s. 376(1), IPC for committing the offence of rape. The prosecutrix mentioned in the categorical manner how the offence of rape had been committed on her. Defence had put no specific suggestion to prosecutrix in cross-examination that accused did not indulge himself in such obnoxious act. The OC during the course of investigation visited the place of occurrence, prepared hand sketch map with index, arranged medical examination of the victim and also arranged chemical examination of the vaginal swab of the prosecutrix. Held, it was not material whether the

14 *Santosh Kumar* v *State of M.P.* (2006) 10 SCC 595.

15 *Dhanesh* alias *Konda Banjare* v *State of Chhattisgarh* 2007 CrLJ 3328.

penetration was full or partial. It is not even material whether marks of injury were present in the body or not. It was evident from the medical report and reading of evidence of victim, that there was no vaginal penetration. Medical evidence proved that victim was in state of virginity having found her hymen intact. Inexperienced in sex and terrified by violent sexual assault by accused, victim took vulval penetration for vaginal one and stated so in a little exaggeration which must not be branded as false evidence so as to treat it as untrustworthy or unreliable. Therefore the court dismissed the petition and upheld the conviction.[16]

9.1.4 Corroboration of prosecutrix version with other evidences

Appellant was convicted for commission of offence under s. 376(2)(*f*) of IPC. Prosecutrix was 7 years old and she consistently stated that she was raped by the accused. Statement of prosecutrix was also corroborated by medical evidence. Salwar and kameez were taken from the victim and handed over to the police. Duration could not be ascertained and the opinion was reserved to be given after chemical examination of the vagina swabs. Further, no allegation of bias was made against the investigating agency. Thus, prosecution case was established beyond reasonable doubt. Accordingly, conviction of appellant was affirmed.[17]

9.1.5 Doctor's statement is not ultimate to prove case of rape

Present appeal had been remanded by Apex Court wherein accused's special leave appeal was admitted and order of conviction under s. 376 and s. 511, IPC and s. 57 of the Bombay Children Act 1948, passed in State appeal by this court was set aside and directed to decide afresh. There was no doubt that other witnesses including report of Chemical Analyzer had fully corroborated statement of victim in its entirety. Merely because there were some small discrepancies or improvement in statements would be no ground to disbelieve statement of victim and give advantage of acquittal to accused. Doctor's

16 *Ratan Acharjee* v *State of Tripura* 2008 CrLJ 4419.
17 *Sahun* v *State of Haryana* 2009 CrLJ 2035.

statement was not ultimate test to prove case of rape. Doctor, had nowhere stated that upon examination, he was of opinion that there was no penetration of any nature whatsoever in relation to victim. Merely because hymen was not torn and there was no bodily injury by itself, would be no ground to reject case of prosecution particularly in view of unequivocal and trustworthy statement of victim and other witnesses and more particularly in view of statement of panchas and Chemical Analyzer's report. As found accused was guilty of offence under s. 376 of IPC and s. 57 of the Bombay Children Act 1948.[18]

9.1.6 Trustworthy testimony of prosecutrix overrides corroboration with other evidences

An appeal was preferred against the judgment whereby appellant was convicted for offence punishable under ss. 363 and 376 of the Ranbir Penal Code 1989. *Held,* the testimony of the prosecutrix was trustworthy and did not require corroboration. Although chemical examination was performed there was no trace of semen on the vaginal swabs. Defence could not take advantage of bad investigation where there was clinching evidence available to the prosecution. Hence, the prosecution had been able to prove its case beyond reasonable doubt.[19]

9.1.7 Prosecution proved guilt beyond reasonable doubt

The appellant was convicted under ss. 342, 506(II), 376(2)(*a*) & (*b*) of IPC. Medical evidence of the prosecutrix, revealed that she might have been subjected to incomplete sexual intercourse. Medical evidence supported version of the prosecutrix that she was raped by the accused. Although chemical examination was conducted, but due to the negative report of the chemical analyzer it was opined, the doctor that there might be possibility of incomplete sexual intercourse.

18 *State of Maharashtra* v *Suresh Shankar Jadhav* 2009 SCC OnLine Bom 702.

19 *Sanjay Kumar* v *State* (2010)2 AIR Jhar R 826; AIR 2010 NOC 71 (Jhar).

Testimony of one witness supported version of prosecutrix. Deposition of a friend of prosecutrix was also considered and though he was a chance witness, his presence at spot was proved by his testimony as well as testimony of police officers. Accused was under influence of liquor at the time of committing the offence as liquor was found in the blood sample of the accused. Prosecution had proved guilt of the accused beyond reasonable doubt. Hence, the appeal was dismissed and conviction sustained.[20]

9.1.8 Two medical reports contradictory to each other

Rape was committed on the prosecutrix by putting her into fear of death. Consequently, the prosecutrix informed the matter to her mother and she in furtherance informed it to her brother, i.e. the maternal uncle of the prosecutrix. Then they took the victim to the District Hospital at about midnight for medical examination. The Doctor issued the report of the medical examination and also informed the gynaecologist who came to the hospital and took the vaginal swab and smear of the victim which was sent for chemical analysis. The mother also filed a petition in the Court of the Judicial Magistrate, First Class as according to her the District Hospital might not be fair. On the basis of the said petition the investigating officer got the victim examined by another gynaecologist in the Medical Hospital at Calicut. The second gynaecologist took the vaginal swab and smear of the victim and sent the same for chemical analysis. Chemical analysis was conducted from the vaginal swab and smear of the victim to determine the presence of semen as it was an alleged rape case. The court was of the view that although the two reports of the analysis of vaginal swab and the smear were contradictory to each other but the present case clearly proved and established the circumstances which necessitated the second medical examination of the victim and so a second set of sample of vaginal swab and smear had been taken and sent for chemical analysis. The second analysis was conducted on the basis of the application filed by

20 *Sunil Atmaram* v *State and Ms. X* 2011 CrLJ 3281.

the mother of the victim as she had serious doubts with regard to the fairness of the doctors of the District Hospital who had carried out the first medical examination. The application by the mother was filed without delay and the second round of the medical examination and taking of the samples was completed within two days. No motive and interest could be attributed to gynaecologist who had conducted the second round of medical examination and had taken the second set of sample for chemical analysis. From the evidence of him, it was also clear that after sexual intercourse, though active spermatozoa would be present for 36 hours, the same would remain in the vaginal canal for as long as 17 days. There was also no evidence to the contrary. In the aforesaid circumstances, the court did not get any reason as to how could the second report of the analysis be ignored. Moreover, the first medical examination also revealed that the victim was suffering from pain, there were bite marks on the private parts of the body and laceration on the lower lip. The court did not find any merit in the appeal, accordingly it was dismissed and the judgment of the High Court was affirmed.[21]

9.2 Rape and murder

9.2.1 Motive and vital links of chain to bring home guilt of the accused were missing

Appellants and three others were charged and convicted under ss. 376, 302 and 34 of IPC for allegedly committing rape of an insane lady and murdering her. The seized articles were sent for chemical analysis and the chemical analyzer's report regarding blood group of the accused/appellant and other accused persons were obtained and were brought on record. The semen, blood and pubic hair of the accused were collected and were sent for chemical analysis. As regards the semen and blood of the accused, the Chemical Analysis (C.A.) showed that the blood of the accused was of 'A' group. Chemical analyzer's report further showed that neither semen nor spermatozoa was detected on the pubic hair of the accused. Clothes of the

21 *O.M. Baby* v *State of Kerala* (2012)11 SCC 362.

accused were seized and the analysis of all the items revealed that no blood was detected on any of these articles nor any semen was found. On the other hand, the clothes of the deceased which were seized revealed that they were stained with blood of group 'O' as well as blood group 'B'. Undisputedly, the blood group of accused was 'A' but the victim's clothes had blood stains of group 'O' and semen of blood group 'O' and 'B'. These facts created doubt about the involvement of the accused in the crime. Vital links of chain to bring home guilt of appellant under s. 376(2)(g) beyond reasonable doubt was missing. Therefore benefit of doubt was given to the accused and the accused was acquitted.[22] Motive is an essential ingredient of the crime, the absence of which results in acquittal of the accused. In *Babu* v *State of Kerala*,[23] although by chemical analysis it was revealed that the deceased died due to cyanide poisoning but since the motive of the accused could not be proved, it resulted in acquittal.

9.2.2 Material particulars of the chemical analyzers report and the prosecution case did not corroborate but conviction awarded as rarest of rare cases

The accused was convicted under ss. 376 and 302, IPC for raping and murder of a child of tender years and awarded with death penalty. In the instant case, legality and correctness of the Chemical Analyzer's Reports had not at all been disputed by the defence. As per that Report, the nail clippings of the deceased were found stained with blood. C.A. Report revealed that earth, half manila under frock, frock, and handkerchief were stained with human blood. Similarly, C.A. Report revealed that the stone was stained with human blood. These factors did corroborate the material particulars of the prosecution case and cannot be ignored altogether from the arena of consideration. The crime committed by the accused did not only shock the judicial mind, but also the mind of the society and therefore, the crime in question was not only against the

22 *Anil Motibaba Barokar* v *State of Maharashtra* 1996 CrLJ 494.
23 *Babu* v *State of Kerala* (2010)9 SCC 189.

individual but against the entire society. After proper evaluation in this regard, the case in hand was undoubtedly within the rarest of rare kind and thus, the capital punishment was affirmed.[24]

9.2.3 Chemical examiner's report revealed same blood group of both the deceased woman and the accused

The accused was convicted under ss. 366, 376(2), 302 and 201, IPC and he filed an appeal against the conviction whereas the State filed a reference for the confirmation of the death sentence. The sealed seized articles were sent for chemical examination in intact condition. This fact was evident from the testimony of the IO, and the head constable, who deposed that nine sealed packets kept intact in Malkhana were sent to FSL. As per the FSL report dried blood of the deceased woman was of Group 'A' and blood found on pubic hair of the accused was also of Group 'A'. Held, court would have re-appreciated entire evidence on record to make decision of appeal on merit. Accused on date of offence was major, as was evident from his medical examination report. Therefore, looking to young age of accused court did not think that present case was to be one of rarest of rare cases warranting death sentence. Court was of view that punishment should have deterrent effect as well as no further chance to accused for relapsing into crime and becoming danger to society. Therefore court upheld conviction of accused under s. 302, IPC but commuted death sentence imposed to imprisonment for life. Court also confirmed the conviction of accused under ss. 376, 363 and 201, IPC .[25]

9.2.4 Chemical analyzer's report and the medical report corroborated the prosecution version

Sessions Judge convicted appellant for commission of offences of rape and murder under ss. 376, 377 & 302, 201, IPC. Post mortem report revealed that there was not only attempt to rape but also sodomy committed on girl. Materials which were

24 *State of Maharashtra* v *Amit* 2003 CrLJ 600.
25 *State of Rajasthan* v *Gopal* (2006)1 RLW 604.

collected were sent for chemical analysis. The chemical analysis report and the medical report also corroborated the prosecution version. Circumstances established on record according to law was consistent only with guilt of accused and wholly inconsistent with his innocence. Thus, prosecution was able to establish its case beyond all reasonable doubt that appellant had committed rape and murder of deceased punishable under ss. 376, 377, 302 and 201.[26]

9.2.5 Chemical examiner's determination on the stained earth and sample earth objectively determined the spot of occurrence

The accused was convicted under ss. 302 and 376(2)(*f*) of IPC and sentenced to death by the Sessions Judge. The Investigating Officer, proceeded to the spot and collected blood-stained earth sample, straw stained with blood, a half pant and printed lungi of the deceased. These material objects were sent for chemical examination. The chemical examination revealed that the sample earth and the blood stained earth taken from the spot were similar with respect to their physical characteristics. Further human blood was found on the blood-stained earth, the blood-stained straw and other articles. The scientific finding very objectively determined the spot of occurrence. A death reference was made by the State and the accused filed an appeal against the conviction. In view of mitigating circumstances, namely, convict had no criminal background, during his detention no adverse report had been submitted by Jail Authority, accused had a family to support and had small children and there appears to be no premeditation or previous planning to commit offence and giving maximum weightage to mitigating circumstance, the Court held that the severest of punishment, i.e death penalty was not proper in this case. Thus, the accused was convicted under ss. 302 and 376(2)(*f*), IPC but the conviction of death penalty imposed on him was modified to punishment of imprisonment for life.[27]

26 *Satgun Paswan* v *State of Orissa* 2010 CrLJ (NOC) 225.
27 *State of Orissa* v *Ardhu Chendreya* 2010 SCC Online Ori 215 .

9.2.5.1 *Courts are to assess the value of the evidence given by experts and cannot sideline the same as opinion evidence unless there are reasons to suspect the opinion*

The appellant was convicted under ss. 302, 376, 394 and 397 and 511 of IPC. I.O. took over investigation. He procured the assistance of the Scientific Assistant and had blood samples collected along with the samples of soil from the spot. The statements of the witnesses were recorded. Meanwhile, the accused was arrested. The materials that were collected during investigation were sent for chemical examination to the Forensic Science Laboratory and the report was obtained. The court held that expert opinion does not require corroboration in all cases to form the basis of conviction. Courts have to assess the value of the evidence given by experts, but it will not be proper for any Court to sideline the expert's evidence as opinion carrying a little value unless there are reasons to suspect the opinion on other grounds to show that the same cannot be accepted. The conviction was upheld.[28]

9.3 Rape and assault

9.3.1 Pending the chemical analysis report it is not proper to release the petitioner on bail

The appellant was convicted under ss. 376 and 354, IPC. Hence, this petition for bail was made. The bare statement by a person, aged 16 years, that she was "raped" alone may not be sufficient for the court to come to a finding that an offence under s. 376, IPC was committed. The investigation was not complete in this case. In the nature of allegations made by the victim that she was raped and in the light of the medical evidence that there were findings to suggest evidence of penetration, it would be premature for the court to arrive at a reasonable belief that the accused was not guilty of rape, merely because of a seemingly inadvertent omission on the part of the investigating agency to ascertain the required

28 *Chellappan* v *State of Kerala* MANU/KE/2361/2012.

details by questioning the relevant witnesses. Though in the certificate given by the doctor there were "findings suggestive of evidence of penetration" but the final opinion was reserved by the expert, pending the chemical analysis report on the sample of vaginal swab, smear etc. Hence, it was not proper to release petitioner on bail, holding that the offence was only under s. 354, IPC. If he was released on bail at that stage it was likely that he might influence or intimidate witness or tamper with the evidence.[29]

9.4 Murder

9.4.1 Chemical examiner's report corroborated with other evidences

The accused persons were convicted under ss. 302/34, IPC. The dead body was sent to the hospital for post-mortem. The material objects which were seized during investigation were sent to the Chemical Examiner and his report was obtained. The post-mortem examination revealed that undigested rice particles were found in the stomach of the deceased. The trial court acquitted the accused persons on one of the grounds that since the deceased had not taken any food after 3.30 p.m., such undigested rice particles could not have been found if the deceased had died at 9.30 p.m. The High Court did not accept the opinion of the trial court and convicted the accused persons. The Supreme Court also supported the view of the High Court that presence of undigested food particles did not raise any serious doubt about the time of the incident. Moreover the absence of any bloodstain on the knife of accused could be reasonably explained. It was on evidence that the knife was thrown away by accused. It was not unlikely that the bloodstain of the knife had been wiped off when the knife was thrown in the field. Therefore, according to the court the evidence adduced in the case had clearly established the complicity of both the accused in causing the murder of the deceased. Thus, the appeal was dismissed and the conviction was upheld.[30]

29 *Santhosh Madhavan* v *C.I. of Police* 2008 CrLJ 4246.
30 *Krishnan* v *State of Kerala* (1996)10 SCC 508.

9.4.1.1 *Discrepancies and contradictions in the evidence of witnesses is not a ground to discard the entire prosecution*

The accused was convicted under s. 302, IPC. It was held by the High Court that merely because there were discrepancies and contradictions in the evidence of some or all of the witnesses, it did not mean that the entire evidence of the prosecution had to be discarded. The report of the chemical examiner showed that the blood stained earth collected from the spot was found to be stained with human blood. Further the doctor, found that the post mortem lividity was well established all over the dead body of the deceased. Under the cross-examination, the defence had elicited from the doctor that the post mortem lividity would not appear in general on a dead body, if it was moved from one position to another position after the death. Thus, it was clear from the above material placed on record that the incident in question took place in the land of the complainant. Even the defence did not dispute the fact that the incident in question took place in the land in question. It is only if, after exercising caution and care and sifting the evidence to separate the truth from untruth, exaggeration, embellishments and improvement, the court came to the conclusion that what could be accepted implicated the accused. Hence the appeal was dismissed and the conviction upheld.[31]

9.4.1.2 *Medical evidence, chemical examination and viscera report corroborated and proved circumstances*

Death reference arose out of judgment of conviction and sentence of capital punishment was awarded by Additional Sessions Judge against the accused for murdering his wife and two children. Motive, *mens rea,* conduct and behavior, handwriting in diary of accused and all circumstances were proved by the prosecution. Circumstances were in chain and there was no missing link in circumstances proved by prosecution. Medical evidence, chemical examination and viscera report totally corroborated and proved circumstances. Accused was disturbed with a fear psychosis completely

31 *Jyotiba Laxman Patel* v *State of Karnataka* 2001 Kar 2175.

demurring all his fine and pleasing normal instincts which made him a cruel murderer. Held, case did not come within purview of rarest of rare cases. Therefore same was converted to rigorous imprisonment for life.[32]

9.4.1.3 *Corroboration with Chemical Examiners report and Doctor's report regarding poisoning but absence of motive*

The accused was convicted under s. 302 for causing death of his wife by administering poison. Post-mortem was performed and the doctors opined that it was a suspected case of celphos poisoning. The stomach as a whole was preserved. Parts of the small and large intestines and parts of the liver, spleen and kidneys were preserved. All these samples duly sealed, were handed over to the police for being sent to the Chemical Examiner. All the samples which were collected and preserved for chemical examination were forwarded to the FSL, whereby the Deputy Director-cum Assistant Chemical Examiner of FSL opined that the samples had presence of aluminium phosphide (celphos). On receipt of the report the same was shown to Doctor who initially sought for some clarification from FSL. After receipt of the clarification from FSL, the Medical Board opined that it was a case of suspected aluminium poisoning. Although the courts below convicted the appellant relying on the incriminating circumstances. The Supreme Court did not support the view of the courts below as there was no evidence that the accused had poison in his possession prior to the time of the incident. In all probability the tablet administered by the accused to the deceased was not celphos. There was also doubt about the genuineness of samples of vomit seized from inside and outside the house. Held, it could not be doubtlessly conclude to be a case of celphos poisoning. Further, accused had neither any opportunity nor clear motive for administering poison. Thus in all probability the deceased had consumed something before coming to meet the accused or may be she had suffered food poisoning or virus infection. On facts, prosecution failed in proving such chain of circumstantial evidence as would fasten the guilt of the accused leaving no

32 *Manik Mukherjee* v *State of Bihar* 2000 CrLJ 3661.

room for doubt. Therefore, the accused appellant was acquitted.[33]

9.4.2 Chemical examination detected no poison in the deceased stomach

This is a death reference case by the State along with an appeal against conviction. Accused was convicted and sentenced to death under ss. 302 and 201, IPC. Exact cause of quarrel not found due to want of evidence. Illicit relationship between accused and deceased was disclosed. Deceased used to maintain illicit relationship with other person and put hurdle in marriage life of accused. The viscera of the deceased were sent for chemical analysis. In the report of chemical analysis, no poison was detected. Hence the doctor opined that the cause of death was head injury. Accused had no criminal antecedent. Held, appellant had been given an opportunity to reform considering peculiar facts of the circumstances. Appeal was dismissed and the conviction and sentence under s. 302 was converted to life imprisonment.[34]

9.4.2.1 *CFSL report proved on record that sulphuric acid was mixed with whisky*

The accused were convicted under ss. 302, 304 and 34, IPC. Dying declaration was made in fit state of mind. The viscera of the deceased was subjected to chemical analysis. The CFSL report proved on record that sulphuric acid was found in viscera which established that acid was mixed with whisky and was forcibly poured down the throat of the deceased. Post-mortem report also supported the prosecution case. There was no material to indicate deliberate delay on part of police officers in dispatching report. No prejudice was found on part of police. Accused had no intention to cause death but had knowledge that inflicted injury was likely to cause death. There accused was convicted under s. 304.[35]

33 *Jaipal* v *State of Haryana* (2003)1 SCC 169.
34 *Manoharsingh* v *State of Maharashtra* (2003) SCC Online Bom 768.
35 *Dharampal* v *State of Delhi* ILR (2004)2 Del 317.

9.4.3 Toxicology report corroborated the testimony of witnesses

Principal Sessions Judge convicted accused for offence of murder under s. 302, IPC. It was clear from evidence of witnesses that the accused had a grudge against deceased because deceased had illicit intimacy with his wife which had been established by evidence of witnesses. However, witnesses saw the deceased with accused immediately before occurrence and within half hour. They again saw deceased running, shouting that accused gave him a drink and he drank same and his stomach was burning. Toxicology report made it clear that monocrotophos with ethyl alcohol was found in the brandy bottle. It was thus clear that the deceased consumed poisonous drink given by the accused as was evident from the medical report and prosecution witnesses. Therefore prosecution had brought home guilt of accused beyond all reasonable doubts.[36]

9.4.4 Chemical examination corroborated the facts of the case

Trial court convicted appellant for offence of murder under s. 302, IPC. It was found that accused did not kill the victim immediately after she rejected his proposal. However, accused started hurting himself with intention to die, so that at least at that stage, deceased would be soft and turn towards him. Even victim tried to save the accused but she failed. Accused started bleeding profusely and victim shouted and at that stage, accused lost all his self-control and committed crime resulting in death of the victim. Further, in no time, he made attempt on his life by not only cutting his right hand wrist but also his neck, in which attempt he failed. All the recovered articles were sent for chemical examination. Hence, Exception 1 to s. 300 of IPC was attracted. Therefore court set aside conviction of accused under s. 302 and instead brought his act under s. 304, Part I of Act.[37]

36 *Kuppusamy* v *Inspector of Police* (2005)5 CTC 666.

37 *Mohd. Fazluddin* v *State represented by Inspector of Police* (2007)1 MWN (Cri) 155 (DB).

9.4.5 Doctor gave his report basing on the chemical examiner's report

Sessions Judge acquitted respondents for offence of murder committed by them under s. 302 along with s. 341, IPC. Held, medical evidence of doctor showed that cause of death of deceased was vagal inhibition. The doctor gave his report basing on the chemical examiners report. However, accused had neither intention nor knowledge that kicking could result into death of deceased; hence, it was termed as accidental death and not homicidal death. Hence no case under s. 302 of IPC could be made out.[38]

9.4.6 Chemical examiner's report corroborated other evidences to prove the prosecution case

The appellant herein was tried and convicted for the murder of his niece, under s. 302, IPC and was awarded the death penalty. In addition he was convicted for an offence punishable under s. 376, IPC and sentenced to undergo rigorous imprisonment for 10 years and a fine of ₹5000. The story of unknown assailants entering the house and causing murder of the victim etc. as contended by the appellant was ruled out and the prosecution story was that it was the appellant who first shot the victim and then attempted to commit suicide, stood proved. The learned State counsel emphasized that the prosecution case stood proved from various factors including medical evidence, the reports of the FSL, the chemical examiner's report, the post-mortem reports and the recovery of the gun and cartridges. The court first took up for consideration the question of the conviction under s. 376, IPC. From the medical evidence and from the chemical examiner's report the court found that the vaginal swab and clothes taken from the dead body indicated the presence of semen. There was however absolutely no evidence to suggest (even assuming that the intercourse had been committed by the appellant) that he had done so without victim's consent or against her will. Some suspicions of rape could perhaps been raised had some injuries been detected on victim's person but no injuries except

38 *State of Karnataka by the Police Inspector* v *R. Raju* 2007 CrLJ 920.

gunshot injuries were found on her person which indicated attempt to rape or the commission of rape. The investigators had also made no attempt to medically examine the appellant to ascertain his capacity to perform sexual intercourse. Thus, the conviction of the appellant under s. 376 could not be sustained. Accordingly, the Supreme Court acquitted the appellant of the charge under s. 376, IPC.[39]

9.4.7 Identification of the dead body was confirmed by the chemical examiner's report

The appellant was convicted for the commission of murder of his wife under ss. 302 and 201 of IPC. On the confessions made by appellant accused the dead body was recovered from a canal. The dead body was identified on the basis of the mangalsutra, saree and also the silver ring on the toe of the deceased which was not disputed. The dead body was also sent for opinion of a chemical examiner who opined that skull, could very well have belonged to the female individual seen in photograph. The said report was also roved and its veracity was not disputed. Therefore, the court had no reason to differ with the findings of the learned trial judge and also the High Court that the extra-judicial confession was voluntary or truthful. Consequently, the appeal was dismissed and the conviction was upheld.[40]

9.4.7.1 *In spite of the Chemical Examiner's report prosecution failed to prove complete chain of circumstances*

Accused persons were alleged to have murdered deceased. Two of the accused persons were acquitted of all charges framed against them, while three other accused were convicted under s. 302/34 by the trial court which was affirmed by the High Court. Hence the present appeal was preferred. The case of the prosecution rested on circumstantial evidence. The prosecution relied upon the following circumstances. Illicit relations of the deceased with one of the accused, the dead body of deceased was found in the courtyard of the house of

39 *Ujjagar Singh* v *State of Punjab* (2007)13 SCC 90.
40 *Ponnusamy* v *State of Tamil Nadu* (2008)5 SCC 587.

accused persons, but two of the accused persons were not present in their house on the day of occurrence, one of the witnesses had seen accused persons going towards the bus-stand in the evening. Recovery of clothes of some accused from their house and the clothes which were recovered by the police at the instance of one of the accused from their house were found bloodstained with human blood of Group 'O' in the chemical analyzer's report. Regarding illicit relationship the Supreme Court held that had there been any such illicit relations, entire village would come to know about such fact. Besides, parents of the deceased and some other village people were not examined in support of this circumstance. *Secondly,* merely because dead body of deceased was found in open space in front of their house which was a public road, it would not be safe to connect the accused persons with the death of deceased. *Thirdly* and *fourthly,* the absence of the accused from their house and their movement towards the bus stand on the relevant day was not proved by the prosecution beyond reasonable doubt. *Fifthly,* no evidence was led to prove that axe, alleged weapon of offence, found on spot in open place that belonged to the accused persons. *Sixthly* and *seventhly,* the prosecution failed to prove that the clothes, which were allegedly seized by police at instance of one of the accused was lying in the open space, were stained with blood group 'O' of deceased found on deceased clothes and on articles which were seized by IO from place of occurrence. Hence, held prosecution failed to complete chain of circumstances to prove, accused persons were guilty beyond reasonable doubt and the High Court was not justified in upholding their conviction on surmises and hypothesis. Hence, the conviction was set aside and acquittal was recorded.[41]

9.4.7.2 *CFSL report was not provided to accused and was not corroborated by prosecution*

An appeal was filed against order by which appellant had been convicted for offence punishable under ss. 302 and 307, IPC.

41 *Shantabai* v *State of Maharashtra* (2008) 16 SCC 354.

Held, no witness had come forward to prove CFSL report and it also appeared that CFSL report had not been made available to accused. In such context, prosecution had to establish as to whether deceased died due to kaner poisoning and not on account of any other poisoning. For determining the question CFSL report was of significant importance. If such report was not given to accused, it would certainly cause serious prejudice to her. Cause of death was not indicated in the post-mortem report and it was noted therein that cause of death will be given after receipt of chemical analysis report. CFSL report merely indicated that stomach, intestine with contents and liver, spleen and kidneys and also 5 ml blood sample tested positive for active constituents of kaner. Such a condition may or may not be caused by poisoning and there might be other reasons. Thus, CFSL report did not enable the court to conclude that deceased died of poisoning or to any specific conclusion with regard to kind of poison which caused his death. This circumstance, i.e. inconclusiveness with regard to poison was in itself sufficient to lead to benefit of doubt being given to appellant and her consequent acquittal.[42]

9.4.8 Chemical analysis revealed cyanide poisoning but motive could not be established

The appeal had been preferred against the judgment and order passed by the High Court of Kerala, reversing the judgment of acquittal recorded by the Sessions Court wherein the appellant was charge-sheeted for murdering his wife by giving her sodium cyanide. The victim died under mysterious circumstances within fifteen days of her marriage in her parent's house. The accused had been employed in the Gulf in a firm dealing with golden jewellery. The couple after marriage stayed for two days with the brother of the appellant at Ollur and they came back to Chalakudy as the parents of victim arranged a reception for them at their house. After that, the appellant left victim at her parent's house and went to see his mother as she had undergone a surgery. On returning to victim's place at 10.30 p.m. he found that the door of her room

42 *Smt. Karpai* v *State (Delhi Admn)* 2009 SCC OnLine Del 1775.

was bolted from inside and there was no response on calling to her. When the door was broken by the appellant and her father, the victim was found unconscious lying on the floor. She was taken to Government Hospital where she was declared dead. The Deputy Superintendent of Police while conducting the investigation of the case received information that just few days prior to the incident the appellant had procured cyanide, thus he was arrested. Chemical analysis was conducted during post mortem as the post mortem report revealed that the victim died of cyanide poisoning. This case was based on circumstantial evidence, and according to the court in cases of circumstantial evidence, motive of the accused must be established at least to a certain extent. But motive could not be established in this case as if the appellant intended to murder the victim he could have administered the poison much before as he procured the poison many days before the death of the victim. Therefore the judgment and order of the High Court was set aside and judgment and order of the trial court was restored.[43]

9.4.8.1 *Chemical Analysis was corroborated with other evidences*

Accused persons were convicted under ss. 341 and 302 read with s. 34, IPC for wrongful restraint and murder. Evidence of one of the witnesses had clearly narrated incident and made mention of name of one of the accused in the FIR. Therefore his evidence was accepted since it was trustworthy. Moreover criminal jurisprudence did not require quantity of evidence but only quality of evidence. Other piece of evidence was medical evidence and recovery which stood fully corroborated with ocular testimony. All the material objects were sent for chemical analysis. Chemical analysis report, serology report and toxicology report were received. Hence the accused was found guilty under s. 302 read with s. 34, IPC. Insofar as other persons who were present at time of occurrence were concerned and they were not known to that witness. Thus, prosecution had failed to prove its case insofar as charge leveled

43 *Babu* v *State of Kerala* (2010)9 SCC 189.

against other accused persons was concerned and that part of judgment had got to be set aside. Therefore Criminal Appeal was allowed in respect of other accused persons and the same were dismissed.[44]

9.4.8.2 *Eyewitness's version corroborated by medical evidence, chemical examiner's report and dying declaration*

The accused was convicted under s. 302, IPC and sentenced to RI for life. The doctor who conducted autopsy on the dead body opined that victim died due to gunshot injuries. The pant, shirt, baniyan and earth which were stained with blood were sent for chemical examination. The chemical examiner gave report. Entire incident of shooting was graphically described by witnesses. They narrated the previous incident of disharmony between the accused and the deceased. They also adverted to previous attempts by accused to harm deceased. Eyewitnesses version corroborated by medical evidence, chemical examiner's report and dying declaration. Trial court as well as the High Court, upon consideration of entire ocular evidence had concluded that both witnesses had given a consistent version of various incidents and enmity between deceased and appellant. Held, the conviction of the courts below was upheld.[45]

9.4.8.3 *Death of the deceased was due to shock and toxaemia due to burns by fire which was corroborated by other evidences*

The High Court confirmed the judgment passed by Additional Sessions Judge convicting the appellant under s. 302 and sentencing him to rigorous imprisonment for life and a fine of ₹2000. The appeal by special leave was preferred before the Supreme Court to question the legality of the judgment of the said High Court.

The marriage of deceased was solemnized with the accused, after which the deceased started living with the accused at his place of residence. Thereafter the deceased gave

44 *Killer Thiayagu* v *State* (15.12.2010 – MADHC) MANU/TN/3660/2010.

45 *Om Pal Singh* v *State of U.P.* (2010)14 SCC 200; AIR 2011 SC 1562.

birth to a girl child after which the deceased went to Chandigarh to reside with the accused. After a few months the accused with his wife and child came to Delhi, where they visited the parents of both. After taking dinner in the house of the parents of the deceased, all of them returned to the house of the parents of the accused and retired to bed at about 11.30 p.m. At 2.30 a.m. shrieks of the deceased were heard and she was found engulfed in the flames. At about 2.45 a.m. deceased was admitted to the hospital at New Delhi by her husband where the duty constable posted informed the ASI. The ASI along with one constable went to the hospital and collected MLC of injured wherein it was mentioned that the injured got admitted at 2.45 a.m. by her husband. It was also mentioned therein that the accident occurred due to the exploding of the stove. It was further mentioned in the said certificate that her clothes smelled of kerosene oil and she had received extensive burns all over the body and face. The deceased ultimately succumbed to her burn injuries after which the father of the deceased submitted a written complaint against the appellant and his family members for burning his daughter to death. On the basis of the complaint the appellant and his mother were charge sheeted under ss. 302 and 34 of IPC. Medical evidence on record confirmed that soot particles were present in the stomach of the deceased. According to the doctor, the approximate area of burn was about 90%. On internal examination, it was found that all the organs were congested. According to the doctor, the death of the deceased was due to shock and toxaemia due to burns by fire. The presence of soot particles in the stomach indicates that the injuries could have been sustained by the deceased only in a conflagration and that too in a closed area. The instinct of survival would have made the deceased to run in an open place but in this case, the record does not indicate such attempts were made by the deceased to run towards any open space and positively establishes that she was found at the end of the passage which hardly measures 12′ x 3′.

From the facts and circumstances of the case, the court was of the opinion that no error was committed either by the trial court or the High Court in convicting the appellant under s. 302, IPC for committing murder of his wife. Therefore, the appeal was dismissed as it lacked merit.[46]

9.4.8.4 *The report of the chemical examiner opined that death was due to chloroform and pentazocine poisoining which was proved by the testimonies of the prosecution witnesses*

The accused were convicted under ss. 302, 364-A, 120B and 201, IPC for the offence of kidnapping for ransom and murder of a young boy aged about 16 years. Testimonies of witness were found credible and corroborating each other. Witness had no animosity against accused. The post mortem of the dead body was carried out by a team of two doctors but no conclusive report as to the cause of death was given but after the report of the chemical examiner the doctors opined that the cause of death was chloroform and pentazocine poisoning. Purchase of chloroform by accused from his shop was proved by one of the witnesses, while other witness proved purchase of fortwin injections. Factum of overdose of chloroform and pentazocine, which was a lethal combination administered to deceased was proved. Death penalty of two accused persons was upheld. Sentence of other accused was reduced to life.[47]

9.4.9 Chemical analysis report corroborated other evidences to confirm the types of arms used in the massacre

The present reference came for confirmation of death sentence and appeal was filed against order of death sentence. Held it appeared that appellant used places for prohibited arms. Prosecution proved that appellant had taken part in and committed unlawful activities. It was proved that appellant maliciously caused explosion. It was established that appellant had imported, possessed, used and transported explosives. It was established that appellant committed terrorist act that resulted in death of 166 persons. During the post mortem, the bullets from the bodies of the victims were recovered and sent

46 *Vijay Kumar Arora* v *State* (2010)2 SCC 353.

47 *Vikram Singh* v *State of Punjab* (2010)3 SCC 56.

for chemical analysis. The Chemical Analyzer had stated that the bullets which was recovered was a deformed copper jacketed bullet fired from 7.62 mm short rifle. Appellant along with other co-accused who were acquitted, smuggled prohibited arms, pistols and ammunitions and possessed said contrabands which they knew or had reason to believe to be liable to be confiscated. With regard to other accused persons prosecution failed to establish its case beyond reasonable doubt against them. Therefore conviction of appellant was confirmed and for all offence appellant was sentenced to death. Therefore appeal against conviction was dismissed and the death sentence reference was allowed.[48]

9.4.9.1 *The viscera were preserved to be sent to the FSL and there was defective investigation still conviction was upheld as it could not prove to be of any disadvantage to the accused*

The trial court found the accused guilty under s. 302/34 of IPC and awarded them life imprisonment and a fine of ₹5000. Challenging the legality and correctness of the judgment of the trial court, the accused persons preferred an appeal before the High Court. The High Court has also dismissed the appeal. Therefore appeal was preferred before the Supreme Court. The accused was married to the deceased and they were staying together. Deceased was three months pregnant. During her last visit to her parental home, she wailed and was not willing to go back to her husband's house stating that her husband and her brother-in-law would kill her if their demands of dowry were not met. However, the wishes of her parents prevailed and she was sent back to her matrimonial home. After four months of her marriage, the elder brother-in-law of the deceased informed her uncle that she fell down in the kitchen due to dizziness. After few minutes the elder brother-in-law of the deceased came back and informed that the deceased fell down and froth was coming out of her mouth and thereafter she died. Uncle of deceased along with the mother of the deceased reached the place of occurrence and found their

48 *State of Maharashtra* v *Mohammad Ajmal Mohammad Amir Kasab* (2012)3 SCC (Cri) 481.

daughter was lying dead. Suspecting it was not a natural death and that there had been some foul play on the part of the accused persons, i.e. the husband and the brother-in-law of the deceased, an FIR was lodged. Although the FIR was lodged under s. 304B of IPC but the trial court on the basis of the police report and upon hearing both the parties found a *prima facie* case under s. 302/34 of IPC against the accused. The viscera of the deceased were preserved to be sent to the FSL, forensic and for chemical analysis. The doctor who conducted post mortem stated that the injuries in the body were ante-mortem and there were multiple bruises on the lower abdomen. The neck was swollen and the face was congested and swollen. Although the cause of the death could not be ascertained, the viscera were preserved to be sent to the FSL. The doctor also deposed that the bruises resemble to black spots. Usually black spots are not noticeable on a dead person but it might cause due to poisoning or suffocation. Bruises and swollen face being congested might be due to some physical assault.

The court after examining the case in the light of circumstances held that there was a clear defect in the investigation or omission on the part of the investigating officer, as well as the doctor but that could prove to be of any disadvantage to the accused. The appeal was dismissed and the conviction of the courts below was upheld.[49]

9.4.9.2 *Chemical analysis report corroborated by medical evidence*

The accused was convicted under s. 302, IPC for the murder of his wife on suspicion of illicit relationship. Accused contended that burn injuries on his wife were caused by an accident, by a burning kerosene lamp, kept by her side. The accused has purchased petrol from the petrol pump in a bottle. The chemical analysis report had clearly mentioned that kerosene was not detected in any of the material objects sent for chemical analysis. In the dying declaration the deceased had suspected that her husband might have set her ablaze. Although in his statement under s. 313, CrPC, the accused

49 *Sahabudddin* v *State of Assam* (2012)13 SCC 213.

stated that it was an accidental fire and he tried to save his wife but no burn injuries were found on his body and it had also been clearly established by the medical evidence that the possibility of causing burn injuries from a small kerosene lamp was impossible. Therefore, it was evident that the accused had given a false statement. Consequently the appeal was dismissed and the conviction was confirmed. Court accepted the chemical analysis report.[50]

9.5 Murder and hurt

9.5.1 Chemical examiner's report cannot be relied upon and lack of common intention

The appellants were convicted by the trial court for the offences under ss. 302, 324, 34 of IPC for murder of one Rajeswaran and causing injury to another person. Both of them were sentenced to life imprisonment. The High Court confirmed the conviction imposed by the trial court.

The two accused were prosecuted for the murder of the deceased Rameswaram by setting him on fire. The victim was admitted to Government Hospital with 90% burn injuries and he died in the hospital within a span of three days from the incident. The accused persons were also charged for attempting to murder a person, the brother of the deceased by stabbing him.

Chemical examination was conducted from the skin taken by the doctor from body of deceased which was preserved in sodium chloride.

Post mortem was conducted by the Civil Surgeon of the Government Hospital. He took out the skin from the body and preserved it in sodium chloride solution for chemical analysis. The post mortem report and the opinion given by him after the receipt of skin test from the chemical examiner according to which Rajeshwaram was died on account of shock resulting from deep burn injuries. According to the chemical examiner's report petrol was detected on the pieces of black lumps.

50 *Jose* v *State of Kerala* (2013) 14 SCC 172.

Although the chemical analyzer detected petrol from the black lumps, the doctor who conducted post mortem could not find the smell of kerosene or petrol or any other inflammable liquid on the body of the deceased. Moreover, the skin which was taken from the body of the deceased was sent for chemical examination about three months after post mortem examination. It was, therefore, not safe to rely on the chemical examiner's report to reach a conclusion that petrol was splashed on the deceased before the burning lamp was thrown at him.[51]

9.5.2 Chemical examiner's report disclosed presence of celphos poison which resulted in acquittal

The appellant was convicted under s. 302/328, IPC for committing murder of her husband by administering poison. In a case of murder by poisoning, it was necessary to prove that death was caused by poison, that poison in question was in possession of accused and the poison was administered by the accused to the deceased. The reason for the murder as contended by the prosecution that there was illicit relationship of accused wife with acquitted co-accused was not proved. Conviction by trial court was based primarily on the evidence of child witness. Deceased died in course of treatment at hospital. Only chemical examination report disclosed presence of celphos poison. Celphos has a pungent smell and characteristics and such poison cannot be administered deceitfully or openly. No direct evidence was found to show that any of the accused administered poison to deceased. Thus conviction and sentence was set aside and acquittal was recorded.[52]

9.5.2.1 *Chemical examination revealed the content of poison but it does not give an opinion as to cause of death*

The appellant had been convicted under ss. 302 and 328, IPC. It is held that Aluminium Phosphide poison cannot be administered by deceit. Two persons cannot commit suicide at the same time and in the same manner. The recovery

51 *Sree Vijayakumar* v *State* (2005)10 SCC 737.
52 *Ranju Devi* v *State of Bihar* 2008 CrLJ (NOC) 117.

effected from the house of the appellant on the same day containing the remaining tea and the utensils showed the poison to be Organophosphorus. Therefore the chain of circumstances was complete, which proved the prosecution case without any reasonable doubt. Report of the scientific experts may be used as evidence in any enquiry, trial or other proceedings of the court in terms of s. 293, CrPC but the chemical examiner does not, as a rule, give an opinion as to cause of death, but merely gives report of chemical examination of the substance sent to him. FSL report could not be relied upon so as to cast a doubt on the prosecution story. Thus in view of the eyewitness and the medical evidence, reliance on the FSL report was not tenable. Appeal was thus dismissed. Conviction upheld.[53]

9.5.2.2 *Scientific evidence relied upon by the courts*

The accused and other appellants were tried and convicted by the Sessions Judge under several sections like 120B, 302, 307, 326, 328 and 201 read with s. 34 of IPC and also under ss. 55(*a*), (*g*), (*h*), (*i*), 57-A and 58 of the Kerala Abkari Act. The accused persons were sentenced to suffer rigorous imprisonment for life, and also have been slapped with fines. Some were also subjected to lesser punishments and subjected to heavy fines. They appealed against this verdict to High Court. The High Court acquitted many appellants leaving behind the present appellants. Hence this appeal has been preferred to the Supreme Court.

Illicit and spurious liquor consumption had taken the lives of 31 persons, 6 persons became blind and 500 people suffered serious injuries due to the said incident. After receiving information the sub-inpector of police reached the hospital and recorded the first information statement. Later he registered a case under ss. 302, 307 read with s. 34 of IPC and under s. 57-A of the Abkari Act. Similar cases were also registered in different police stations. Similar cases were registered and consolidated.

53 *Anita* v *State of Haryana* (2010)3 RCR (Cri) 112 (DB).

The investigation machinery quickly responded to the happenings and a Special Investigation Team (SIT) was constituted as per the directions of Director General of Police. The prosecution alleged that methyl alcohol which is a poisonous substance used to be brought from Karnataka and mixed with ethyl alcohol. At times, this concoction was mixed with toddy and other essences resulting in a drink called "kalapani".

Chemical analysis was conducted to confirm the chemicals that were present in the spurious liquor. It was therefore clear from the chemical analyzer's evidence that scientific evidence collected by the prosecution was rightly relied upon by the courts below and the Supreme Court therefore found no reason to reject the said evidence. So, it was crystal clear that methyl alcohol which was the main culprit, was not only dangerously poisonous substance but was also used in mixing the liquor which was under the control of accused, the kingpin of business, who had been helped by his brothers, servants and relatives. The court dismissed the appeals of subject to modification of the sentences of some of the accused who had already undergone ten years of imprisonment.[54]

9.5.2.3 *Forcible administration of poison corroborated by only the appellant's presence in the bedroom and his failure to answer the causes for the injuries*

The Division Bench of Kerala High Court confirmed the judgment and order of sentence of trial court under ss. 323 and 302 of IPC and gave the accused life imprisonment. Against the said order of the High Court the appeal have been preferred to the Supreme Court.

On the fateful day, the victim Raji was sleeping in the bedroom with her husband. Suddenly at 2 a.m. on hearing a scream from the victim, the inmates rushed to the bedroom to find the victim dead. The body was sent for post-mortem.

The post-mortem report itself revealed signs of poisoning. The case of the prosecution was that the death of the victim

54 *Chadran* v *State of Kerala* (2011)5 SCC 161.

was caused by cyanide poison which was highly corrosive poison and is obtained by distilling potassium cyanide or potassium ferrocyanide with dilute sulphuric acid.[55] The Forensic Laboratory Expert also deposed that the injuries could be because of forcible administration of poison. According to the court the injuries found, would not be there in case of suicidal poisoning. Moreover, apart from the appellant no one else was there in the bedroom to apply force on the victim. Court also relied on the statements of Forensic Laboratory Expert where he revealed that the injuries were fresh in nature and could be due to the forcible administration of poison. Therefore, the court concluded that the prosecution had rightly proved that it was a clear case of murder. Above all the appellant also failed to answer the causes for the injuries when enquired by the trial court.[56]

9.6 Murder and unnatural offence

9.6.1 Chemical analysis corroborated by other evidences

The accused appellant was convicted under ss. 302, 377 and 201 of IPC. The case was based on circumstantial evidence and the accused committed pederasty (unnatural intercourse between a man and a boy) and murder of a 10 year old boy in most barbaric manner. The accused was referred for medical examination and the blood sample was taken from him. On the disclosure of the accused, the shirt worn by him, was recovered. The seized articles were referred for chemical analysis. DNA test was conducted by an expert who was having an experience of 14 years as a chemical analyst and she had examined thousands of samples including DNA tests. The prosecution was able to prove its case beyond reasonable doubt. The Supreme Court partly allowed the appeal and applied the R-R test and as the accused submitted that he had no previous criminal history and would not be a menace to

55 Modi's *Medical Jurisprudence and Toxicology*, 24th Ed. 2011, p. 260 (Nagpur: LexisNexis ButterworthsWadhwa).

56 *Shanmughan* v *State of Kerala* (2012)2 SCC 788.

society, the court commuted the death sentence to life imprisonment.[57]

9.7 Dowry death

9.7.1 Chemical analysis revealed insecticide poisoning but demand for dowry could not be proved

The appellants were convicted under s. 304B read with s. 34, IPC by the Sessions Court and High Court. Demand was made by accused-appellants from parents of deceased to meet domestic expenses and for purchasing manure. Thereafter the deceased was found dead. Post-mortem examination on the body of the deceased was conducted by a team of two doctors who opined that the cause of death was insecticide poisoning. The viscera were preserved for chemical analysis. The appeal before the Supreme Court had been preferred by the appellants challenging their conviction under s. 304-B read with s. 34, IPC. It was held by the apex court that demand made by accused cannot be said to be a demand for dowry since correlation between giving or taking of property or valuable security with the marriage of the parties was essential. But, demand for money on account of some financial stringency or for meeting some urgent domestic expenses or for purchasing manure cannot be termed as a demand for dowry. Hence, since an essential ingredient of s. 304-B, IPC viz. demand for dowry was not established, the conviction of the appellants could not be sustained. Thus the appeal was allowed and the appellants were acquitted. Although it was a case of suspected dowry death but since the demand for dowry could not be proved the appellants were acquitted.[58]

9.8 Murder and cruelty by husband and relatives of husband

9.8.1 Chemical analyzer's report was referred to point out how the kerosene lamp was used to murder the accused

Appellant was married to deceased and started ill-treating her on the ground that she should bring money from her parents

57 *Anil* v *State of Maharashtra* (2014)4 SCC 69.

58 *Appasaheb* v *State of Maharashtra* (2007)9 SCC 721.

and one day appellant threw kerosene lamp on deceased and her sari started burning resulting which she died subsequently. The learned APP, referred to the fact that there were quarrels between the parties in the past one year. She further referred to the Chemical Analyzer's Report to point out that in spite of throwing the kerosene lamp on to the deceased; some kerosene had still remained therein. The lamp was meant for lighting the room since there was no power. It was obviously a sufficiently big lamp and it was thrown from such a near position that there was no question of missing the target. The wife of accused had died within less than 48 hours from the time when she suffered burn injuries. Hence, the present case, clearly fell in defining murder and thus the conviction and sentence of the trail court was upheld.[59]

9.8.2 Non-explanation of the blood stain found by chemical analysis coupled with other evidences completed the chain of circumstances

Additional Sessions Judge convicted appellant for offence of murder under s. 302, IPC, cruelty by husband under s. 498A and causing disappearance of evidence of offence under s. 201, IPC. It is held that evidence of medical officer was that death was caused by cardio respiratory failure due to asphyxia by strangulation. Evidence and findings of post mortem report of the medical officer mentioned that death was due to strangulation by ligature as opposed to hanging. The accused had not explained the blood stain on his shirt, which was seized and sent for chemical analysis. The false plea of alibi set up by the appellant coupled with failure to explain the circumstances of the death of the deceased, who was his wife and with whom the appellant resided alone in the flat and with whom he was last seen together becomes an additional link in the chain of circumstances to make it complete and unerringly pointing to the guilt of the accused. Thus there was circumstantial evidence to hold accused guilty of murder of deceased and death of deceased was homicidal.[60]

59 *Sayaji Hanmant Bankar* v *State of Maharashtra* 2005 CrLJ 412.

60 *Deepak Revachand Talreja* v *State of Maharashtra* 2008(1) Bom CR (Cri) 510.

9.8.3 Chemical analysis ruled out death by poison at the circumstances proved that death was due to strangulation and resultant asphyxia

The trial court after consideration of the evidence on record held that the offences under ss. 498A, 302 and 201 of the IPC had been sufficiently substantiated and proved against accused, the sole appellant herein for murdering his wife and causing the disappearance of evidence. The remaining accused were acquitted as evidence on record could not sufficiently prove the charges against them. Being aggrieved, the appellant perused the matter before the High Court but the court affirmed the judgment of the trial court where the appellant was sentenced to life imprisonment and fine with two years rigorous imprisonment with fine and another two years for the respective offences noticed. An appeal was filed against the judgment of the Division Bench of the High Court.

Deceased wife was married to appellant husband for ten years and had no children. Relationship between the two, except the initial few years was not cordial. The deceased were also subjected to such acts as would sufficiently constitute cruelty to pressurize her to concede to divorce to facilitate a second marriage. Deceased died an unnatural death and was found lying with her body covered with a quilt upto her face. Door of the room was locked from inside but there was recess of 4 inches between two planks of the door so that one could put chain inside standing from outside or one could remove the chain put from inside by putting a hand inside the door through the recess while standing outside. Two small containers of insecticide and two cups found near the body.

The viscera of the deceased were sent for chemical analysis in order to ascertain the cause of death. The post mortem report indicated that the death was due to strangulation and resultant asphyxia. All the injuries were ante-mortem in nature. Some injuries on the body were found and according to the doctor, the injuries mentioned in the post-mortem report could be caused by fingers of the hands, by pressure. The doctor opined in the case there could be possibility of throttling. The examination of the viscera sent for chemical analysis also ruled out death by poison, thereby strengthening the opinion of the doctor who conducted the post-mortem.

The court held that the present case was an illustrative case to justify the usual saying that though witness might lie, the circumstances would not. Although the accused tried to mislead the court through clear maneuverings by manipulating the presence of some insecticides and cups on the spot to divert the attention of the investigating agencies, through the medical examination his guilt and cunningness was totally exposed. The court reasoned that a person who consumed such kind of poison could not have died, in the manner the body of the deceased was found inside the room, but the deceased should have suffered severe convulsions in the process and the quilt could not have remained on the body so perfectly laid and neatly covering her body upto the face. The court was wholly satisfied by overall consideration of the circumstances of the case as the motive part of the crime also got reinforced and the concurrent findings recorded by the courts below were merited and were shown not to suffer from any infirmity as to call for the interference in an appeal under Art. 136 of the Constitution of India. The appeal therefore failed and was dismissed.[61]

9.8.4 Death due to asphyxia was not proved and presence of poison bottle

The appellant was charged under ss. 302 and 498A of the IPC. The trial court recorded acquittal. The High Court, while affirming acquittal under s. 498A, IPC and s. 4 of the Dowry Prohibition Act, however convicted him under s. 302, IPC. Post mortem of the deceased was conducted and the viscera were preserved for chemical analysis. Opinion of doctor regarding death due to asphyxia did not satisfy the test laid down in Modi's *Medical Jurisprudence.* No mark of violence was present. Conclusion that husband alone was responsible for death of deceased was difficult to accept. The prosecution story,

61 *Vithal* v *State of Maharashtra* (2009)11 SCC 637; AIR 2009 SC 2067.

suggesting strong motive on part of appellant to commit murder, thus ruled out. Conclusion that because of plastic bottle, which at some point of time contained poison, was found near cot of deceased did not imply that the appellant husband deliberately kept it to raise a false plea, which might lead to surmise and conjecture. Therefore, the appellant husband was acquitted and the appeal was allowed.[62]

9.9 Cruelty by husband and relatives and dowry death

9.9.1 Chemical examination revealed death by insecticide poison which was not substantiated and non-consideration of that portion of the evidence which was taken into consideration by the trial court

The appellant along with four others was tried for the charges punishable under ss. 498A and 304B of IPC and ss. 3 and 4 of the Dowry Prohibition Act 1961. All of them were acquitted of the said charges by the trial court. The State preferred appeal against acquittal in the High Court, The High Court confirmed the order of acquittal of all the other accused except the appellant. The High Court accordingly convicted the appellant under s. 498A and sentenced him to undergo rigorous imprisonment for two years with a fine of ₹5000 and he was sentenced to rigorous imprisonment for ten years under s. 304B of IPC. The High Court also convicted the appellant for the offence punishable under s. 3 of the Dowry Prohibition Act 1961 and sentenced him to undergo rigorous imprisonment for five years and to pay a fine of ₹15000 and sentenced him to a rigorous imprisonment for six months and to pay a fine of ₹1000. The substantive sentences of imprisonment were directed to run concurrently. Hence this appeal have been preferred.

The deceased Poonam was married to the appellant. Soon after the marriage, the appellant and the other accused allegedly started harassing and torturing the deceased to bring more dowry. She was subjected to mental and physical cruelty repeatedly. The deceased gave birth to a male child about four months before the occurrence and the same constituted

62 *Subramanium* v *State of Tamil Nadu* (2009)14 SCC 415.

another occasion for the appellant and the other accused to demand cash and other valuable articles. One day, the victim called her near relation that she was subjected to torture and requested him to see her. When her said relative reached her house he heard shrieks of the deceased Poonam, coming out of the house. The appellant and the other respondents were shouting inside the house loudly and they did not allow the victim to meet her relative. The relative then informed father of the victim about the incident. On the next day when the complainant father of the victim reached the house along with his sons and the relative, the neighbours informed that the deceased had been taken by the accused and others to the hospital in a serious condition and the deceased was crying that she had been given poison by the appellant and others. When the father and others reached the hospital they came to know that the deceased had expired and her body was lying in the hospital. No accused were present in the hospital. Father of the victim therefore lodged an FIR.

Chemical examination of the viscera was conducted after post-mortem. The serologist reported that the viscera contained insecticide poison.

In this case the report of the serologist was not considered by the Supreme Court, although it was considered by the High Court as according to the court although the High Court concluded that the deceased died an unnatural death by poisoning within 14 months of her marriage with the appellant and there was consistent demand of dowry by him after the marriage, but the court did not discuss that portion of the evidence which was taken into consideration by the trial court. Moreover, the High Court did not record any findings that the trial court has misread the evidence or its findings were perverse. Therefore, the Supreme Court was satisfied that the trial court, for good and cogent reasons, acquitted all the accused including the appellant and it is the High Court which committed error in reversing the well considered judgment of the trial court. It was also noted by the Supreme Court that on the same evidence the High Court agreed with the trial court to acquit the other accused by refusing to rely on the prosecution story but a different yardstick had been applied so far as the appellant was concerned solely on the ground of the appellant's proximity with the victim on the fateful night.

The appeal was therefore allowed by the Supreme Court setting aside the impugned judgment of the High Court and acquitting the appellant from all the charges restoring the judgment of the trial court.[63]

9.9.2 Chemical examination revealed Aluminium Phosphide poison as cause of death corroborated by other evidences

The trial court convicted the appellant, under ss. 304B and 498A of IPC, and sentenced him and his parents to seven years rigorous imprisonment which was upheld by the High Court. Hence the appeal is preferred before the Supreme Court. Appellants prayed for sympathetic view regarding sentence as appellant, father-in-law was about 80 years old and his legs were amputed for severe diabetes and that other appellant, mother-in-law was about 78 years of age and she needed to look after her husband.

Rachhpal Kaur, the deceased married the appellant Kulwant Singh. Although she brought sufficient dowry she had been subjected to harassment and maltreatment by her husband and in-laws for bringing insufficient dowry. This resulted in the intervention of the panchayat so that the couple could lead a normal married life, which ultimately did not yield any positive result as after a month later the deceased was found lying dead in suspicious circumstances. The deceased had been taken to the hospital after rigor mortis had set in and froth was coming out from her mouth and nose. The post-mortem conducted on the deceased also revealed that she was carrying a 26-week foetus. Some parts of her body were then removed, sealed and sent for chemical examination to the chemical examiner.

Chemical examination was conducted to reveal the cause of death. The report of the chemical examiner received much later indicated the presence of aluminium phosphide (a pesticide) in the stomach of the deceased and phosphine, a constituent of aluminium phosphide, detected in her liver,

63 *Anil Kumar Gupta* v *State of Uttar Pradesh* (2011)11 SCC 24.

spleen, right kidney and right lung. According to Medical Officer, the contents that were found in the body were sufficient to cause the death of deceased.

The view of the court was that as far as the present case was concerned, the deceased was harassed by her husband and in-laws for dowry and that she died under abnormal circumstances due to aluminium phosphide poisoning. So, according to the court there were sufficient evidence to hold the appellants guilty of offences punishable under the aforesaid sections of IPC. [64]

9.10 Murder and unlawful assembly

9.10.1 Chemical examination corroborated the objective findings of the IO fitted in with the prosecution case

The accused persons were convicted under ss. 302/149, 147 and 148, IPC by the trial court. Post mortem of the deceased persons were conducted. In the opinion of the doctor, the injuries caused to the three deceased persons were sufficient to cause death in the ordinary course of nature. Apart from the medical evidence, the prosecution case was supported by the objective findings of the police. The IO, when visited the place of occurrence found bloodstained earth inside the bhusaura (a storeroom of cattle fodder) where all the three deceased persons were working on the fodder-cutting machine at the time of the alleged occurrence. He further found cut fodder in the said room with stains of blood thereon, seized the same and sent it to the chemical examiner. The serologist reported that the same contained human blood. Apart from that, the IO recovered four empty cartridges and three pellets from the place of occurrence and prepared seizure memos thereafter. Thus the objective findings of the IO fitted in with the prosecution case that the occurrence had taken place where the three deceased persons were working. Hence, the order of acquittal was set aside and convictions and sentence recorded by the trial court was restored.[65]

64 *Kulwant Singh* v *State of Punjab* (2013)4 SCC 177.
65 *State of U.P.* v *Sheo Sanehi* (2004)12 SCC 347.

9.10.2 Chemical examination conducted but prosecution had not ruled out possibility of articles, could have been tampered with, on account of absence of any evidence regarding sealing of articles

Present appeal was filed against order whereby appellants were convicted under ss. 143, 146, 147, 148, 149, 201, 302 and 452 of IPC. It was held that material contradictions pertaining to place of finding of right leg slipper created strong doubt about its real presence at spot of offence. Prosecution had not ruled out possibility of articles, could have been tampered with, on account of absence of any evidence regarding sealing of articles. But the seized articles were sent for chemical examination. Evidence adduced by prosecution was not cogent, convincing and sufficient to hold that accused were only persons who were responsible for commission of crime. Therefore setting aside the conviction, acquittal was given and the appeal was allowed in the process.[66]

9.11 Attempt to murder

In the instant appeal by special leave, the appellant had challenged his conviction under s. 307 of IPC. The trial court sentenced him to undergo 4 years rigorous imprisonment and to pay a fine of ₹500 and in default to undergo two months rigorous imprisonment. The High Court by its impugned judgment upheld the conviction but reduced the sentence to two years rigorous imprisonment maintaining the sentence of fine.

Chemical examination of the blood found on the knife was conducted to determine the commission of the offence. On chemical examination of the knife, it was found that the knife had human blood on it of 'AB' blood group which was also the blood group of the injured.

The court held that the arguments of the appellant were not supported by any evidence on record, therefore it could not be accepted. Submission of the appellant that he had also received injuries in the course of the said occurrence remained

66 *Manoj Mahadev Gawade* v *State of Maharashtra* 2014 SCC OnLine Bom 913.

unexplained by the prosecution, is not an excuse. According to the court although the burden on the prosecution is heavy while the defence only needed to probabilise the defence taken, yet there must be at least some materials on record to support the defence plea and probabilise its case. The court found it was completely lacking in this case. Moreover, one of the witnesses was the injured witness who was the victim of the assault and another witness was accompanying him. The two courts below, have concurrently found, the evidence of the prosecution as acceptable and the Supreme Court did not find any reason to take a separate view.

The appeal was dismissed. Since the appellant was released on bail during the pendency of the present appeal, the bail bonds were cancelled and it was directed to take the appellant into custody forthwith to serve out the remainder of the sentence.[67]

9.12 Rape and robbery

An appeal was filed against the acquittal of respondents for offences under s. 376 and s. 392 read with s. 34 of the IPC. Statement of prosecutrix was implicitly reliable. Statement of prosecutrix was corroborated by recordings in recovery panchnama. Prosecutrix was medically examined after 72 hours. The underwear of the prosecutrix and clothes of the respondents along with sample of their blood and semen were sent to the Chemical Analyst. Absence of serious injuries on her private parts would not rule out her being subjected to rape. Delay of 60 hours in lodging FIR was plausibly explained. Hence both the respondents were convicted under s. 376 and second respondent was also convicted for offence under s. 379, IPC.[68]

9.13 Rape and hurt

The accused duo were convicted by the trial court under ss. 376(2)(g) and 323 of IPC. Prosecutrix who was a widow aged about 55 years and having two grown-up children, alleged that

67 *Nasir Sikander Shaik* v *State of Maharashtra* (2005)10 SCC 585.
68 *State of Maharashtra* v *Savala Sagu Kokare* 1997 CrLJ 786.

respondents grappled with her and made her lie down on the earth and then committed rape and in that process she received injuries. Allegations were corroborated by medical evidence and the chemical analyzer's report. The FIR was submitted by her on the next day against the respondents. She was medically examined and her torn salwar was sent for chemical analysis. On medical examination various injuries were found on her person. The doctor was of the opinion that those reflected signs of a struggle. It was also not denied by the respondents that the seized salwar had stains of blood and semen on it. The mere fact that some different marks were noted on the sealed packet was by itself no ground to discard the otherwise reliable evidence of the prosecutrix. Under the circumstances, the appeal was allowed by setting aside the judgment of the High Court as it had acquitted the respondents. The conviction and sentence of the trial court was thus upheld.[69]

9.14 Penalty for illegal cultivation of poppy etc.

The respondent was charge-sheeted by the police for the offence under s. 9 of the Opium Act 1878. He was found in possession of 4.5 kg of opium wrapped in glazed paper, the sample of which was forwarded to the Chemical Examiner, who after testing the same, reported that it was opium. Two police personnel produced affidavits regarding the role played by them in forwarding the sample to the Chemical Examiner. The trial Magistrate found that the evidence of the prosecution was enough to convict him of the offence under s. 9 of the Opium Act. The Sessions Court upheld the conviction and sentence passed by the trial court. In revision, the High Court quashed the conviction and sentence by rejecting the evidence of policemen tendered by means of affidavit. The prosecution challenged the said verdict of the High Court in the instant appeal. Setting aside the impugned judgment, the Supreme Court held that in the present case, the facts stated in the affidavit were purely of a formal character. At any rate,

69 *State of H.P.* v *Lekh Raj* (2000)1 SCC 247.

even the defence could not dispute that aspect because no request or motion was made on behalf of the accused to summon the deponents of the affidavits to be examined in court. In such a situation, it was quite improper that the High Court used such a premise for setting aside the conviction and sentence passed on the respondent. The appeal was thus allowed. Therefore the Supreme Court accepted the Chemical Examiner's Report and allowed the appeal of the State by upholding conviction.[70]

9.15 Possession of charas under Narcotics Drug and Psychotropic Substances Act 1985

9.15.1 Chemical examination of the substance recovered from the accused was found to be a narcotic drug

The accused was convicted for the offence punishable under s. 8 of the NDPS Act 1985, by the trial court for possession of charas. He challenged the conviction before the High Court. The Division Bench of High Court acquitted him on the ground that the person who analyzed the narcotic drug was not an examiner as defined in r. 2(*c*) read with ss. 17 to 22 of the NDPS Act.

A superior officer of police being informed that a man who was sitting near the bus stand is suspected to be a dealer of "charas" went to the spot along with two witnesses to the spot. Another witness also joined them. When they reached the spot and interrogated the accused, the accused revealed his name as Jaswant Kumar. One of the witnesses told the appellant that he was suspected of having in possession of charas and whether he would like to be examined in the presence of a gazetted officer or a Magistrate. The SHO recorded the same in writing and obtained his signatures thereon from the accused. The accused replied that he would like to be searched in presence of a Magistrate. Accordingly, he was taken to Sub-Divisional Magistrate, Banjar. The accused was holding a greenish-coloured polythene packet and this polythene packet

70 *State of Punjab* v *Naib Din* (2001)8 SCC 578.

was unwrapped and 750 grams of charas was found. The ASI took samples and the appellant was taken into custody. The sample taken was sent to the Composite Testing Laboratory.

Chemical Examination of the sample was performed by the Chemical Analyst. The substance recovered from the accused was found to be a narcotic drug from the chemical examination. A certificate was furnished by the Testing Laboratory after the chemical examination of the recovered article. Although the appellant raised the contention that the article recovered from him was sent for chemical analysis to the testing laboratory, the same was not an authorized laboratory and therefore the certificate produced by the prosecution was not reliable. Although this contention of the accused was accepted by the High Court but the Supreme Court held that chemical examination carried out by the Testing Laboratory was valid in law therefore the finding of the court is not sustainable.

The appeal of the State was thus allowed setting aside the finding of the High Court and the finding of the Sessions Judge was upheld. The accused was directed to surrender to serve out the remaining period of sentence.[71]

9.15.2 Delay in sending the sample to the FSL for chemical analysis

An appeal was directed against the judgment and order of the High Court whereby the High Court dismissed the appeal filed by the accused and upheld the conviction and sentence passed against him under the provisions of s. 18 of the NDPS Act inflicting a rigorous imprisonment for a period of ten years and with rupees one lakh as fine.

The police party conducted a search of a truck where the accused was sitting beside the driver. Before the search was conducted the police party prepared consent memos to show compliance with s. 50 of the NDPS Act, which were signed/thumb marked by the appellant and attested by the witnesses. On the instruction, the DPS, Inspector conducted search of

71 *State of H.P.* v *Jaswant Kumar* (2004)13 SCC 516.

the appellant and upon such search one bag was found in the right hand of the accused and on search of the said bag, it was found to contain opium wrapped in a glazed paper. The aforesaid opium was thereafter weighed and it was found that that was 7 kg of opium out of which 250 gm was taken as a sample in one parcel and the remaining quantity was put in another parcel. After preparing two separate parcels, the same were sealed. The sealed parcels were taken into possession vide recovery memo, attested by the witnesses. After that the two samples were sent to the office of the Chemical Examiner. The learned senior counsel appearing on behalf of the accused submitted that mandatory provisions of s. 55 of the Act, were not complied with after the effective recovery of the accused. He also strongly urged that since the sample had been sent to the analyst for chemical examination after a lapse of 40 days the appellant should have been acquitted on the ground that the entire case of the prosecution was doubtful.

Chemical examination was conducted to determine the nature of the two samples seized from the appellant. As per the report of the chemical analyst, the contents of the sample were found to be of opium.[72]

The court forwarded its view that the question regarding delay in sending the samples of the opium to the Forensic Science Laboratory (FSL) had no relevance as the fact that the recovery of the said sample from the possession of the appellant stood proved and established by cogent and reliable evidence led in the trial, that opium was seized from the appellant and seals put on the sample were intact till it was handed over to chemical examiner. That itself proves and establishes that there was no tampering with the aforesaid seal in the sample at any stage and the sample received by the analyst for chemical examination contained the same opium which was recovered from the possession of the appellant.[73]

72 *Karnail Singh* v *State of Rajasthan* (2000)7 SCC 632.
73 *Hardip Singh* v *State of Punjab* (2008)8 SCC 557 .

9.15.3 Material sent for examination should reach the FSL with intact seals

An appeal had been filed in order to challenge the order directing acquittal of the respondent who was tried for allegedly committing the offences under s. 8 read with s. 18 of the Narcotic Drugs and Psychotropic Substances Act 1985 (NDPS Act). The learned Special Judge, NDPS found him guilty and sentenced him to undergo imprisonment for 10 years and to pay a fine of ₹1 lakh.

The SHO, was conducting a routine check of the vehicles on the road. In the evening, the accused along with another came riding on a motorcycle, which had no number plate and when they were asked to stop they did not stop. They were chased by the police jeep and ultimately the motorcycle was stopped. According to the prosecution, the motorcycle was searched and large quantity of opium was seized. Both were arrested and a case under the abovementioned section of NDPS Act, was registered. The trial court acquitted the other accused but not the appellant. Hence, the appellant preferred an appeal to the High Court on the ground that the samples which were allegedly collected at the time of recovery did not reach the Forensic Science Laboratory, intact and on that ground the accused was entitled to acquittal. The High Court however held that there was non-compliance with respect to s. 55 of NDPS Act and the evidence of witnesses clearly shows that the requisite procedures under s. 55 were not followed.

The samples which were collected from the spot were sent for chemical examination to determine the nature of the chemical. As per the chemical examination report the material sent for examination was found to be opium containing morphine. The Supreme Court held that the effect of samples reaching with the intact seals had been considered by it in a large number of cases,[74] therefore, on the basis of such experience the impugned judgment of the High Court was set aside.[75]

74 *State of Rajasthan* v *Daul* (2009)14 SCC 387.
75 *State of Rajasthan* v *Bhiya Ram* (2009)14 SCC 390 .

9.15.4 FSL Report clearly stated that the seals were intact and matched with the specimen seals hence issue raised regarding tampering of seals is baseless

An appeal was directed by the State against the judgment of the High Court acquitting the respondent who was convicted under ss. 8 and 18 of the NDPS Act 1985 by the Sessions Judge and sentenced the accused to undergo ten years rigorous imprisonment and to pay a fine of ₹1 lakh with default stipulation.

The police party on getting information that the accused having opium in possession would pass through a place on foot from the village, proceeded towards the spot in a Government vehicle and caught hold of the person who was carrying gunny bag on his head. Thereafter, the accused was informed about the secret information and that he was to be searched. Before making the search, the respondent-accused was given a notice under the provisions of s. 50 of the NDPS Act, asking him whether he wanted to be searched before the Magistrate or a gazetted officer upon which the accused consented for being searched. Thereafter the accused was searched in presence of two witnesses. During search, from the gunny bag, a plastic bag containing black-brown substance was recovered and it was assessed as nothing but contraband opium and on being asked the accused told he had no valid licence to keep the opium. On weighing, it was found to be 6 kg out of which two samples of 30gm each were taken for the purposes of chemical analysis. Thereafter those samples were deposited in FSL.

Chemical examination of the substance was conducted as it was assessed to be contraband opium. The FSL Report stated that the sample gave positive tests for the chief constituents of the coagulated juice of opium poppy having 3.6% morphine. In appeal the only stand of the respondent was that the samples were in the custody of one Jamnalal, who was not examined which rendered the prosecution version unacceptable. On the basis of this point only, the High Court had set aside the conviction passed by the trial court. The learned counsel for the appellant State pointed out that non-examination of

Jamnalal could not be fatal to the credibility of the prosecution version. The entire scenario, starting from the seizure of the sample till their receipt at the FSL and the report thereafter clearly proves that the samples were not only sealed but were also kept in proper and safe custody. According to him if the seal was intact, there was no question of possibility of any tampering. The Supreme Court also justified the version of the learned counsel for the State and held that the conclusion attempted by the High Court was unsustainable in the view of the FSL Report which clearly stated that the seals were intact and matched with the specimen seals. Hence the issue raised by the learned counsel for the respondent accused that if Jamnalal was not examined, there was possibility of the sample being tampered is baseless. Again the court relied on the case of *Hardip Singh,*[76] to explain the circumstances of the case and held that the present case was on a much better footing.

The judgment of the High Court was set aside and the judgment of the trial court was restored. The respondent was directed to surrender to serve out the remainder of sentence.[77]

9.15.5 Seizure and taking of samples for the purpose of chemical examination were doubted

Aggrieved and dissatisfied with the decision of the High Court for recording acquittal of the respondent, the Union of India filed this appeal before the Supreme Court. The trial court charged the respondents under ss. 8 and 18 of the NDPS Act.

Secret information was received by a sub-inspector that two people would be carrying about 20 kg of opium. A preventive party was formed and it reached the place where it found the two respondents were carrying cement gunny bags. On their search, 10 kg of opium packed in five polythene bags of 2kg each from each of them were said to have been recovered.

The contraband article recovered from the respondents was sent for chemical analysis. The report of the Assistant Chemical

76 *Hardip Singh* v *State of Punjab* (2008)8 SCC 557.
77 *State of Rajasthan* v *Daul* (2009)14 SCC 387.

Examiner, Government Opium and Alkaloid Works showed presence of 01.68% and 02.05% of morphine by B.P. extraction from the first sample and the second sample respectively. The High Court acquitted the accused on many grounds, among which one of the grounds was that the sample of the narcotics were not taken in terms of the Standing Instruction and by complying with s. 55 of the NDPS Act. The Supreme Court explained that the Standing Instruction which had been issued under the Act, lays the procedure for taking samples. The High Court has noticed that the person who took the samples of 25 gm each from all the five bags, mixed them and then sent them to the laboratory but there was nothing to show that adequate quantity from each bag had been taken. Regarding compliance with s. 55 the court reasoned that the person who took the samples did not testify as to which of the bags seized had been sent for analysis, neither any statement was made by him that the bags produced were the bags in question which were seized or the contraband was found in them. The court was of the view that High Court had arrived at proper finding in respect of all the points of issue including seizure and taking of samples for the purpose of chemical examination which were doubted.

Impact of forensic evidence. On the basis of the aforementioned reasons the court did not see any reason to interfere with the judgment of acquittal. Hence the appeal was dismissed accordingly.[78]

9.15.6 Doubt regarding delay of more than two months for sending the sample to CFSL required to be removed by prosecution

Whether conviction of appellant under s. 20 of the Narcotic Drugs and Psychotropic Substances Act 1985 was justified. It is held that Court found when sample was redeposited with MHC, as stated by Constable then it was not understood as to why there was delay of more than two months for sending it for analysis to CFSL. This doubt was required to be removed by prosecution by adducing reliable evidence on that behalf,

78 *Union of India* v *Bal Mukund* (2009)12 SCC 161 .

more specifically when there was contradiction with respect to samples having resealed at three or four places as aforesaid and seal used by Police at the time of recovery and re-sealing remained with police and NCB forms, which allegedly contained facsimile of seal, were withheld. Thus report of analysis of sample could not be connected with recovery of alleged contraband from appellant. Court found that report issued by Director of Forensic Science Laboratory, fell short of requisite particulars. Chemical Examination Report stood not connected with recovered stuff and it also did not prove that stuff recovered were charas within meaning of the Act. Accordingly, conviction and sentence of appellant passed by trial court was unsustainable and was therefore set aside. Thus appeal was allowed and acquittal was given.[79]

9.15.7 Delay in sending the sample to the office of the chemical examiner

An order of conviction of the trial court passed against the appellant under s. 18 of the Narcotic Drugs and Psychotropic Substances Act 1985 (NDPS Act) and sentenced him to undergo a rigorous imprisonment for ten years and to pay a fine of rupees one lakh and in default of payment of the same, to undergo rigorous imprisonment for another two years, for having being found in possession of 1 Kg and 750 gm of opium without any permit or license.

The sample which was recovered from the appellant was sent to the chemical examiner for chemical examination and determination of the same. The report of the chemical examiner marked indicated the sample as opium whose seals were intact when it was received and tallied with the sample impression of the seal. The report of the chemical examiner was admissible under s. 293 of CrPC. Although it was pointed out by the learned counsel for the appellant that there was a delay of twelve days in sending the sample for chemical examination, the court held the submission as baseless or without factual basis. According to the court, the trial court as

79 *Renu Gogar* v *State of H.P.* 2010 SCC Online HP 101.

well as the High Court, on examination of the entire material, concluded that there was sufficient independent evidence produced by the prosecution regarding the completion of link evidence. Therefore, the delay in sending the sample to the office of the chemical examiner becomes not worth mentioning. The court was of considered view that mere delay in sending the sample of the narcotic to the office of the chemical examiner would not be sufficient to conclude that the sample had been tampered with. There was sufficient evidence to indicate that the delay, if any, was totally unintentional. Moreover, after considering the clear evidence of the chemical examiner, the Supreme Court held that there could not be any infirmity in the link evidence merely because there was a delay of few days in sending the sample to the chemical examiner's office.

The court was unable to find any perversity or any miscarriage of justice in the findings of the courts below. So, the appeal was dismissed on the basis of no merit and the conviction was upheld considering the entire material on record and on the basis of the concurrent findings of the said two courts.[80]

80 *Jarnail Singh* v *State of Punjab* (2011)3 SCC 521.

Chapter 6

Cyber Forensics

1 Introduction

Cyber forensics is a wide term that includes *inter alia* computer forensics and network forensics. Computer forensics means gathering evidence from computer media and network forensics means gathering digital evidence[1] that is distributed across networks.[2] As per the definition provided by the Computer Emergency Response Team of the Asian School of Cyber Laws:

1 Digital evidence is information stored or transmitted in binary form that may be relied on in court. It can be found on a computer hard drive, a mobile phone, a personal digital assistant (PDA), a CD, and a flash card in a digital camera, among other places. Digital evidence is commonly associated with electronic crime, or e-crime, such as child pornography or credit card fraud. However, digital evidence is now used to prosecute all types of crimes, not just e-crime. For example, suspects' e-mail or mobile phone files might contain critical evidence regarding their intent, their whereabouts at the time of a crime and their relationship with other suspects. Available at <https://www.nij.gov/topics/forensics/evidence/digital/Pages/welcome.aspx> accessed on 17.11.2018.

2 A network consists of multiple devices that communicate with one another. It can be as small as two computers or as large as billions of devices. While a traditional network is comprised of desktop computers, modern networks may include laptops, tablets, smartphones, televisions, gaming consoles, smart appliances, and other electronics. Available at <https://techterms.com/definition/network> accessed on 17.11.2018.

Cyber forensics is the discovery, analysis, and reconstruction of evidence extracted from and/or contained in a computer, computer system, computer network, computer media and computer peripheral. Therefore, cyber forensics involve finding and decrypting password protected information, encrypted information and steganographic[3] content, tracing the source of email, tracking software piracy, recovering deleted data, matching information and floppy disks to computers that created them, remotely monitoring computers and preserving digital evidence for presentation in court.

Digital evidence is the foundation of any case involving computers. Even a traditional offence like homicide and rape may involve a computer either directly or indirectly. So cyber forensic may be used in the investigations of both traditional as well as cyber crimes. Searching, examining, collecting and preserving digital evidence should be done to make the evidence admissible.

2 Cyber forensic and investigation process

The basic principle behind cyber forensic is that every activity on computer leaves their trace, derived from the rule of ordinary evidence based on Locard's Principle that every crime scene contains evidence. Thus, collecting evidences from Digital Medias, analysis of evidences, opinion or report writing are the stages through which cyber forensics and cyber crime investigation process passes goes on. Cyber Forensic Analysis involves four basic steps. They are (1) identifying sources of evidence, (2) securing evidences and preserving identified evidences, (3) analyzing the evidences, (4) documenting found

3 Steganography (pronounced STEHG-uh-NAH-gruhf-ee, from Greek *steganos*, or "covered," and *graphie*, or "writing") is the hiding of a secret message within an ordinary message and the extraction of it at its destination. Steganography takes cryptography a step farther by hiding an encrypted message so that no one suspects it exists. Ideally, anyone scanning your data will fail to know it contains encrypted data. Available at <https://searchsecurity.techtarget.com/definition/steganography> accessed on 17.11.2018.

and analyzed evidences. The evidence must be extracted and presented in a way that preserves its "integrity".[4]

Cyber Forensics Expert never works on Original or Evidence media. He first creates forensic image of the original hard disk, and then follow all the investigation on forensic image.[5] Unless completely unavoidable, data should never be analyzed using the same machine it is collected from. The forensic examiner renders an opinion, based upon the examination of the material that has been recovered. An opinion and report is rendered by the forensic examiner, to determine whether they have been used for criminal, civil or unauthorized activities. Computer Forensics is done in a fashion that adheres to the standards of evidence that are admissible in a court of law. Thus, computer forensics must be techno-legal in nature rather than purely technical or purely legal.

Section 79A of the Information Technology Act deals with Examiner of Electronic Evidence. It gives a power on the Central Government, for providing expert opinion on electronic form evidence before any court or other authority if necessary.

3 Cyber forensic and cyber crime

As cyber forensics is the discovery, analysis, and reconstruction of evidence such discovery, analysis and reconstruction of evidence is made when there is a commission of cyber crime or any other traditional crime using computers. An understanding of the application of cyber forensic to cyber crimes would also clarify the application of cyber forensics in traditional crimes.

Cyber crimes has not been defined in the Information Technology Act. It may be defined as unlawful acts where the computer is used either as a tool or target or both. The enormous growth of electronic commerce or e-commerce and online share trading has led to a phenomenal increase in

4 Santosh Raut, *Cyber Forensics*, Amity University, Noida, India, viewed on 12.05.2011 available at <https://www.all-about-forensic-science.com/cyber-forensics.html>.

5 Rohas Nagpal, *Cyber Crime and Corporate Liability*, 1st Ed., p. 209.

incidents of cyber crime. Cyber crime also encompasses infringement of Intellectual Property Rights.

4 Legal provisions under which cyber crimes are prosecuted/ referred

In India, the Information Technology Act 2000 and the Indian Penal Code 1860 are the principal statutes containing provisions relating to computer related crime. The primary purpose of the IT Act 2000, is to provide legal recognition to electronic commerce and to facilitate filing of electronic records with the Government. The Act also penalizes various cyber crimes and provides strict punishments. The Act is made effective with the operation of various Rules. Some of the rules are the Information Technology (Certifying Authorities) Rules 2000, the Cyber Regulation Appellate Tribunal (Procedure) Rules 2000, etc.

The Indian Penal Code penalises several cyber crimes like forgery of electronic records, cyber frauds, destroying electronic evidence etc. The Indian Evidence Act, also provides laws for making electronic evidence admissible. Section 65B was the most important amendment that was introduced in the Indian Evidence Act 1872, which made electronic evidences admissible in courts. The Copyright Act 1970 is also applicable in certain cases involving Intellectual Property violations.

Cyber Crimes investigation and adjudication are guided by the provisions of the Code of Criminal Procedure 1973 and IT Act 2000.

5 Judicial pronouncements on IT Act 2000

In *Shreya Singhal* v *Union of India,*[6] the Supreme Court struck down s. 66A of the IT Act 2000 as unconstitutional. This public interest litigation was filed to challenge the Constitutionality of s. 66A of the IT Act 2000 as being arbitrary, ambiguous and violative of fundamental right to free speech guaranteed under Art. 19 of the Constitution of India. The court held that

6 *Shreya Singhal* v *Union of India* (2013)12 SCC 73.

s. 66A of the IT Act 2000 is arbitrary, ambiguous, and violative of right to freedom of speech and it takes within its sweep the speech that is innocent as well. The court took the view that no part of it was severable and section as a whole was struck down as unconstitutional.

In *Anwar P.V.* v *P.K. Basheer,*[7] it was held that when digital evidences like CD, VCD, chip are produced, they are required to be accompanied by certificate in terms of s. 65B of the Indian Evidence Act,[8] at time of taking document.

6 Use of cyber forensic for collection and analysis of electronic evidence/admissibility of cyber forensics in the decision making process

There is no iota of doubt regarding admissibility of electronic evidence. Even what would be the presumption regarding electronic documents have been explained by the Indian Evidence Act 1872 under ss. 85A, 85B, 85C and s. 88A. But, it is evident that electronic evidence needs to be collected to make itself admissible. Collection of electronic evidence requires cyber forensics. Computer forensics, is a branch of forensics wherein an expert, collects, stores, preserves, analyses and produces data from a computer. Cyber forensics may also be

7 *Anwar P.V.* v *P.K. Basheer* AIR 2015 SC 180.

8 Section 65B(4). In any proceedings where it is desired to give a statement in evidence by virtue of this section, a certificate doing any of the following things, that is to say,—
(*a*) identifying the electronic record containing the statement and describing the manner in which it was produced;
(*b*) giving such particulars of any device involved in the production of that electronic record as may be appropriate for the purpose of showing that the electronic record was produced by a computer;
(*c*) dealing with any of the matters to which the conditions mentioned in sub-section (2) relate,
and purporting to be signed by a person occupying a responsible official position in relation to the operation of the relevant device or the management of the relevant activities (whichever is appropriate) shall be evidence of any matter stated in the certificate; and for the purposes of this sub-section it shall be sufficient for a matter to be stated to the best of the knowledge and belief of the person stating it.

categorized like mobile forensics, email forensics, wireless forensics, disk forensics etc. The data which had been analyzed may be used as electronic evidence in civil, criminal and other matters in court or tribunals. The process analyzing, collection and preservation of the electronic evidence is made by maintaining the authenticity and correctness of the electronic data. Along with collection cyber forensics also include retrieving any deleted or hidden encrypted files. It can be made both on original medium and on mirror image replica.

In *State* v *Mohhammad Afzal,*[9] more commonly known as the *Parliament Attack* case, the laptop seized from the accused contained several evidences that confirmed motives of the two terrorist. The sticker of the Ministry of Home affairs were forged on laptop and pasted on the Ambassador car, which they used to gain entry into the Parliament House. Another terrorist forged the ID card with a Government of India emblem and seal using the same laptop for the same purpose of gaining entry into the Parliament. Similarly, in *Mohd. Ajmal Amir Kasab* v *State of Maharashtra,*[10] cyber forensics were used to trace the conspiracy from the intercepted mobile phone call recordings of the accused. Through cyber forensics, it was revealed that the terrorists who attacked hotel Oberoi in Mumbai belonged to Pakistan and during the attack were regularly in contact with co-conspirators in Pakistan through mobile phones.[11]

Cyber forensics has now been acclimatized in our culture which is very evident from the judgments of courts. In *Shafhi Mohammad* v *State of Himachal Pradesh,*[12] the Supreme Court has acknowledged the importance of videography and directed the Central Government for implementation of the action plan for installing CCTV cameras in all police stations and prisons to check human rights abuse.

9 *State* v *Mohhammad Afzal* (2003) DLT SCC 1.

10 *Mohd. Ajmal Amir Kasab* v *State of Maharashtra* (2012)9 SCC 1.

11 Karnika Seth, *Computers, Internet and New Technology Laws*, 2nd Ed., pp. 451 and 452.

12 *Shafhi Mohammad* v *State of Himachal Pradesh* (2018)5 SCC 311.

7 Offences under Information Technology Act 2000

7.1 Access related crimes

The following can be referred to as access related crimes: (1) Unauthorized access, (2) Hacking.

7.1.1 Unauthorized access

The term 'access' has been defined under s. 2(1)(*a*) of the Information Technology Act. "Access" with its grammatical variations and cognate expressions means gaining entry into, instructing or communicating with the logical, arithmetical, or memory function resources of a computer, computer system or computer network.

Section 43(*a*) of the IT Act 2000 interprets unauthorized access.

Section 70 of the same Act explains "Accessing protected Systems". According to it:

(1) The appropriate Government may, by notification in the Official Gazette, declare that any computer, computer system or computer network to be a protected system.

(2) The appropriate Government may, by order in writing, authorise the persons who are authorised to access protected systems notified under sub-sec. (1).

(3) Any person who secures access or attempts to secure access to a protected system in contravention of the provisions of this section shall be punished with imprisonment of either description for a term which may extend to ten years and shall also be liable to fine.

7.1.1.1 *Challenge to Constitutional validity of s. 70 of the Information Technology Act 2000*

The Government of Kerala issued a notification under s. 70 of the Information Technology Act 2000 declaring a project idea namely 'FRIENDS' software (Fast, reliable, instant, efficient network for disbursement of services) as a protected system. The project envisaged development of a software, for single window collection of bills payable to Government, local authorities, various statutory agencies, Government corporations etc. Towards tax, fees, charges for electricity, water etc. A person by making a consolidated payment in a computer counter served through 'FRIENDS' system could discharge all his liabilities due to the Government, local authorities and various agencies.[13]

The work of developing the 'FRIENDS' software was entrusted to Firos. The software was first established at Tiruvanthapuram, free of cost and since the project was successful, the Government decided to set up the same to all other 13 district centres. The Government of Kerala entered into a contract with Firos for setting up and commissioning 'FRIENDS' software system in 13 centres all over Kerala for providing integrated services to the customers through a single window for a total consideration of ₹13 lakh. Firos set up 'friends' service centres in all the 13 centres and they were paid the agreed remuneration.

The Government arranged to modify the 'FRIENDS' software to suit its further requirements through another agency. Regarding this a dispute arose between Firos and the Government with regard to Intellectual Property Rights (IPR) and the 'FRIENDS' software.

Thereafter, the Government of Kerala, issued a notification under s. 70 of the IT Act, declaring the 'FRIENDS' software installed in the computer system and computer network established in all centres in Kerala as a protected system.

Firos filed a Writ Petition challenging s. 70 of the Information Technology Act 2000.

The court concluded that there is no conflict between the provisions of the Copyright Act and s. 70 of the Information Technology Act 2000. Section 70 of the Information Technology Act 2000 is not unconstitutional. While interpreting s. 70 of the

13 *Firos* v *State of Kerala* AIR 2006 Ker 297.

Information Technology Act 2000, a harmonious construction with the Copyright Act is needed. Government cannot unilaterally declare any system as 'protected' other than 'Government work' falling under s. 2(*k*) of the Copyright Act 1957 on which Government's copyright is recognized under s. 17(*d*) of the said Act.[14]

7.1.1.2 *Cases on unauthorized access*

JURISDICTION OF CIVIL COURTS IN ACTS INVOLVING UNAUTHORIZED ACCESS. In *JCB India Ltd.* v *I.P. Address: 122.163.98.166,*[15] there was a data theft and copyright infringement. The court considered whether in the light of the provisions of s. 61 which bars the jurisdiction of civil courts, could the plaintiff file a suit for injunction against infringement of copyright and confidential information in a civil court when such acts involved unauthorized access and downloading of such matter using computers or should approach the Adjudicating Authority.

The court relied on the case of *Secretary of State* v *Mask and Co.*[16] Wherein it was held that it is settled law that 'the exclusion of jurisdiction of civil courts is not to be readily inferred, but that such exclusion must either be explicitly expressed or clearly implied'. Further the court observed in *Dhulabhai* v *State of M.P.,*[17] that where there is an express bar of the jurisdiction of the court, the Act must be to analyze the adequacy or the sufficiency of the remedies provided but the same are not decisive to establish the jurisdiction of the civil courts.

The court also considered rulings of the Supreme Court in *Roop Lal Sathi* v *Nachhattar Singh Gill,*[18] and *Raptakos Brett*

14 Rohas Nagpal, *Cyber Crime and Corporate Liability,* CCH India, Wolters Kluwer (India) Pvt. Ltd., First Ed., pp. 324-326.

15 *JCB India Ltd.* v *I.P. Address: 122.163.98.166* decided by Delhi High Court in CS (OS) 1021/2008 on 25th August 2008.

16 *Secretary of State* v *Mask and Co.* AIR 1940 PC 105.

17 *Dhulabhai* v *State of M.P.* AIR 1969 SC 78.

18 *Roop Lal Sathi* v *Nachhattar Singh Gill* (1982)3 SCC 487; AIR 1982 SC 1559.

and Co. Ltd v *Ganesh Property*[19] and took the view where issues involved two Acts, only a part of the plaint cannot be rejected on ground of lack of jurisdiction. The court finally held that if some of the causes pleaded by the suit are seemingly barred, still the court should not reject the plaint because some of the reliefs may be barred in law that can be decided in the final stage considering the 'composite nature of the claims' in the pleadings.

Provisions of IT Act 2000 do not exclude the jurisdiction of civil courts. In *Super Cassettes Industries Ltd.* v *Myspace Inc.*,[20] the High Court of Delhi dealt with a case for copyright infringement wherein plaintiff alleged that infringing songs and videos were uploaded on defendant's website that directly infringed its copyright in the said works. The court yet again held that provisions of the IT Act 2000, do not exclude the jurisdiction of civil courts in copyright infringement cases in view of s. 81 of the IT Act 2000.[21]

Defendant restrained from using data, letting it or deleting the same. In *Shashank Shekhar Mishra* v *Ajay Gupta*,[22] a suit for permanent injunction restraining defendant from using software or letting it or creating third party interest therein, seeking damages from defendants alleging that defendants have illegally snatched his laptop, that contained copyrighted materials including a new programme he had designed named Quizpro Wordpress plugin. The defendant who was proceeded against, *ex parte* was restrained from using any data, letting it or deleting the same with direction to return the laptop or pay the amount equal to value of laptop and damages of ₹10 lakh. The court observed that jurisdiction of civil courts was not barred.[23]

19 *Raptakos Brett and Co. Ltd.* v *Ganesh Property* (1998)7 SCC 184.

20 *Super Cassettes Industries Ltd.* v *Myspace Inc.* 2011(48) PTC 49.

21 Section 81. The provisions of this Act shall have effect notwithstanding anything consistent therewith contained in any other law for the time being in force.

22 *Shashank Shekhar Mishra* v *Ajay Gupta* 2011(184) DLT 675.

23 Karnika Seth, *Computer Internet and New Technology Laws*, 2nd Ed., pp. 410–411.

7.1.2 Hacking

According to s. 66 of the Information Technology Act 2000:

> "If a person, dishonestly, or fraudulently, does any act referred to in section 43, he shall be punishable with imprisonment for a term which may extend to three years or with fine which may extend to five lakh rupees or with both."

7.1.2.1 *Denial of service*

A 'Denial of Service' (DoS) is any type of attack where the attackers (hackers) attempt to prevent legitimate users from accessing the service. In a DoS attack, the attacker usually sends excessive messages asking the network or server to authenticate requests that have invalid return addresses. The network or server will not be able to find the return address of the attacker when sending the authentication approval, causing the server to wait before closing the connection. When the server closes the connection, the attacker sends more authentication messages with invalid return addresses. Hence, the process of authentication and server wait will begin again, keeping the network or server busy. Hence, the attacker destroys information residing in a computer resource or diminishes its value or utility to the public.

7.1.2.2 *Denial of Service Attack (DoS)*

A DoS attack can be done in a several ways. The basic types of DoS attack include:

1. Flooding the network to prevent legitimate network traffic.
2. Disrupting the connections between two machines, thus preventing access to a service.
3. Preventing a particular individual from accessing a service.
4. Disrupting a service to a specific system or individual.

DoS attacks can cause the following problems:

1. Ineffective services;
2. Inaccessible services;
3. Interruption of network traffic;
4. Connection interference;[24]

7.1.2.3 *Cases on hacking*

ACT OF TRANSFERRING SENSITIVE CONFIDENTIAL INFORMATION OF PAST EMPLOYER AMOUNTS TO HACKING An employee was alleged to have stolen confidential information and copyrighted materials from his past employer and disclosed the same to a competitor entity where he took employment later. The accused filed a petition under s. 438, Code of Criminal Procedure 1973 by which he sought an anticipatory bail as an FIR was lodged against him by the J.C.B. India, Private Limited, his past employer under s. 66 of the IT Act 2000 and ss. 420 and 406 of the Indian Penal Code. J.C.B. produced screenshots of accused e-mail inbox that showed that he had transferred sensitive confidential secrets of his past employer to his personal e-mail id and then transferred the said information to his new employer.

The Court was of the view that such acts *prima facie* amounted to hacking under s. 66 of the IT Act 2000 and rejected his bail petition as it did not accept his submission that the information was transferred in exercise of his duties. The court observed that transfer of information further to a competitor company where he joined cannot be justified. Also, as per his appointment letter he was required to destroy company related documents from his personal computer when he left his previous employer. [25]

FIR QUASHED WHEN DISPUTE WAS OF CIVIL NATURE AND DID NOT INFRINGE ANY OTHER INDIVIDUAL'S RIGHT. In *Nirav Navinbhai Shah* v *State of Gujarat*,[26] the Gujarat High Court dealt with a petition for

24 Denial-of-Service Attack (DoS) available at <https://www.techopedia.com/definition/24841/denial-of-service-attack-dos> accessed on 07.11.18.

25 *Abhinav Gupta* v *State of Haryana* 2008 CrLJ 4536.

26 *Nirav Navinbhai Shah* v *State of Gujarat* (2006)26 GLH 711.

quashing of FIR under s. 438 of the Code of Criminal Procedure 1973 registered for offence of hacking and data theft under ss. 66 and 72 of IT Act 2000 on ground that dispute between the parties was only of civil nature which was amicably settled between the parties A the offence did not infringe any other individual's right and dispute was of civil nature which had been settled by parties, court quashed the FIR as its continuance would not be in the interest of justice.

7.2 Cyber pornography

Section 67 of the Information Technology Act 2000 is the most serious Indian Law penalising Cyber Pornography. There are also other laws in India that deal with pornography which include the Indecent Representation of Women (Prohibition) Act 1986 and the Indian Penal Code 1860.

According to s. 67 of the Information Technology Act 2000:

> Whoever publishes or transmits or causes to be published or transmitted in the electronic form, any material which is lascivious or appeals to the prurient interest or if its effect is such as to tend to deprave and corrupt persons who are likely, having regard to all relevant circumstances, to read, see or hear the matter contained or embodied in it, shall be punished on first conviction with imprisonment of either description for a term which may extend to three years and with fine which may extend to five lakh rupees and in the event of second or subsequent conviction with imprisonment of either description for a term which may extend to five years and also with fine which may extend to ten lakh rupees.

Section 67B of the Information Technology Act 2000:

> *Punishment for publishing or transmitting of material depicting children in sexually explicit act, etc., in electronic form.* Whoever—
>
> (*a*) publishes or transmits or causes to be published or transmitted material in any electronic form which depicts children engaged in sexually esplicit act or conduct; or

(*b*) creates text or digital images, collects, seeks, browses, downloads, advertises, promotes, exchanges or distributes material in any electronic form depicting children in obscene or indecent or sexually explicit manner; or

(*c*) cultivates, entices or induces children to online relationship with one or more children for and on sexually explicit act or in a manner that may offend a reasonable adult on the computer resource; or

(*d*) facilitates abusing children online, or

(*e*) records in any electronic form own abuse or that of others pertaining to sexually explicit act with children,

shall be punished on first conviction with imprisonment of either description for a term which may extend to five years and with fine which may extend to ten lakh rupees and in the event of second or subsequent conviction with imprisonment of either description for a term which may extend to seven years and also with fine which may extend to ten lakh rupees:

Provided that provisions of s. 67, s. 67A and this section does not extend to any book, pamphlet, paper, writing, drawing, painting representation or figure in electronic form—

(i) the publication of which is proved to be justified as being for the public good on the ground that such book, pamphlet, paper, writing, drawing, painting representation or figure is in the interest of science, literature, art or learning or other objects of general concern; or

(ii) which is kept or used for *bona fide* heritage or religious purposes.

Explanation. For the purposes of this section "children" means a person who has not completed the age of 18 years.

7.2.1 Cases on publishing obscene material

7.2.1.1 *Criminal petition under s. 482, CrPC dismissed in view of obscene electronic evidence transmitted*

In *Dr. Katari Sunil Kumar* v *Dr. B. Hemanalini*,[27] the respondent, *Dr. B. Hemanalini* filed a private complaint in the Court of the Judicial Magistrate, First Class, contending the emails received by her were generated from the laptop/computer of the petitioner/accused. She also enclosed the hard copies of the mails received by her to her complaint. It evidence reported that the mails were sent from the laptop of the accused. A particular word 'HAAI' was used in all the mails, which was unique. The mails were sent in chain to each other. The above factors established that the mails were generated from the computer of the accused and they were sent by the accused to the complainant. The learned Magistrate recorded the sworn statement of Dr. B. Hemanalini and proceeded to take cognizance of the offences punishable under s. 67 of the Information Technology Act 2000 and s. 509[28] of the Indian Penal Code 1860. Hence the criminal petition was instituted under s. 482, Code of Criminal Procedure 1973[29] by the accused Dr. Katari Sunil Kumar to quash the proceeding instituted by the complainant. The court dismissed the petition in view of the electronic evidence found in the case.

7.2.1.2 *Bail granted as no prima facie evidence found regarding publication of pornography*

Bazee.com is a customer to customer website, which facilitates the online sale of property. Bazee.com receives commission

27 *Dr. Katari Sunil Kumar* v *Dr. B. Hemanalini* 2013(1) ALD (Cri) 251.

28 *Word, gesture or act intended to insult the modesty of a woman.* Whoever, intending to insult the modesty of any woman, utters any word, makes any sound or gesture, or exhibits any object, intending that such word or sound shall be heard, or that such gesture or object shall be seen, by such woman, or intrudes upon the privacy of such woman, shall be punished with simple imprisonment for a term which may extend to three years, and also with fine.

29 *Saving of inherent powers of High Court.* Nothing in this Code shall be deemed to limit or affect the inherent powers of the High Court to make such orders as may be necessary to give effect to any order under this Code, or to prevent abuse of the process of any Court or otherwise to secure the ends of justice.

from such sales and also generates revenue from advertisements carried on in its web pages. Avinash Bajaj, the CEO of Bazee.com was arrested under s. 67 of the Information Technology Act 2000 for distributing Cyber Pornography. His bail application was rejected by the trial court. He then approached the Delhi High Court for bail. The charges stemmed from the fact that someone had sold copies of a pornographic CD through the Bazee.com website. The major factors considered by the court were there was no *prima facie* evidence that Mr. Bajaj directly or indirectly published the pornography. The actual obscene recording/clip could not be viewed on Bazee.com website. The court granted him bail subject to furnishing two sureties of ₹1 lakh each. The court ordered Mr. Bajaj to surrended his passport and not to leave India without the permission of the Court. The Court also ordered Mr. Bajaj, to participate and assist in the investigation.[30]

7.2.2 Case on child pornography

7.2.2.1 *Supreme Court directed the Government to block porn sites including child pornographic materials*

Innocent children cannot be made prey to these kinds of painful situations and a nation by no means, can afford to carry any kind of experiment with its children in the name of liberty and freedom of expression. The court also referred to ss. 13 to 15 of the Protection of Children from Sexual Offences Act 2012. A Cyber Regulation Advisory Committee was constituted under s. 88 of the Information Technology Act 2000 and *inter alia* assigned with brief regarding availability of child pornography on internet. The court ordered for complete prohibition of child pornography except the extent of right to view pornography other than child pornography as part of freedom of expression. The Central Government was directed to block certain websites. The matter was posted for further hearing.[31]

30 *Avnish Bajaj* v *State (N.C.T.) of Delhi* 116(2005) DLT 427.

31 *Kamlesh Vaswani* v *Union of India* (2016)7 SCC 592.

7.3 Computer fraud

Section 43(*h*) of the Information Technology Act 2000:

If any person without permission of the owner or any other person who is in charge of a computer, computer system or computer network—

(*h*) Charges the services availed of by a person to the account of another person by tampering with or manipulating any computer, computer system, or computer network;

.... he shall be liable to pay damages by way of compensation not exceeding one crore rupees to the person so affected.

In a computer fraud, a computer is used to commit cheating or deception to cause a wrongful loss to a person or wrongful gain to a cyber criminal. In India, the IT Act 2000 read with the Indian Penal Code 1860 provided description of the acts or omissions that amount to computer fraud which is a punishable offence including s. 66 for hacking, punishment for identity theft in s. 66C and for cheating by personification under s. 66D.

Sometimes computer frauds include data thefts, denial of service attacks, which causes system failure by over spamming, forgery and virus attacks. Nowadays, corporate entities are suffering huge losses through digital theft of data rather than physical or conventional means of stealing. As a result of growing computer frauds, auditor's role is no more limited to verifying financial statements but also use of Computer Assisted Audit Techniques (CAAT) and digital methods to detect computer frauds. CAAT involves two different categories namely applications such as Excel. MS Access, SQL and the Second comprises of Generalized Audit Software, PC based file interrogation software like IDEA, ACKL.[32]

32 Dalal, Chetan, *Novel and Conventional'Methods of Audit, Investigation, and Fraud Detection*, CCH Wolters Kluwer, p. 433.

Section 66 of the IT Act 2000:

Computer related offences. If any person, dishonestly or fraudulently, does any act referred to in section 43, he shall be punishable with imprisonment for a term which may extend to three years or with fine which may extend to five lakh rupees or with both.

Explanation. For the purposes of this section,—

(*a*) the word "dishonestly" shall have the meaning assigned to it in section 24 of the Indian Penal Code (45 of 1860);

(*b*) the word "fraudulently" shall have the meaning assigned to it in section 25 of the Indian Penal Code (45 of 1860).

Section 66C of the Information Technology Act:

Punishment for identity theft. Whoever, fraudulently or dishonestly make use of the electronic signature, password or any other unique identification feature of any other person, shall be punished with imprisonment of either description for a term which may extend to three years and shall also be liable to fine which may extend to rupees one lakh.

7.3.1 Cases on identity theft

7.3.1.1 *Complaint may be quashed in case of commission of non-compoundable offences*

A petition has been filed in the Madhya Pradesh High Court, under s. 482, CrPC against the order of the trial court. Whereby it accepted the compromise filed by the parties in regard to commission of offence punishable under s. 420 of the IPC. However, the trial court refused to accept the compromise in regard to commission of offence punishable under ss. 66C and 66D of the Information Technology Act. The allegation against the accused was that he received ATM Card of the complainant and also got information about code number of the ATM card and thereafter he had withdrawn an amount of ₹17,700 from the account of Sonam Sharma through ATM Card by using facility of Internet bank. During the pendency of the petition the complainant filed an application for compromise. The permission was also granted. However the trial court refused to grant permission for compromise in regard to commission of offence punishable under ss. 66C and 66D of the Information Technology Act on the ground that no compromise is permissible for commission of offence punishable under the aforesaid sections as the impugned sections are non-compoundable in nature. The High Court observed that the dispute between the parties is of private nature and had no adverse effect to others and even resolved by the compromise.[33] Referring the case of *Gian Singh* v *State of Punjab*,[34] decided by the Apex Court, the High Court of Madhya Pradesh, held that the compromise settlement arrived at between the parties in form of compromise petition is a sensible step that will benefit the parties. Continuation of criminal proceeding would amount to abuse of process of law. There was no possibility of conviction in view of compromise entered between the parties. The petition filed by the accused petitioner was allowed setting aside the order passed by the trial court.[35]

7.3.1.2 *FIR quashed when the accused persons are not proclaimed offender and there is a genuine, voluntary compromise*

A prayer in a petition was filed under s. 482, CrPC was for quashing of FIR under ss. 66, 66A, 66C and 66D of the Information Technology Act and s. 201 of IPC, registered at Police Station, North Chandigarh and all subsequent proceedings arising therefrom on the basis of a compromise. The complainant had appeared before the trial court on 18.1.2017 and had specifically stated that he has no objection if the application for compounding the offences is allowed and the accused are discharged as they have sought an unconditional apology.[36]

33 *Abhishek Mishra* v *State of Madhya Pradesh* decided on 14.1.2016.

34 2012 AIR SCW 5333.

35 Available at <https://indiankanoon.org/doc/125921697/> accessed on 13.11.2018.

36 *Aatir Khan* v *U.T. of Chandigarh* decided on 14.12.2017.

Taking into consideration the report as forwarded by learned Judicial Magistrate, Ist Class, Chandigarh, wherein it had been reported that neither of the accused has been declared as proclaimed offender nor the compromise so entered into between the parties were genuine, voluntarily and without any coercion or undue influence, the High Court did not hesitate in quashing the aforesaid FIR, as, no useful purpose would be served to continue with the proceedings before the trial Court in the instant FIR.[37]

Section 66D of the Information Technology Act 2000:

> 66D. *Punishment for cheating by personation by using computer resource.* Whoever, by means for any communication device or computer resource cheats by personating, shall be punished with imprisonment of either description for a term which may extend to three years and shall also be liable to fine which may extend to one lakh rupees.

7.3.2 When offences are bailable bail cannot be denied[38]

This was an application for bail under s. 439 of the Code of Criminal Procedure filed on behalf of the petitioner Bhola in Crime No. 850/2016, registered by Police Station Adhartal, District Jabalpur under ss. 66D and 67 of the Information Technology Act and s. 292 of the IPC.[39]

37 Available at <https://indiankanoon.org/doc/12734806/> accessed on 13.11.18.

38 *Bhola* v *State of Madhya Pradesh* MCRC-20225-2016. Available at <https://indiankanoon.org/doc/31434357> accessed on 22.11.2018.

39 Section 292(2) of the IPC states: Whoever—sells, lets to hire, distributes, publicly exhibits or in any manner puts into circulation, or for purposes of sale, hire, distribution, public exhibition or circulation, makes, produces or has in his possession any obscene book, pamphlet, paper, drawing, painting, representation or figure or any other obscene object whatsoever, or imports or exports such materials shall be punished on the first conviction with imprisonment of either conviction for a term which may extend to two years, and with fine which may extend to two thousand rupees, and in the event of second or subsequent conviction, with imprisonment of either description for a term which may extend to five years, and also fine which may extend to five thousand rupees.

As per the prosecution case, petitioner Bhola, who was a sweeper in a hotel, gave his mobile phone to co-accused Deepak, who created a fake face-book account and from that account sent obscene messages and photographs to the face-book account of the victim, who is an MBA student. She was also threatened with defamation. Thus, the role ascribed to the petitioner is that he made his mobile available to co-accused Deepak, who sent the offending, messages. The offence was registered under ss. 66D and 67 of the Information Technology Act 2000 and s. 292 of the IPC. As per s. 77B of the Information Technology Act, the offences punishable with imprisonment of three years and are bailable. Thus, the offences punishable under ss. 66-D and 67 of the Information Technology Act 2000, are bailable. The offence under s. 292 of the IPC is also bailable.

In aforesaid circumstances, the application for bail under s. 439 of the CrPC filed on behalf of the petitioner Bhola was allowed. It was directed that the petitioner shall be released on bail on furnishing a personal bond of ₹30,000 with a solvent surety in the same amount to the satisfaction of the trial court for his appearance before the concerned Court on all dates fixed in the case and for complying with the conditions enumerated under s. 437(3) of the CrPC.

7.3.3 At the time of framing charge, court is to see whether prima facie charge exist under s. 66D of IT Act 2000

The present petition was filed in the Punjab and Haryana High Court or quashing the order dated 6.8.2015 passed by Additional Sessions Judge, Chandigarh whereby revision petition against the framing of the charges under ss. 66A and 66D of the Information Technology Act 2000 (hereinafter referred to as 'the Act') was partly accepted and charge was ordered to be framed under s. 66D of 'the Act'.[40]

40 *Manish Singla* v *U.T. Chandigarh* CRM No. M-32648 of 2015, date of decision 23.9.2015. Available at <https://indiankanoon.org/doc/9561678/> accessed on 22.11.18.

Relevant facts of the case that on 27.7.2013 complainant Archna Kaura reported to the police that present petitioner misused her photograph on facebook profile to create a fake account in her name and thereafter sent a friend request to her children. While her children were still viewing the request, the account was deleted. The same incident had earlier occurred on 12.6.2013 and yet another incident occurred in October 2012 when a fake account was created in the name of Vikram Thakur and her photograph was sent to her husband's account and after three hours the same person hacked her husband's account and deleted the email.

Having considered the submissions made by learned counsel for the petitioner, the court was of the considered view that it had come in the investigation that petitioner had also made a phone call on 8.7.2013 from his mobile No. 97806-22167 to Mobile No. 92166-28891 giving threat to the husband of complainant of dire consequences.

As per order dated 6.8.2015 passed by Additional Sessions Judge, Chandigarh, petitioner was then to face trial for offence under s. 66D of the Information Technology Act 2000 and s. 415 of the IPC which explains 'Cheating'.

The High Court was of the view that the provisions of law made it ample clear that certainly there were allegation of causing harm to the reputation by creating a false facebook account and sending the same to the children of the complainant. In that process complainant was unnecessarily upset and damage was caused to her. Learned Additional Sessions Judge, Chandigarh had rightly observed that it was not a simple case of friendship request but the result of such an act could be devastating. That way there was certainly a *prima facie* case for framing of charge under s. 66D of 'the Act' for which petitioner had been ordered to face trial. Law on the point is settled that at the time of framing of charge, Court must see whether a *prima facie* case exist, so as to ask anybody to face the trial. In the present case, Court below had observed that there is *prima facie* case for framing of charge against petitioner for commission of offence under s. 66D of 'the Act'.

Resultantly the present petition was without any merit and were dismissed.

7.4 Computer based forgery

Computer frauds also involve forging documents which are sensitive and important documents. Section 463 of the Indian Penal Code explains 'Forgery'.[41] The offence of forgery is committed when a false document or false electronic record is made with intent to cause damage or injury according to s. 464 of IPC.[42] Section 465 of IPC provides punishment for

41 Whoever makes any false documents or false electronic record or part of a document or electronic record, with intent to cause damage or injury, to the public or to any person, or to support any claim or title, or to cause any person to part with property, or to enter into any express or implied contract, or with intent to commit fraud or that fraud may be committed, commits forgery.

42 A person is said to make a false document or false electronic record—

First—Who dishonestly or fradulently—

(a) makes, signs, seals or executes a document or part of a document;
(b) makes or transmits any electronic record or part of any electronic record;
(c) affixes any electronic signature on any electronic record;
(d) makes any mark denoting the execution of a document or the authenticity of the electronic signature,

with the intention of causing it to be believed that such document or part of document, electronic record or electronic signature was made, signed, sealed, executed, transmitted or affixed by or by the authority of a person by whom or by whose authority he knows that it was not made, signed, sealed, executed or affixed; or

Secondly—Who, without lawful authority, dishonestly or fraudulently, by cancellation or otherwise, alters a document or an electronic record in any material part thereof, after it has been made, executed or affixed with electronic signature either by himself or by any other person, whether such person be living or dead at the time of such alteration; or

Thirdly—Who dishonestly or fraudulently causes any person to sign, seal, execute or alter a document or an electronic record or to affix his electronic signature on any electronic record knowing that such person by reason of unsoundness of mind or intoxication cannot, or that by reason of deception practised upon him, he does not know the contents of the document or electronic record or the nature of the alteration.

forgery and s. 468 says, whoever commits forgery, intending that the document or electronic record forged shall be used for the purpose of cheating, shall be punished with imprisonment of either description for a term which may extend to seven years, and shall also be liable to fine.

Section 477A of the Indian Penal Code 1860 provides punishment for falsification of accounts including electronic records of accounts.

In addition to the conventional commission of forgery, s. 65 of the Information Technology Act, explains 'Tampering with Computer Source Code', Counterfeiting,[43] Data Diddling[44] or Salami Attack[45] are various forms of application of s. 65 of IT Act 2000.

7.5 Tampering with computer source code

Section 65 explains *Tampering with computer source documents*. Whoever knowingly or intentionally conceals, destroys or alters or intentionally or knowingly causes another to conceal, destroy, or alter any computer source code used for a computer, computer programme, computer system or computer network, when the computer source code is required to be kept or maintained by law for the time being in force, shall be punishable with imprisonment up to three years, or with fine which may extend up to two lakh rupees, or with both.

Explanation. For the purposes of this section, "computer source code" means the listing of programmes, computer commands, design and layout and programme analysis of computer resource in any form.

43 Counterfeiting is Fraudulent imitation, as in the Parliament Attack Case [*State* v *Md. Afzal* 107(2003) DLT 385] the accused were found to have created fake entry passes to the Parliament.
44 Data Diddling involves illegal or unauthorized data alteration.
45 Salami Attack is alteration of computer source code.

7.5.1 Cases on tampering with computer source code

7.5.1.1 *When the alleged offences are tried by a Magistrate's court and they are not exclusively punishable with death or life imprisonment, anticipatory bail may be granted*[46]

The facts of the prosecution case were that on 9.7.2012 Sharanappa Neeralagi, Regional Manager, KVG Bank filed complaint alleging that the complainant bank migrated to core banking solutions as per the RBI directives on 31.3.2011. The service provider M/s. C-Edge Technologies Limited, Wellspring Godrej and Boyce Complex, Mumbai has outsourced the contract to M/s. Tykon System Solutions, Bangalore. On 19.3.2012 during tallying physical cash in hand with that of CBS system, two suspicious transactions for sum of ₹4,00,000 and ₹10,00,000 on 25.6.2011 and 22.7.2011 were credited to savings bank account No. 89001798234. The said amount was withdrawn by Belagavi Branch. Senior Manager, I.T. Division was deputed to Belagavi Branch to verify the suspected transaction. He submitted that ₹14,00,000 was fraudulently withdrawn from S.B. Account No. 89001798234. It is stated that SB Account at Jainapur Branch was opened without following KYC norms in the name of Farhan Mohammad. It was known that same named person was working in Tykon System Solutions, Bangalore but bank does not have any information about him. The present petitioner was Manager at Jainapur Branch and alleged that he violated the KYC norms, not obtained proper documents while opening SB Account and thereby authorized fraudulent transaction and committed dereliction of duties. On the basis of all these allegations case came to be registered for the above said offences.

The High Court of Karnataka, considering the averments of the petitioner that he is innocent and not involved in committing the offence and that he will not abscond or flee

46 *Basavaraj S/O Mallappa Kutakoli* v *State of Karnataka* Criminal Petition No. 100301/2017. Available at: <https://indiankanoon.org/doc/193836616/> accessed on 22.11.2018.

from trial or investigation and he is ready to furnish adequate surety and security for his release on bail, concluded that alleged offences were triable by the Magistrate Court and they were not exclusively punishable with death or life imprisonment. Hence, by imposing reasonable conditions petitioner can be considered for releasing on anticipatory bail. Accordingly, petition was allowed. Petitioner was ordered to be released on bail with some conditions.

7.5.1.2 *Manupulations with computer source code amounted to tampering*[47]

Reliance Infocom launched a scheme under which a cell phone subscriber was given a digital handset worth ₹10,500 as well as service bundle for 3 years with an initial payment of ₹3,350 and monthly outflow of ₹600. The subscribers were also provided a 1 year warranty and 3 year insurance on the handset. The condition was that the handset was technologically locked so that it would only work with Reliance Infocom Services. If the customer wanted to leave Reliance services, he would have to pay some charges including the true price of the handset. Since the handset was of high quality, the market response to the scheme was phenomenal. Unidentified persons contacted Reliance customers with an offer to change to a lower price in Tata Indicom Scheme. As part of the deal, their phone would be technologically 'unlocked' so that the exclusive reliance handsets could be used for the Tata Indicom service.

Reliance officials came to know about this 'unlocking' by 'Tata Employees' and lodged a FIR under various provisions of IPC, IT Act 2000 and the Copyright Act. The police then raided some officials of Tata Indicom in Andhra Pradesh and arrested a few Tata Tele Services Limited officials for re-programming the Reliance handsets. These arrested persons approached the High Court requesting the Court to quash the FIR on the ground that their acts did not violate the said legal provisions.

47 *Syed Asifuddin* v *State of Andhra Pradesh* 2005 CrLJ 4314.

The findings of the court were that as per s. 2(*i*) of the IT Act 2000, any electronic, magnetic, or optical device, used for storage of information received through satellite, microwave, or other communication, media and the devices which are programmable and capable of retrieving any information by manipulations of electronic, magnetic or optical impulses is a computer which can be used as computer system in a computer network.

The instructions or programme given to computer in a language known to the computer are not seen by users of the computer/consumers of computer functions is known as source code.

Based on the above finding, the court held that such manipulation amounted to tampering with computer source code as envisaged by s. 65 of the IT Act 2000.

7.6 Cyber terrorism

Section 66F of the Information Technology Act 2000 deals with cyber terrorism which states as follows:

66F. *Punishment for cyber terrorism.* (1) Whoever,—

(A) with intent to threaten the unity, integrity, security or sovereignty of India or to strike terror in the people or any section of the people by—

(*i*) denying or cause the denial of access to any person authorised to access computer resource; or

(*ii*) attempting to penetrate or access a computer resource without authorisation or exceeding authorised access; or

(*iii*) introducing or causing to introduce any computer contaminant,

and by means of such conduct causes or is likely to cause death or injuries to persons or damage to or destruction of property or disrupts or knowing that it is likely to cause damage or disruption of supplies or services essential to the life of the community or adversely affect the critical information infrastructure specified under section 70; or

(B) knowingly or intentionally penetrates or accesses a computer resource without authorisation or exceeding authorised access, and by means of such conduct obtains access to information, data or computer database that is restricted for reasons of the security of the State or foreign relations; or any restricted information, data or computer database, with reasons to believe that such information, data or computer database so obtained may be used to cause or likely to cause injury to the interests of the sovereignty and integrity of India, the security of the State, friendly relations with foreign States, public order, decency or morality, or in relation to contempt of court, defamation or incitement to an offence, or to the advantage of any foreign nation, group of individuals or otherwise, commits the offence of cyber terrorism.

(2) Whoever commits or conspires to commit cyber terrorism shall be punishable with imprisonment which may extend to imprisonment for life.

7.6.1 Case on cyber terrorism

7.6.1.1 *The challenger who questions the accuracy of the computer evidence has to establish the challenge*[48]

Several terrorist had attacked the Parliament House on 13th December 2001 intending to take as hostage or kill the Prime Minister, Central Ministers, Vice President of India and Members of Parliament. Several Terrorist were killed by the police in the encounter and several persons were arrested in connection with the attack. The Designated Judge of the Special Court constituted under s 23 of the Prevention of Terrorist Activities Act 2002 (POTA) had convicted several accused

48 *State* v *Mohd. Afzal* 107(2003) DLT 385.

persons. They filed an appeal in the Delhi High Court challenging the legality and validity of the trial and the sustainability of the judgment. Digital evidence played an important role in this case. Computerized cell phone, call logs were heavily relied upon. A laptop, several smart media storage disks and devices were recovered from a truck intercepted at Srinagar pursuant to information given by two of the suspects. These articles were deposited in the police 'malkhana' on 16th December 2001. Although the laptop was deposited in the 'malkhana' some files were written onto the laptop on 21st December. The laptops were forensically examined by a private computer engineer and the Assistant Government Examiner of Questioned Documents, Bureau of Police Research, Hyderabad. The laptop contained files relating to identity cards and stickers that were used by the terrorist to enter the Parliament premises. Cyber forensic examination showed that the laptop was used for creating, editing and viewing image files (mostly identity cards). The issue *inter alia* raised by defence was in the absence of verified time setting and reliable information about the hard disc being original, there is no certainty that the material found on a latter date, was exactly the material, which may have existed on a previous date. The court concluded that if someone challenges the accuracy of computer evidence on the ground of misuse of system or operating failure or interpolation, then the challenger has to establish the challenge. Mere theoretical or generic doubt cannot be cast on the evidence.

7.6.2 Hate speech

Hate Speech may be classified under the broad spectrum of terrorism. It is an act of making oral communications, writing something or posting on the internet which are aimed at defaming, intimidating or inciting violence or riots written against an individual or a specific group of individuals with a bias towards religion, nationality, sect, region, gender, class, profession or physical attributes.

In India, Art. 19(2) of the Constitution allows imposition of reasonable restrictions on the right to freedom of speechand expression in the interest of protecting the sovereignty and interest of India, relations with foreign States, security of State, public order, decency or morality or in relation to contempt of court, defamation or incitement to offence. Section 66A of the IT Act 2000 prescribed punishment for sending offensive messages through communication services using internet or computers. Section 66A reads as:

> "Any person who sends, by means of a computer resource or a communication device,—
>
> (*a*) any information that is grossly offensive or has menacing character; or
>
> (*b*) any information which he knows to be false, but for the purpose of causing annoyance, inconvenience, danger, obstruction, insult, injury, criminal intimidation, enmity, hatred or ill will, persistently by making use of such computer resource or a communication device,
>
> (*c*) any electronic mail or electronic mail message for the purpose of causing annoyance or inconvenience or to deceive or to mislead the addressee or recipient about the origin of such messages,
>
> shall be punishable with imprisonment for a term which may extend to three years and with fine.
>
> *Explanation*. For the purpose of this section, terms "electronic mail" and "electronic mail message" means a message or information created or transmitted or received on a computer, computer system, computer resource or communication device including attachments in text, images, audio, video and any other electronic record, which may be transmitted with the message."

But in the recent landmark judgment of *Shreya Singhal* v *Union of India*,[49] the Supreme Court of India struck down s. 66A of the IT Act 2000 as unconstitutional. This public interest

49 *Shreya Singhal* v *Union of India* (2013)12 SCC 73.

litigation was filed to challenge the constitutionality of s. 66A of the IT Act 2000 as being arbitrary, ambiguous and violative of fundamental right to free speech guaranteed under Art. 19 of the Constitution of India. The court held that s. 66A of the IT Act 2000 is arbitrary, ambiguous, and violative of right to freedom of speech and it takes within its sweep the speech that is innocent as well. The court took the view that no part of it was severable and section as a whole was struck down as unconstitutional.

7.7 Liability of intermediaries

Section 79 of the Information Technology Act 2000:

> 79. *Exemption from liability of intermediary in certain cases.* (1) Notwithstanding anything contained in any law for the time being in force but subject to the provisions of sub-sections (2) and (3), an intermediary shall not be liable for any third party information, data, or communication link made available or hasted by him.
>
> (2) The provisions of sub-section (1) shall apply if—
>
> (*a*) the function of the intermediary is limited to providing access to a communication system over which information made available by third parties is transmitted or temporarily stored or hosted; or
>
> (*b*) the intermediary does not—
>
> (*i*) initiate the transmission,
>
> (*ii*) select the receiver of the transmission, and
>
> (*iii*) select or modify the information contained in the transmission;
>
> (*c*) the intermediary observes due diligence while discharging his duties under this Act and also observes such other guidelines as the Central Government may prescribe in this behalf.
>
> (3) The provisions of sub-section (1) shall not apply if—
>
> (*a*) the intermediary has conspired or abetted or aided or induced, whether by threats or promise

or outhorise in the commission of the unlawful act;

(b) upon receiving actual knowledge, or on being notified by the appropriate Government or its agency that any information, data or communication link residing in or connected to a computer resource, controlled by the intermediary is being used to commit the unlawful act, the intermediary fails to expeditiously remove or disable access to that material on that resource without vitiating the evidence in any manner.

Explanation. For the purpose of this section, the expression "third party information" means any information dealt with by an intermediary in his capacity as an intermediary.

7.7.1 Case on liability of intermediary[50]

The appellant had directed the appeal before the State Consumer Dispute Redressal Forum against order dated 7.8.2015 of District Consumer Disputes Redressal Forum, Jalandhar (in short the 'District Forum), vide which, the complaint of the complainant was accepted. The appellant of this appeal is the opposite party in the original complaint before the District Forum and respondent of this appeal is complainant therein and they be referred as such hereinafter for the sake of convenience.

The factual backdrop of the complaint, filed by the complainant before the District Forum under s. 12 of the Consumer Protection Act 1986 (in short, "the Act") against the OPs was that he placed an order with OP on its e-commerce website, for purchasing a Panasonic Split Air Conditioner 1.5 ton, 3 star, bearing model No. UC18QKY3, which was confirmed by it, vide order No. 4939226590. The product was in stock and

50 *Jasper Infotech Pvt. Ltd.* v *Kewal Krishan* First Appeal No. 1042 of 2015. Available at <https://indiankanoon.org/doc/37889787/> accessed on 22.11.2018

an email regarding confirmation of order and a copy of bill was sent by OP on email ID of the complainant. It was further averred that complainant was agreed to pay an amount of ₹28,519 for product at the time of delivery at his address. Opposite party mentioned the estimated dispatch date, i.e. 16.2.2015 and estimated delivery date, i.e. 25.2.2015 of the product. The complainant contacted the customer care centre of OP on 17.2.2015, 20.2.2015, 23.2.2015 and it was assured by representative that its delivery would be made very soon. The product was not supplied to him on one pretext or the other. The complainant received phone call from customer care, on 1.3.2015, informing that order has been cancelled by OP due to non-availability of the product and email was also sent by OP in this regard. The complainant enquired from customer care, as how the product was shown available on the website, if the same was out of stock, but the phone connection of complainant was disconnected without giving any reply by the representative. The price of the ordered product increased in the meanwhile and OP stopped the delivery of the product on the same price to him. Since, complainant was pressed by the urgent need of air conditioner, hence he purchased the same Panasonic Split Air Conditioner from M/s. Supreme Radios, GT Road, Jalandhar on the increased price of ₹33,200, vide invoice No. 25123 on 3.3.2015. The OP harassed the complainant for a long time. He prayed that OP be directed to refund the excess amount of ₹4,681 paid by him for the purchase of above Air Conditioner at increased rate and further to pay ₹50,000 as compensation for mental harassment and ₹10,000 as cost of litigation.

Upon notice, OP filed written reply averring that OP Company operates the online website www.snapdeal.com and it is an online market place, facilitating the online sale and purchase of goods/merchandise offered by various merchants/ sellers to third parties, who visit/log onto snapdeal. It was averred that OP company does not sell any product to any consumer and is only doing the business under the brand/ trademark snapdeal, through above website. In an online market place, consumer transactions are processed by online market place operator and then delivered by the participating sellers. The OP company only act as an intermediary, through its above website by providing a medium to various sellers all over India to offer for sale and sell their product(s) to the general public at large. It is submitted that the sellers are separate entities, being controlled and managed by different persons/stakeholders. It does not directly or indirectly sell any products on its website, which is an online market place. The sellers directly raise invoices to the final customers for the products sold and bear all commercial risks and warranty on the products is provided either by the manufacturing companies or by the sellers selling the products. Under the provision of s. 79 of the Information Technology Act 2000, the complaint is liable to be dismissed immediately. It was further contended that the order placed to the seller Wow Deals, through OP by the complainant. The seller took the order and was responsible for checking the stock/verification/availability of the product, as he was alone responsible for sending the product to the complainant. The estimated dispatch date and the delivery date was given by the seller, i.e. Wow Deals. The mail sent to the complainant on 23rd February clearly stipulated that it was informed to the seller that there was an issue at the sellers end. When the courier partner went to pick up the product from the seller, the seller failed to hand over the product due to which the OP had to cancel the order. It was further averred that discretion of purchasing the AC at a higher price lay with the complainant and OP could not be penalized for the fault of the seller. The answering OP denied the averments of the complainant and prayed for dismissal of the complaint.

On conclusion of evidence and arguments, the District Forum accepted the complaint by directing OP to pay ₹10,000 to the complainant as compensation and to pay ₹3,000 as litigation expenses. Aggrieved by above order, the OP now appellant, has preferred this appeal against the same.

The forceful submission of counsel for the appellant was that in view of s. 79 and s. 2(*w*) of the Information Technology Act, the appeal cannot be filed against OP.

As, the point in issue was of the matter pertaining to internet transactions which are to be disposed of under the Information Technology Act, the State Commission interpreted s. 13(3) of the IT Act 2000 which is as under:

> Save as otherwise agreed to between the originator and the addressee, an electronic record is deemed to be dispatched at the place where the originator has his place of business, and is deemed to be received at the place where the addressee has his place of business.

Section 13(3) of the Information Technology Act 2000 has to be read with s. 11(2) of Consumer Protection Act 1986. The District Forum has correctly observed that where the contract of services or goods entered into on internet or online, then for the purpose of consumer complaints, part of cause of action arises, *inter alia* at complainant's place of business provided the contract is communicated to him through the internet including email. The cause of action arises despite the fact that the contract is made over internet in the below noted cases:

(*a*) where the contract is performed or is to be performed;

(*b*) where money under the contract is either payable or paid; or

(*c*) where repudiation of the contract is received, if any.

Consumer Forum is competent to entertain the consumer complaint, even if infinitesimal cause of action arose within its jurisdiction. The complaint can be filed before the Consumer Forum, where part of cause of action arises, provided the complaint is within the pecuniary competence of the District Forum. Here in this case, the order was booked online by the complainant. It was accepted at the other end and the communication of acceptance was conveyed to complainant at Jalandhar, where he placed the order and has place of business. Consequently, the reasoning of the District Forum Jalandhar is sustainable to entertain the complaint. Even, the Contract Act recognizes it to be giving part of cause of action, where the acceptance of offer is conveyed to the proposer. We are in agreement with the reasoning of the District

Forum on this point that it has territorial jurisdiction to try the complaint.

The Consumer Protection Act 1986 has been enacted by the legislature to provide for protection of interest of consumers and different Forums have been constituted under the Act to meet with these eventualities. The Act has been designed to advance the case of protection of consumers and to provide speedy disposal of the matters. The complainant placed order from Jalandhar and confirmation was also received by him at Jalandhar from OP end. Goods were to be delivered at Jalandhar and payment was to be made by the complainant at Jalandhar therefor. Cause of action certainly accrues within the territorial jurisdiction of Jalandhar Forum and the same is, thus, competent to entertain the complaint. The District Forum relied upon in this regard, which was sent by OP stating that the order of complainant has been received and email would be sent and SMS and movement of his order items were dispatched. Even receiving address is also mentioned to be at Jalandhar for delivery of the ordered A.C. Even dispatch date 16.2.2015 and estimated delivery date, i.e. 25.2.2015 are also recorded in it with payment of an amount of ₹28,519. From the information of this website of OP, it is evident that OP confirmed the proposal of the complainant and communicated it to complainant at Jalandhar. Opposite party suddenly cancelled the order vide Ex. C-5 due to non-availability of stock with their seller and it was conveyed to complainant at Jalandhar.

The forceful submission of the appellant was that the appellant was only an intermediary without any pro-acting role in the matter and is protected by s. 79 of the Information Technology Act 2000. We find that there is no delivery of the goods to the complainant by OP. The complainant was compelled to purchase the A.C. at higher rate from other seller, which fact was proved by Ex. C-9. Opposite Party conveyed cancellation of the ordered A.C., vide Ex. C-5. Surprisingly, the complainant again placed order for the same product of ₹33,849, which was confirmed by the website of OP, as is plain by Ex. C-7 and Ex. C-8 on the record. All the website of OP confirmed the products for which complainant again placed an order for ₹33,850 which is rather a mysterious factor. The District Forum has justifiably held that this is an act of unfair trade practice on the part of OP. Unfair trade practice has been defined under s. 2(1)(*r*) of the CP Act that "unfair trade practice means a trade practice which, for the purpose of promoting the sale, use or supply of any goods or for the provision of any service, adopts any unfair method or unfair or deceptive practice including any of the following practices .... (2) permits the publication of any advertisement whether in any newspaper or otherwise, for the sale or supply at a bargain price, of goods or services that are not intended to be offered for sale or supply at the bargain price, or for a period that is and in quantities that are, reasonable, having regard to the nature of the market in which the business is carried on, the nature and size of business, and the nature of the advertisement." It, thus, makes it evident that even the permission to give publication of any advertisement on website regarding the supply of any good on bargain price, which are not intended to be offered at the bargain price is an unfair trade practice. The OP certainly gained some monetary advantage from publication of sale on its website with regard to Panasonic A.C. in question. The same was not supplied to the complainant at bargained price of ₹28,519 in agreed time. OP certainly gained monetarily by publishing this advertisement on its website, which was never intended to be brought into practice. This is certainly unfair trade practice, as rightly concluded by the District Forum in this regard. We rely upon law laid down by the Meghaleya State Consumer Commission as held in *M.D., Air Deccan* v *Ram Gopal Aggarwal.*[51]

As a result of our above discussion, The State Commission at Chandigarh held that the District Forum rightly found the appellant guilty of unfair trade practice by permitting the publication of the advertisement on its website, which was never intended to be practiced; we find no illegality or

51 2014(1) CLT 179/180.

perversity in the order of the District Forum under challenge in this case and the same is affirmed in this appeal. We find no merit in the appeal and the same is hereby dismissed.

The appellant had deposited an amount of ₹7,000 in this Commission at the time of filing the appeal and further deposited ₹6,000 in compliance with order of this Commission. After calculating the interest on these amounts, which accrued thereon, if any, the amount of ₹13,000 be remitted by the registry to the respondent of this appeal, being complainant, by way of crossed cheque/demand draft after expiry of period of 45 days and the remaining amount thereafter, if any, be remitted by the registry to the appellant of this appeal by way of crossed cheque/demand draft.

7.8 Liability of company

Section 85 in the Information Technology Act 2000:

> 85. *Offences by companies.* (1) Where a person committing a contravention of any of the provisions of this Act or of any rule, direction or order made thereunder is a company, every person who, at the time the contravention was committed, was in charge of, and was responsible to, the company for the conduct of business of the company as well as the company, shall be guilty of the contravention and shall be liable to be proceeded against and punished accordingly: Provided that nothing contained in this sub-section shall render any such person liable to punishment if he proves that the contravention took place without his knowledge or that he exercised all due diligence to prevent such contravention.
>
> (2) Notwithstanding anything contained in sub-section (1), where a contravention of any of the provisions of this Act or of any rule, direction or order made thereunder has been committed by a company and it is proved that the contravention has taken place with the consent or connivance of, or is attributable to any neglect on the part of, any director, manager, secretary or other officer of the company, such director, manager, secretary or other officer

shall also be deemed to be guilty of the contravention and shall be liable to be proceeded against and punished accordingly.

Explanation. For the purposes of this section,—

(*i*) "company" means any body corporate and includes a firm or other association of individuals; and

(*ii*) "director", in relation to a firm, means a partner in the firm.

7.8.1 Cases on liability of company

7.8.1.1 *Director's liability when company is not arraigned as an accused*

The Supreme Court held that s. 85 of the Information Technology Act 2000 provides for deemed liability of Directors in case of offences committed by companies, therefore a Director cannot be held liable without impleading the company as an accused.[52]

52 *Aneeta Handa* v *M/s. Godfather Travels & Tours (P) Ltd.* (2012)5 SCC 661.

Index

